A. D. T. (Adeline Dutton Train) Whitney

Faith Gartney's Girlhood

A. D. T. (Adeline Dutton Train) Whitney

Faith Gartney's Girlhood

ISBN/EAN: 9783337128685

Printed in Europe, USA, Canada, Australia, Japan

Cover: Foto ©ninafisch / pixelio.de

More available books at **www.hansebooks.com**

FAITH GARTNEY'S GIRLHOOD

BY

MRS. A. D. T. WHITNEY,

AUTHOR OF "HITHERTO," "THE GAYWORTHYS," "PATIENCE STRONG'S OUTINGS"
ETC., ETC.

WITH ILLUSTRATIONS BY C. G. BUSH.

'To do my duty in that state of life to which it shall please God to call me.'

BOSTON:
HOUGHTON, MIFFLIN AND COMPANY.
The Riverside Press, Cambridge.
1882.

Entered according to Act of Congress, in the year 1868, by
A. K. LORING,
In the Clerk's Office of the District Court of the District of Massachusetts.

PREFACE.

I BEGAN this story for young girls. It has grown, as they grow, to womanhood. It makes no artistic pretension. It is a simple record of something of the thought and life that lies between fourteen and twenty.

I dedicate it, as it is, to these young girls, who dream, and wish, and strive, and err; and find, perhaps, little help to interpret their own spirits to themselves. I believe and hope that there is nothing in it which shall hinder them in what is noblest and truest.

May there be something that shall lift them — though by ever so little — up!

A. D. T. W.

CONTENTS.

CHAPTER		PAGE
I.	"Money, Money!"	7
II.	Sortes	12
III.	Aunt Henderson	17
IV.	Glory McWhirk	24
V.	Something Happens	35
VI.	Aunt Henderson's Girl-Hunt	55
VII.	Cares; and What Came of Them	65
VIII.	A Niche in Life, and a Woman to Fill It	71
IX.	Life or Death?	78
X.	Rough Ends	82
XI.	Cross Corners	90
XII.	A Reconnoissance	100
XIII.	Development	110
XIV.	A Drive with the Doctor	118
XV.	New Duties	131
XVI.	"Blessed be Ye, Poor"	138
XVII.	Frost-Wonders	152
XVIII	Out in the Snow	160
XIX.	A "Leading"	174

CONTENTS.

CHAPTER		PAGE
XX.	Paul	183
XXI.	Pressure	194
XXII.	Roger Armstrong's Story	204
XXIII.	Question and Answer	211
XXIV.	Conflict	229
XXV.	A Game at Chess	238
XXVI.	Lakeside	245
XXVII.	At the Mills	253
XXVIII.	Locked In	258
XXIX.	Home	272
XXX.	Aunt Henderson's Mystery	280
XXXI.	Nurse Sampson's Way of Looking at It	291
XXXII.	Glory McWhirk's Inspiration	300
XXXIII.	Last Hours	308
XXXIV.	Mrs. Parley Gimp	314
XXXV.	Indian Summer	320
XXXVI.	Christmas-tide	328
XXXVII.	The Wedding Journey	343

FAITH GARTNEY'S GIRLHOOD.

CHAPTER I.

"MONEY, MONEY!"

*"Shoe the horse and shoe the mare,
And let the little colt go bare."*

EAST or West, it matters not where,—the story may, doubtless, indicate something of latitude and longitude as it proceeds,—in the city of Mishaumok, lived Henderson Gartney, Esq., one of those American gentlemen of whom, if she were ever canonized, Martha of Bethany must be the patron saint,—if again, feminine celestials, sainthood once achieved through the weary experience of earth, don't know better than to assume such charge of wayward man,— born, as they are, seemingly, to the life-destiny of being ever "careful and troubled about many things."

We have all of us, as little girls, read "Rosamond." Now, one of Rosamond's early worries suggests a key to half the worries, early and late, of grown men and women. The silver paper won't cover the basket.

Mr. Gartney had spent his years, from twenty-five to forty, in sedulously tugging at the corners. He had had his share of silver paper, too,— only the basket was a little too big.

In a pleasant apartment, half library, half parlor, and used in the winter months as a breakfast room, beside a table still covered with the remnants of the morning meal, sat Mrs. Gartney and her young daughter, Faith; the latter with a somewhat disconcerted, not to say rueful, expression of face.

A pair of slippers on the hearth and the morning paper thrown down beside an arm-chair, gave hint of the recent presence of the master of the house.

"Then I suppose I can't go," remarked the young lady.

"I'm sure I don't know," answered the elder, in a helpless, worried sort of tone. "It don't seem really right to ask your father for the money. I did just speak of your wanting some things for a party, but I suppose he has forgotten it; and, to-day, I hate to trouble him with reminding. Must you really have new gloves and slippers, both?"

Faith held up her little foot for answer, shod with a partly-worn bronze kid, reduced to morning service.

"These are the best I've got. And my gloves have been cleaned over and over, till you said yourself, last time, they would hardly do to wear again. If it were any use, I should say I must have a new dress; but I thought at least I should freshen up with the 'little fixings,' and perhaps have something left for a few natural flowers for my hair."

"I know. But your father looked annoyed when I told him we should want fresh marketing to-day. He is really pinched, just now, for ready money, — and he is so discouraged about the times. He told me only last night of a man who owed him five hundred dollars, and came to say he did n't know as he could pay a cent. It don't seem to be a time to afford gloves and shoes and flowers. And then there 'll be the carriage, too."

"Oh dear!" sighed Faith, in the tone of one who felt herself checkmated. "I wish I knew what we really *could* afford! It always seems to be these little things that don't cost much, and that other girls, whose fathers are not nearly so well off, always have, without thinking anything about it." And she glanced over the table, whereon shone a silver coffee-service, and up at the mantel where stood a French clock that had been placed there a month before.

"Pull at the bobbin and the latch will fly up." An unspoken suggestion, of drift akin to this, flitted through the mind of Faith. She wondered if her father knew that this was a Signal Street invitation.

Mr. Gartney was ambitious for his children, and solicitous for their place in society.

But Faith had a touch of high-mindedness about her that made it impossible for her to pull bobbins.

So, when her father presently, with hat and coat on, came into the room again for a moment, before going out for the day, she sat quite silent, with her foot upon the fender, looking into the fire.

Something in her face however, quite unconsciously, bespoke that the world did not lie entirely straight before her, and this catching her father's eye, brought up to him, by an untraceable association, the half proffered request of his wife.

"So you haven't any shoes, Faithie. Is that it?"

"None nice enough for a party, father."

"And the party is a vital necessity, I suppose. Where is it to be?"

The latch-string was put forth, and while Faith still stayed her hand, her mother, absolved from selfish end, was fain to catch it up.

"At the Rushleighs'. **The Old** Year out and the New Year in."

"Oh, well, we mustn't 'let the colt go bare,'" answered Mr. Gartney, pleasantly, portmonnaie in hand. "But you must make that do." He handed her five dollars. "And take good care of your things when you have got them, for I don't pick up many five dollars now-a-days."

And the old look of care crept up, replacing the kindly smile, as he turned and left the room.

"I feel very much as if I had picked **my father's** pocket," said Faith, holding the bank-note, half ashamedly, in her **hand**.

Henderson Gartney, Esquire, was a man of no method **in** his expenditure. When money chanced to be plenty with him it was very apt to go as might happen — for French clocks, or whatsoever; and then, suddenly, the silver paper fell short elsewhere, and lo! a corner was left uncovered.

The horse and the mare were shod. Great expenses were incurred; money was found, somehow, **for** grand outlays; but the comfort of **buying**, with a readiness, the little needed matters **of every day, — this** was foregone. "Not **let the colt go bare!**" **It was** precisely the thing he was continually doing.

Mrs. Gartney had long found it to be her only wise way **to** make her hay while the sun was shining, — to buy, when she could buy, what she was sure would be most **wanted,** — and to look forward as far as possible, in her provisions, since her husband scarcely seemed to look **forward at all.**

So she exemplified, over and **over again** in her life, the story of Pharaoh and his fat and lean kine.

That night, Faith, her little purchases and arrangements all complete, and flowers and carriage bespoken for the next evening, went to bed to dream such dreams as only come to the sleep of early years.

At the same time, lingering by the fireside below for a half hour's unreserved conversation, Mr. Gartney was telling his wife of another money disappointment.

"Blacklow, at Cross Corners, gives up the lease of the house in the spring. He writes me he is going out to Indiana with his son-in-law. I don't know where I shall find another such tenant, — or any at all, for that matter."

CHAPTER II.

SORTES.

"How shall I know if I do choose the right?"

"Since this fortune falls to you,
Be content, and seek no new."

MERCHANT OF VENICE.

"Now, Mahala Harris," said Faith, as she glanced in at the nursery door, which opened from her room, "don't let Hendie get up a French Revolution here while I'm gone to dinner."

"Land sakes! Miss Faith! I don't know what you mean, nor whether I can help it. I dare say he'd get up a Revolution of '76, over again, if he once set out. He does train like 'lection. fact, sometimes."

"Well, don't let him build barricades with all the chairs, so that I shall have to demolish my way back again. I'm going to lay out my dress for to-night."

And very little dinner could her young appetite manage on this last day of the year. All her vital energy was busy in her anticipative brain, and glancing thence in sparkles from her eyes, and quivering down in swift currents to her restless little feet. It mattered little that there was delicious roast beef smoking on the table, and Christmas-pies were arrayed upon the sideboard, while up stairs the bright ribbon and tiny, shining, old-fashioned buckles were waiting to be shaped into **rosettes** for the **new** slippers, and the lace hung, half basted, from **the neck of the** simple but **delicate** silk dress, **and** those lovely green-house flowers **stood in a** glass dish on her dressing-table, **to** be sorted for her hair, and into a graceful breast-knot. No,—dinner was a **very** secondary and contemptible affair, compared with these.

Ah, if people **could only** hold **out to live, all the rest of** their days, **on perfume and beauty and** grace and dreamy delights, — **that seem, in the** charmed vision **of** youth, the essential verities of life, — how the worry and care of breakfasts and dinners and butchers' **and** grocers' bills and the trouble of servants **should be** gloriously done away with! To-night, Faith's eyes shine, and her cheek glows with the mere joy **of** life **and** loveliness; **but, to-morrow,** she will be hungry like any other mortal; **and there must** be chickens, or beefsteak, **or even coarser mutton or pork, to feed the very** roses that flush **and crown** her girlish beauty. **We don't** live straight from the spirit impulse yet!

There were few forms or faces, truly, that were pleasanter **to** look **upon in the** group that stood, disrobed of their careful outer wrappings, in Mrs. Rushleigh's dressing-room; their hurried chat and gladsome greetings distracted with **the** drawing **on of** gloves **and the last** adjustment of shining locks, while the bewildering **music was** floating **up from below,** mingled with the hum of voices from the rooms where, as children say, "the party had begun" **already.**

And Mrs. Rushleigh, when Faith paid her timid respects in the drawing-room at last, made her welcome with a peculiar grace and *empressement* that had their own flattering weight and charm; for the lady was a sort of St. Peter **of** fashion, holding its mystic keys, and admitting or rejecting whom she would; and culled, with marvellous tact and taste, the flower of the upgrowing world of Mishaumok to adorn " her set."

After which, Faith, claimed at once by an eager aspirant, and beset with many a following introduction and petition, was drawn to and kept in the joyous whirlpool of the dance, till she had breathed in enough of delight and excitement to carry her quite beyond the thought even of ices and oysters and jellies and fruits, and the score of unnamable luxuries whereto the young revellers were duly summoned at half past ten o'clock.

Four days' anticipation, — four hours' realization, — culminated in the glorious after-supper midnight dance, when, marshalled hither and thither by the ingenious orders of the band, the jubilant company found itself, just on the impending stroke of twelve, drawn out around the room in one great circle; and suddenly a hush of the music, at the very poising instant of time, left them motionless for a moment to burst out again in the age-honored and heart-warming strains of "Auld Lang Syne." Hand joining hand they sang its chorus, and when the last note had lingeringly died away, one after another gently broke from their places, and the momentary figure melted out with the dying of the Year, never again to be just so combined. It was gone, as vanishes also every other phase and grouping in the kaleidoscope of Time.

"Now is the very 'witching hour' to try the Sortes!"

Margaret Rushleigh said this, standing on the threshold of a little inner apartment that opened from the long drawing-room, at one end; and speaking to those nearest her in the scattered groups that had hardly ceased bandying back and forth their tumultuous "Happy New Years."

She held in her hand a large and beautiful volume, — a **gift of** Christmas day.

"Here are Fates for everybody who **cares to find them out!**"

The book was a collection of poetical quotations, arranged by numbers, and to be chosen thereby, and the chance application taken as an oracle.

Everything like fortune-telling, or a possible peering into the things of coming time, has such a charm! Especially with them to whom the past is but a prelude and beginning, and for whom the great, voluminous Future holds enwrapped the whole mystic Story of Life!

"No, no, this won't do!" **cried** the young lady, as circle behind circle closed and crowded eagerly about her. "Fate don't give out her revelations in such wholesale fashion. You must come **up with proper reverence, one by one.**"

As she spoke, she withdrew a little within **the curtained** archway, and, placing the crimson-covered book of destiny upon an inlaid table, brought forward a piano-stool, and **seated** herself thereon, as a priestess upon **a** tripod.

A little shyly, one after another, gaining knowledge of what was going **on,** the company strayed in from without, and, each **in turn** hazarding a number, received in answer the rhyme or stanza indicated; and who shall say how long those chance-directed words, chosen for the **most** part with the elastic ambiguity **of all** oracles of **any** established authority, lingered echoing in the heads **and** hearts of them to whom they were given, — shaping and confirming, or **darkening** with their denial many an after hope and fear?

One only, **of** them all, has an interest for us that needs a record.

Faith Gartney came **up among the very last.**

"How many numbers are there to choose from?" she asked.

"Three hundred and sixty-five. The number of days in the year."

"Well, then, I'll take the number of the day; the last, — no, I forgot, — the first of all."

Nobody before had chosen this, and Margaret read, in a clear, gentle voice, not untouched with the grave beauty of its own words, and the sweet, earnest, listening look of the young face that bent toward her to take them in, —

> "Rouse to some high and holy work of love,
> And thou an angel's happiness shalt know;
> Shalt bless the earth while in the world above;
> The good begun by thee while here below
> Shall like a river run, and broader flow."

Ten minutes later, and all else were absorbed in other things again, — leave-takings, parting chat, and a few waltzing a last measure to a specially-accorded grace of music. Faith stood, thoughtfully, by the table where the book was closed and left. She quietly reopened it at that first page. Unconscious of a step behind her, her eyes ran over the lines again, to make their beautiful words her own.

"And that was your oracle, then?" asked a kindly voice.

Glancing quickly up, while the timid color flushed her cheek, she met a look as of a wise and watchful angel, though it came through the eye and smile of a gray-haired man, who laid his hand upon the page as he said, —

"Remember, — it is *conditional*."

CHAPTER III.

AUNT HENDERSON.

"I never met a manner more entirely without frill."
SYDNEY SMITH.

LATE into the morning of the New Year, Faith slept. Through her half consciousness crept, at last, a feeling of music that had been wandering in faint echoes among the chambers of her brain all those hours of her suspended life, and were the first sensations to stir there, when that mysterious Life flashed back along its channels, and brought a light more subtle than the mere sunshine that through the easterly windows was flooding all her room with its silent arousal.

Light, and music, and a sense of an unexamined, half-remembered joy, filled her being and embraced her at her waking on this New Year's Day. A moment she lay in a passive, unthinking delight; and then her first, full, and distinct thought shaped itself, as from a sweet and solemn memory,—

"Rouse to some high and holy work of love,
And thou an angel's happiness shall know."

An impulse of lofty feeling held her in its ecstasy; a noble longing and determination shaped itself, though vaguely, within her. For a little, she was touched in her deepest and truest nature; she was uplifted to the threshold of a great resolve. But generalities are so grand, — details so commonplace and unsatisfying. What should she do? What "high and holy work" lay waiting for her?

And, breaking in upon her reverie, — bringing her down with its rough and common call to common duty, — the second bell for breakfast rang.

"Oh, dear! It is no use! Who'll know what great things I've been wishing and planning, when I've nothing to show for it but just being late to breakfast? And father hates it so, — and New Year's morning, too!"

Hurrying her toilet, she repaired, with all the haste possible, to the breakfast-room, where her consciousness of shortcoming was in nowise lessened when she saw who occupied the seat at her father's right hand, — Aunt Henderson!

Aunt Faith Henderson, who had reached her nephew's house last evening just after the young Faith, her namesake, had gone joyously off to "dance the Old Year out and the New Year in." Old-fashioned Aunt Faith, — who believed most devoutly that "early to bed and early to rise" was the *only* way to be "healthy, wealthy, or wise!" Aunt Faith, who had never quite forgiven our young heroine for having said, at the discreet and positive age of nine, that "she didn't see what her father and mother had called her such an ugly name for. It was a real old-maid's name!" Whereupon, having asked the child what she would have preferred as a substitute, and being answered, "Well, — Clotilda, I guess; or Cleopatra." — Miss Henderson had told her that she was quite welcome to change it for any heathen woman's that she pleased, and the worse behaved perhaps the better. She would n't be so likely to do it any discredit!

Aunt Henderson had a downright and rather extreme fashion of putting things; nevertheless, in her heart she was not unkindly.

So when Faithie, with her fair, fresh face, — a little apprehensive trouble in it for her tardiness, — came in, there was a grim bending of the old lady's brows; but, below, a half-belying twinkle in the eye, that, long as it had looked out sharply and keenly on the things and people of this mixed-up world, found yet a pleasure in anything so young and bright.

"Why, auntie! How do you do?" cried Faith, cunning culprit that she was, taking the "bull by the horns," and holding out her hand. "I wish you a Happy New Year! Good morning, father, and mother! A Happy New Year! I'm sorry I'm so late."

"Wish you a great many," responded the great-aunt, in stereotyped phrase. "It seems to me, though, you've lost the beginning of this one."

"Oh, no!" replied Faithie, gayly. "I had that at the party. We danced the New Year in."

"Humph!" said Aunt Henderson.

Breakfast over, and Mr. Gartney gone to his counting-room, the parlor-girl made her appearance with her mop and tub of hot water, to wash up the silver and china.

"Give me that," said Aunt Henderson, taking a large towel from the girl's arm as she set down her tub upon the sideboard. "You go and find something else to do."

Wherever she might be, — to be sure, her round of visiting was not a large one, — Aunt Henderson never let any one else wash up breakfast-cups.

This quiet arming of **herself, with** mop and towel, stirred up everybody else to duty. Her niece-in-law laughed, withdrew her feet **from the** comfortable fender, and departed to the kitchen to give her household orders for the day. Faith **removed** cups, glasses, forks, **and spoons from** the table to the sideboard, while the maid, **returning with a** tray, carried off to the lower regions the larger dishes, and the remnants of the meal.

"I have n't told you yet, Elizabeth, what I came to **town for,"** said **Aunt Faith, when** Mrs. Gartney came **back into the** breakfast-room. **"I'm going to** hunt **up a girl."**

"A girl, aunt! Why, what has become of Prudence?"

"Mrs. Pelatiah Trowe. That's what's become of her. More fool she."

"But **why in** the world do you come to the **city for a** servant? It**'s** the **worst** possible place. **Nineteen out of** twenty are utterly good for nothing."

"I**'m going to** look out for the **twentieth."**

"But are n't there girls enough in Kinnicutt who would be glad to step into Prue's place?"

"Of course there are. Plenty. But they're all well enough off where they are. When I have a chance to give **away,** I want to give it to somebody that needs it."

"I**'m** afraid you'll hardly find any efficient girl **who** will appreciate the chance **of** going twenty miles into **the** country."

"I don't want an efficient **girl.** I'm efficient myself, and that's **enough."**

"Going to *train* another, at your **time of life, aunt?"** **asked** Mrs. Gartney, in surprise.

"I suppose I must either train a girl, **or let her train**

me; and, at my time of life, I don't feel to stand in need of that."

"How shall I go to work to inquire?" resumed Aunt Henderson, after a pause.

"Well, there are the Homes, and the Offices, and the Ministers at Large. At a Home, they would probably recommend you somebody they've made up their minds to put out to service, and she might or might not be such an one as would suit you. Then at the Offices, you'll see all sorts, and mostly poor ones."

"I'll try an Office, first," interrupted Miss Henderson. "I *want* to see all sorts. Faith, you'll go with me, by-and-by, won't you, and help me find the way?"

Faith, seated at a little writing-table at the farther end of the room, busied in copying into her album, in a clear, neat, but rather stiff school-girl's hand, the oracle of the night before, did not at once notice that she was addressed.

"Faith, child! don't you hear?"

"Oh, yes, aunt. What is it?"

"I want you to go to a what-d'ye-call-it office with me, to-day."

"An intelligence office," explained her mother. "Aunt Faith wants to find a girl."

"'*Lucus a non lucendo,*'" quoted Faith, rather wittily, from her little stock of Latin. "Stupidity offices, *I* should call them, from the specimens they send out."

"Hold your tongue, chit! Don't talk Latin to me!" growled Aunt Henderson.

"What are you writing?" she asked, shortly after, when Mrs. Gartney had again left her and Faith to each other. "Letters, or Latin?"

Faith colored, and laughed.

"Only a fortune that was told me last night," she replied.

"Oh! 'A little husband,' I suppose, 'no bigger than my thumb; put him in a pint pot, and there bid him drum.'"

"No," said Faith, half seriously, and half teased out of her seriousness. "It's nothing of that sort. At least," she added, glancing over the lines again, "I don't think it means anything like that."

And Faith laid down the book, and went up stairs for a word with her mother.

Aunt Henderson, who had been brought up in times when all the doings of young girls were strictly supervised, and who had no high-flown scruples, because she had no mean motives, deliberately walked over and fetched the elegant little volume from the table, reseated herself in her arm-chair, — felt for her glasses, and set them carefully upon her nose, — and, as her grand-niece returned, was just finishing her perusal of the freshly-inscribed lines.

"Humph! A good fortune. Only you've got to earn it."

"Yes," said Faith, quite gravely. "And I don't see how. There don't seem to be much that I can do."

"Just take hold of the first thing that comes in your way. If the Lord's got anything bigger to give you, he'll see to it. There's your mother's mending-basket brimful of stockings."

Faith couldn't help laughing. Presently she grew grave again.

"Aunt Henderson," said she, abruptly, "I wish something would happen to me. I get tired of living sometimes. Things don't seem worth while."

Aunt Henderson bent her head slightly, and opened her eyes wide over the tops of her glasses.

"Don't say that again," said she. "Things happen fast enough. **Don't you dare** to tempt Providence."

"Providence won't be tempted, nor misunderstand," **replied** Faith, an undertone of reverence qualifying her girlish repartee. "He knows just what I mean."

"**She's a** queer child." said Aunt Faith to herself, afterwards, thinking over the brief conversation. "She'll be something or nothing, I always said. I used to think 't would **be nothing.**"

CHAPTER IV.

GLORY McWHIRK.

> There's beauty waiting to be born,
>   And harmony that makes no sound;
> And bear we ever, unawares,
>   A glory that hath not been crowned.

SHALL I try to give you a glimpse of quite another young life than Faith Gartney's? One looking also vaguely, wonderingly, for "something to happen," — that indefinite "something" which lies in everybody's future, which may never arrive, and yet which any hour may bring?

Very little likelihood there has ever seemed for any great joy to get into such a life as this has been, that began, or at least has its earliest memory and association, in the old poor-house at Stonebury.

A child she was, of five years, when she was taken in there with her old, crippled grandmother.

Peter McWhirk was picked up dead, from the gravelled drive of a gentleman's place, where he had been trimming the high trees that shaded it. An unsound limb — a heedless movement — and Peter went straight down, thirty feet, and out of life. Out of life, where he had a trim, comfortable young wife, — one happy little child, for whom skies were as blue, and grass as green, and buttercups as golden as for the little heiress of Elm Hill, who was riding over the lawn in her basket-wagon, when Peter met his death there, — the hope, also, of another that was to come.

Rosa McWhirk and her baby of a day old were buried the week after, together; and then there was nothing left for Glory and her helpless grandmother but the poor-house as a present refuge; and to the one death, that ends all, and to the other a life of rough and unremitting work to look to for by-and-by.

When Glory came into this world where wants begin with the first breath, and go on thickening around us, and pressing upon us until the last one is supplied to us — a grave — she wanted, first of all, a name.

"Sure what'll I call the baby?" said the proud young mother to the ladies from the white corner house, where she had served four faithful years of her maidenhood, and who came down at once with comforts and congratulations. "They've sint for the praist, an' I've niver bethought of a name. I made so certain 't would be a boy!"

"What a funny bit of a thing it is!" cried the younger of the two visitors, turning back the bed-clothes a little from the tiny, red, puckered face, with short, sandy-colored hair standing up about the temples like a fuzz-ball.

"I'd call her Glory. There's a halo round her head like the saints in the pictures."

"Sure, that's jist like yersilf, Miss Mattie!" exclaimed Rosa, with a faint, merry little laugh. "An' quare enough. I knew a lady once't of the very name, in the ould country. Miss Gloriana O'Dowd she was; an' the beauty o' County Kerry. My Lady Kinawley, she came to be. 'Deed, but I'd like to do it, for the ould times, an' for you thinkin' of it! I'll ask Peter, anyhow!"

And so Glory got her name; and Mattie Hyde, who gave

her that, gave her **many** another **thing that** was no less a giving to the mother also, before she was two years old Then Mrs. **Hyde and** the young lady, having first let the corner house, went away to **Europe to stay for years;** and **when a** box **of** tokens from the far, foreign lands came back to Stonebury awhile **after, there** was a **grand shawl** for Rosa, and a pretty braided frock for the baby, and a rosary **that** Glory keeps to this hour, that had been blessed by the Pope. That was the last. Mattie and her mother sailed out upon the Mediterranean one day from the bright coast **of** France for a far eastern port, to see the Holy Land. **God's** Holy **Land they** did see, though they never touched those Syrian shores, **or** climbed the hills about Jerusalem.

Glory remembered, — for the most part dimly, for some special **points** distinctly, — **her** child-life of three years in Stonebury poor-house. How her grandmother and an old countrywoman from the same county "at home" sat knitting and crooning together in a sunny corner of the common room in winter, or out under the stoop in summer; how she rolled down the green bank behind the **house;** and, when **she grew** big **enough** to be trusted with a knife, was sent out **to dig** dandelions in the spring, and how an older girl went **with** her round the village, and sold them from house to house. How, at last, her old grandmother died, and **was** buried; and how a woman of the village, who had used to buy her dandelions, found a place for her with a relative of her own, in the ten-mile distant city, **who** took **Glory to** "bring up," — "seeing," **as she** said, "**there was nobody** belonging to **her to interfere."**

Was there a day, after that, that did **not** leave its searing **impress upon heart** and memory, **of the** life that was given, in its every young pulse and breath, to sordid toil for others, and to which it seemed nobody on earth owed aught of care or service in return?

Clothed and fed, to be sure, she was; that is, she neither starved, nor went naked; but she was barely covered and nourished as she must be,—as any beast of burden must be,—to do its owner's work.

It was a close little house,—one of those houses where they have fried dinners so often that the smell never gets out,—in Budd Street,—a street of a single side, wedged in between the back yards of more pretentious mansions that stood on fair parallel avenues sloping down from a hill-top to the water-side, that Mrs. Grubbling lived.

Here Glory McWhirk, from eight years old to nearly fifteen, scoured knives and brasses, tended door-bell, set tables, washed dishes, and minded the baby; whom, at her peril, she must "keep pacified,"—*i. e.*, amused and content, while its mother was otherwise busy. For her, poor child, —baby that she still, almost, was herself,—who amused, or contented her? There are humans with whom amusement and content have nothing to do. What will you? The world must go on.

Glory curled the baby's hair, and made him "look pretty." Mrs. Grubbling cut her little handmaid's short to save trouble; so that the very determined yellow locks which, under more favoring circumstances of place and fortune, might have been trained into lovely golden curls like the child's who lived in the tall house opposite the Grubblings' door, and who came, sometimes, to the long back-parlor windows, and unconsciously shone into poor, unknown Glory's life, who watched for her as for a vision,—these locks, I say, stood up continually in their restless reaching after the fairer destiny that had been meant for them, in the old fuzz-ball fashion; and Glory grew more and more to justify her name.

Do you think she did n't know what beauty was, — this child who never had a new or pretty garment, but who wore frocks " fadged up" out of old, faded breadths of her mistress's dresses, and bonnets with brims cut off and topknots taken down, and coarse shoes, and stockings cut out of the legs of those whereof Mrs. Grubbling had worn out the extremities? Do you think she did n't feel the difference, and that it was n't this that made her shuffle along so with her toes in, when she sped along the streets upon her manifold errands, and met gentle-people's children laughing and dancing and skipping their hoops upon the sidewalks?

I tell you the soul shapes to itself a life, whether the outer life conform to it or not. What else is imagination given for?

Did you ever think how strange it is that among the millions of human experiences, — out of all the numberless combinations of circumstance and incident that make the different lives of men and women, — now unfolding their shifting webs upon this earth, you yourself, and that without voluntary choice, have just one, perhaps but a very dull and meagre one, allotted you? With all the divine capacity you find in yourself to enter into and comprehend a life quite other than and foreign to the daily reality of your own, and to feel how it would be to you if it might become tangible and actual, did you ever question why it is that you are kept out of it, and of all else save the one small and insufficient history? The very consciousness of such capacity answers you why.

"No man lives to himself."

Out of all lives, actual and possible, each one of us appropriates continually into his own. This is a world of hints only, out of which every soul seizes to itself what it needs.

This girl, uncherished, repressed in every natural longing to be and to have, took in all the more of what was possible; for God had given her this glorious insight, this imagination, wherewith we fill up life's scanty outline, and grasp at all that might be, or that elsewhere, is. In her, as in us all, it was often — nay, daily — a discontent; yet a noble discontent, and curbed with a grand, unconscious patience. She scoured her knives; she shuffled along the streets on hasty errands; she went up and down the house in her small menial duties; she put on and off her coarse, repulsive clothing; she uttered herself in her common, ignorant forms of speech; she showed only as a poor, low, little Irish girl with red hair and staring, wondering eyes, and awkward movements, and a frightened fashion of getting into everybody's way; and yet, behind all this, there was another life that went on in a hidden beauty that you and I cannot fathom, save only as God gives the like, inwardly, to ourselves.

There are persons who have an "impediment of speech," so that the thoughts that shape themselves in the brain are smothered there, and can never be born in fitting utterance. There are many who have an impediment of life. A something wanting — withheld — that hinders the inner existence from flowering out into visible fact and deed. Flowers it not somewhere? Is there not building somewhere, all the while, that which God hath reserved for them from the foundation of the world?

When Glory's mistress cut her hair, there were always

tears and rebellion. **It was** her one, eager, passionate long-**ing, in those childish days, that** these locks of hers should be let to grow. She thought she could almost bear anything else, if **only this** stiff, unseemly **crop might** lengthen out into waves and ringlets that should toss in the wind like the carefully kempt tresses of children she met in **the** streets. She imagined it would be a complete and utter happiness just once to feel it falling in its wealth about her shoulders or dropping against her cheeks; and to be able to **look** at it **with her** eyes, **and twist her fingers in it at** the ends. And **so,** when it got to be its longest, and began to make itself troublesome **about her** forehead, **and** to peep below her shabby bonnet in **her neck,** she had a brief season of wonderful enjoyment **in it.** Then she could "make believe" it **had** really grown out; **and** the comfort she took in "going through the motions," — pretending to tuck behind her ears what scarcely touched their tips, and tossing **her head continually,** to throw back imaginary masses of curls, was truly indescribable, and such as I **could not begin to make you** understand.

"**Half-witted monkey!**" Mrs. Grubbling would ejacu-**late, contemptuously,** seeing, **with** what she conceived marvellous penetration, the half of her little servant's thought, and so pronouncing from her own half-wit. Then the great shears came out, and the instinct of grace and beauty in the child was pitilessly outraged, and her soul mutilated, as it were, in every clip of the inexorable shears.

Glory lived half her life in that back parlor of the Pembertons. The little golden-haired vision went and came; it sat by its mother's **side in** the firelight, before the curtains were drawn down; **it had a** party, now and then, of other little radiances like unto itself: and Glory, "tending baby" in Mrs. Grubbling's fusty chamber, watched their games through the long, large-paned windows, and reproduced them next day, when the chores were done, and she and baby could go up stairs and "have a party;" bidding thereto, on his solemn promise of good behavior, "Bubby," otherwise Master Herbert Clarence Grubbling; ranging, also, six chairs, to represent or to accommodate invisible "company."

And, for me, I can't help thinking there may have been company there.

She was always glad — poor Glory — when the spring-time came. The water running in the gutters; the blades of grass and tufts of chickweed that grew under the walls; the soft, damp air that betokened the mollifying season, — these touched her with a delight, and gave her a sense of joy and beauty that might have been no deeper or keener if it had come to her through the ministries of great rivers, and green meadows, and all the wide breeze and blue of the circling sky.

She took Bubby and Baby down to the Common, of a May-day, to see the processions and the paper-crowned queens; and stood there in her stained and drabbled dress, with the big year-and-a-half-old baby in her arms, and so quite at the mercy of Master Herbert Clarence, who defiantly skipped off down the avenues, and almost out of her sight, — she looking after him in helpless dismay, lest he should get a splash or a tumble, or be altogether lost; and then what would the mistress say? Standing there so, — the troops of children in their holiday trim passing close beside her, — her young heart turned bitter for a moment, as it sometimes would; and her one utterance of all that swelled her martyr-soul broke forth, —

"Laws a me! Sech lots of good times in the world, and I aint in 'em!"

And then she meekly turned off homeward, lugging the baby in her arms, who peremptorily declined her enticing suggestion when they passed the Common gates, that he should get down, and "go patty, patty, on the sidewalk;" Master Herbert, who had in the midst of his most reckless escapades kept one eye carefully upon her movements, racing after her, vociferating that he would "go right and tell his ma how Glory ran away from him"

Yet, that afternoon, when Mrs. Grubbling went out shopping, and left her to her own devices with the children, how jubilantly she trained the battered chairs in line, and put herself at the head, with Bubby's scarlet tippet wreathed about her upstart locks, and made a May Day!

I say, she had the soul and essence of the very life she seemed to miss.

There were shabby children's books about the Grubbling domicile, that had been the older child's — Cornelia's — and had descended to Master Herbert, while yet his only pastime in them was to scrawl them full of pencil-marks, and tear them into tatters. These, one by one, Glory rescued, and hid away, and fed upon, piecemeal, in secret. She could read, at least, — this poor, denied unfortunate. Peter McWhirk had taught his child her letters in happy, humble Sundays and holidays long ago; and Mrs. Grubbling had begun by sending her to a primary school for awhile, irregularly, when she could be spared; and when she had n't just torn her frock, or worn out her shoes, or it did n't rain, or she had n't been sent of an errand and come back too late, — which reasons, with a multitude of others, constantly recurring, reduced the school-days in the year to a number whose smallness Mrs. Grubbling would have indignantly disputed, had it been calculated and set before her; she being one of those not uncommon persons who regard a duty continually evaded as one continually performed, it being necessarily just as much on their minds; till, at last, Herbert had a winter's illness, and in summer it wasn't worth while, and the winter after, baby came, so that of course she couldn't be spared at all; and it seemed little likely now that she ever again would be. But she kept her spelling-book, and read over and over what she knew, and groped her way slowly into more, till she promoted herself from that to "Mother Goose," — from "Mother Goose" to "Fables for the Nursery," — and now, her ever fresh and unfailing feast was the "Child's Own Book of Fairy Tales," and an odd volume of the "Parents' Assistant." She picked out, slowly, the gist of these, with a lame and uncertain interpretation. She lived for weeks with Beauty and the Beast, — with Cinderella, — with the good girl who worked for the witch, and shook her feather-bed every morning; till at last, given leave to go home and see her mother, the gold and silver shower came down about her, departing at the back-door. Perhaps she should get her pay, sometime, and go home and see her mother.

Meanwhile, she identified herself with—lost herself utterly in—these imaginary lives. She was, for the time, Cinderella; she was Beauty; she was above all, the Fair One with Golden Locks; she was Simple Susan going to be May Queen; she dwelt in the old Castle of Rossmore, with the Irish Orphans. The little Grubbling house in Budd Street was peopled all **through, in** every corner, with her fancies. Don't tell me **she** had nothing but her niggardly outside living there.

And the wonder began to come **up in her mind, as it** did in Faith Gartney's, **whether and when** " something might **happen** " to her.

CHAPTER V.

SOMETHING HAPPENS.

> Athirst! athirst! The sandy soil
>   Bears no glad trace of leaf or tree;
> No grass-blade sigheth to the heaven
>   Its little drop of ecstasy.
>
> Yet other fields are spreading wide
>   Green bosoms to the bounteous sun;
> And palms and cedars shall sublime
>   Their rapture for thee, — waiting one!

"Take us down to see the apple-woman," said Master Herbert, going out with Glory and the baby one day when his school did n't keep, and Mrs. Grubbling had a headache, and wanted to get them all off out of the way.

Bridget Foye sat at her apple-stand in the cheery morning sunlight, red checks and russets ranged fair and tempting before her, and a pile of roasted pea-nuts, and one of delicate molasses-candy, such as nobody but she knew how to make, at either end of the board.

Bridget Foye was the tidiest, kindliest, merriest apple-woman in all Mishaumok. Everybody whose daily path lay across that southeast corner of the Common, knew her well, and had a smile, and perhaps a penny for her; and got a smile and a God-bless-you, and, for the penny, a rosy or a golden apple, or some of her crisp candy in return.

Glory and the baby, sitting down to rest on one of the

benches close by, as their habit was, had one day made a nearer acquaintance with blithe Bridget. I think it began with Glory — who held the baby up to see the passing show of a portion of a menagerie in the street, and heard two girls, stopping just before her to look, likewise, say they'd go and see it perform next day, — uttering something of her old soliloquy about "good times," and why she "warn't ever in any of 'em." However it was, Mrs. Foye, in her buxom cheeriness, was drawn to give some of it forth to the uncouth-looking, companionless girl, and not only began a chat with her, after the momentary stir in the street was over, and she had settled herself upon her stool, and leaning her back against a tree, set vigorously to work again at knitting a stout blue yarn stocking, but also treated Bubby and Baby to some bits of her sweet merchandise, and told them about the bears and the monkeys that had gone by, shut up in the gay, red-and-yellow-painted wagons.

It was between her busy times of trade. The buzz of bigger trade and toil had long ago begun "down town," and the last tardy straggler had passed by, on his way to the day's labor of hand or brain. Children were all in school. Here, in the midst of the great, bustling city, was a green hush and quiet; and from this until noon Bridget had but chance and scattering custom. Nursemaids and babies did n't afford her much. Besides, they kept, for the most part, to the upper walks. There are fashions among nursemaids as among their betters.

Glory had no acquaintance among the smart damsels who perambulated certain exclusive localities, in charge of elegant little carriages heaped up inside with lace, and feathers, and embroideries, in the midst of which peeped out with difficulty the wee human face which served as nucleus and excuse for all the show.

So it became, after this first opening, Glory's chief pleasure to get out with the children now and then, of a sunny day, and sit here on the bench by Bridget Foye, and hear her talk, and tell her, confidentially, some of her small, incessant troubles. It was one more life to draw from, — a hearty, bright, and wholesome life, beside. She had, at last, in this great, tumultuous, indifferent city, a friendship and a resource of her own.

But there was a certain fair spot of delicate honor in Glory's nature that would not let her bring Bubby and Baby in any apparent hope of what they might get, gratuitously, into their mouths. She laid it down, a rule, with Master Herbert, that he was not to go to the apple-stand with her unless he had first put by a penny for a purchase. And so unflinchingly she adhered to this determination, that sometimes weeks went by, — hard, weary weeks, without a bit of pleasantness for her; weeks of sore pining for a morsel of heart-food, — before she was free of her own conscience to go and take it.

Bridget told stories to Herbert, — strange, nonsensical fables, to be sure, — stuff that many an overwise mother, bringing up her children by hard rule and theory, might have utterly forbidden as harmful trash, — yet that never put an evil into his heart, nor crowded, I dare to say, a better thought out of his brain. Glory liked the stories as well, almost, as the child. One moral always ran through them all. Troubles always, somehow, came to an end; good creatures and children got safe out of them all, and lived happy ever after; and the fierce, and cunning, and bad, — the wolves, and foxes, and witches, — trapped themselves in their own wickednesses, and came to deplorable ends.

"Tell us about the little red **hen**," said Herbert, paying his money, and munching his candy.

"An' thin ye'll trundle yer hoop out to the big tree, an' lave Glory an' me our lane for a minute?"

"Faith, an' I will that," said the boy, — aping, ambitiously, the racy Irish accent.

"Well, thin, there was once't upon a time, away off in the ould country, livin' all her lane in the woods, in a wee bit iv a house be herself, a little rid hin. Nice an' quite she was, and nivir did no kind o' harrum in her life. An' there lived out over the hill, in a din o' the rocks, a crafty ould felly iv a fox. An' this same ould villain iv a fox, he laid awake o' nights, and he prowled round shly iv a daytime, thinkin' always so busy how he'd git the little rid hin, an' carry her home an' bile her up for his shupper. But the wise little rid hin nivir went intil her bit iv a house, but she locked the door afther her, an' pit the kay in her pocket. So the ould rashkill iv a fox, he watched, an' he prowled, an' he laid awake nights, till he came all to skin an' bone, on' sorra a ha'porth o' the little rid hin could he git at. But at lasht there came a shcame intil his wicked ould head, an' he tuk a big bag one mornin', over his shouldher, and he says till his mother, says he, 'Mother, have the pot all bilin' agin' I come home, for I'll bring the little rid hin tonight for our shupper.' An' away he wint, over the hill, an' came craping shly and soft through the woods to where the little rid hin lived in her shnug bit iv a house. An' shure, jist at the very minute that he got along, out comes the little rid hin out iv the door, to pick up shticks to bile her tay-kettle. 'Begorra, now, but I'll have yees,' says the shly ould **fox, and in he** shlips, unbeknownst, intil the house, an' hides behind the door. An' in comes the little rid hin, a minute afther, with her apron full of shticks, an' shuts to the door an' locks it, an' pits the kay in her pocket. An thin she turns round,— an' there shtands the baste iv a fox in the **corner.** Well, thin, what did she do, but jist dhrop **down** her shticks, and fly up in a great fright and **flutter to the big bame acrass inside o' the** roof, where the fox could n't get at her?

"'Ah, ha!' says the ould **fox, 'I'll** soon bring yees down out o' that!' An' he began **to** whirrul round, an' **round,** an' round, fashter an' fashter an' fashter, on the floor, afther his big, bushy **tail,** till the little rid hin got so dizzy **wid** lookin', that she **jist** tumbled down off the bame, and the fox whipped her up and popped her intil his bag, and shtarted off home in a minute. **An' he wint up the wood, an'** down the wood, half the **day** long, with the little rid hin shut up shmotherin' in the bag. Sorra a know **she knowd** where she was, at all, at all. She thought she was all biled an' ate up, an' finished, shure! But, by an' by, she remimbered herself, an' pit her hand in her pocket, and tuk out her little **bright** schissors, **and** shnipped a big hole in the bag behind, an' out she leapt, an' picked up a big shtone an' popped it intil the bag, an' rin aff home, an' locked the door.

" **An'** the fox he tugged away **up over the hill, with** the big shtone at his back thumpin' his shouldhers, thinkin' to himself how heavy **the** little **rid hin was, an' what a fine** shupper he'd have. An' whin he came in sight iv his din **in the** rocks, and shpied his ould mother a watchin' for him at the **door, he** says, ' Mother! have ye the pot bilin'?' An' the ould mother says, 'Sure an' it is; an' have ye the little rid hin?' 'Yes, jist here in me bag. Open the lid o' the pot till I pit her in,' says he.

"An' the ould mother fox she lifted the lid o' the pot, and the rashkill untied the bag, and hild it over the pot o' bilin' wather, an' shuk in the big, heavy shtone. Au' the bilin' wather shplashed up all over the rogue iv a fox, an' his mother, an' shealded them both to death. An' the little rid hin lived safe in her house foriver afther."

"Ah!" breathed Bubby, in intense relief, for perhaps the twentieth time. "Now tell about the girl that went to seek her fortune!"

"Away wid ye!" cried Bridget Foye, "Kape yer promish, an' lave that till ye come back!"

So Herbert and his hoop trundled off to the big tree.

"An' how are yees now, honey?" says Bridget to Glory, a whole catechism of questions in the one inquiry. "Have ye come till any good times yit?"

"Oh, Mrs. Foye," says Glory, "I think I'm tied up tight in the bag, an' I'll never get out, except it's into the hot water!"

"An' havint ye nivir a pair iv schissors in yer pocket?" asks Bridget.

"I don't know," says poor Glory, hopelessly. And just then Master Herbert comes trundling back, and Bridget tells him the story of the girl that went to seek her fortune and came to be a queen.

Glory half thinks that, some day or other, she, too, will start off and seek her fortune.

The next morning, Sunday, — never a holiday, and scarcely a holy day to her, — Glory sits at the front window, with the inevitable baby in her arms.

Mrs. Grubbling is up stairs getting ready for church

After baby has his forenoon drink, and is got off to sleep. — supposing he shall be complaisant, and go, — Glory is to dust up, and set table, and warm the dinner, and be all ready to bring it up when the elder Grubblings shall have returned, a hungered.

Out at the Pembertons' green gate she sees the tidy parlor-maid come, in her smart shawl and new, bright ribbons; holding up her pretty printed mousseline dress with one hand, as she steps down upon the street, and so revealing the white hem of a clean starched skirt; while the other hand is occupied with the little Catholic prayer-book and a folded handkerchief. Actually, gloves on her hands, too. The gate closes with a cord and pulley after her, and somehow the hem of the fresh, outspreading crinoline gets caught in it, as it shuts. So she turns half round, and takes both hands to push it open and release herself. Doing so, something slips from between the folds of her handkerchief, and drops upon the ground. A bright half dollar, which was going to pay some of her little church dues to-day. And she hurries on, never missing it out of her grasp, and is half way down the side street before Glory can set the baby suddenly on the carpet, rush out at the front door, regardless that Mrs. Grubbling's chamber window overlooks her from above, pick up the coin, and overtake her.

"I saw you drop it by the gate," is all she says, as she puts it into Katie Ryan's hand.

Katie stares with surprise, turning round at the touch upon her shoulder, and beholding the strange figure, and the still stranger evidence of honesty and good-will.

"Indeed, and I'm thoroughly obliged to ye," says she, barely in time, for the odd figure is already retreating up the street. "It's the red-headed girl over at Grubblings."

she continues to herself. "Well, anyhow, she's an honest, kind-hearted crature, and I'll not forget it of her."

Glory has made another friend.

"Well, Glory McWhirk, this **is very pretty** doings indeed!" began Mrs. Grubbling, in a high key, which had a certain peculiar ring also of satisfaction in it, at finding fair and obvious reason this time for a hearty fault-finding, — meeting the little handmaiden at the parlor door whither she had hurried down to confront her in her delinquency, — "So this is the way, is it, when my back is turned for a minute? That **poor** baby dumped down on the floor, to crawl up to the hot stove, or do any other horrid thing he likes, while you go flacketting out, bareheaded, into the streets, after a topping jade like that? You can't have any high-flown acquaintances while you live in my house, I tell you now, once and for all. Are you going to take up that baby or not?" Mrs. Grubbling had been thus far effectually heading Glory off, by standing square in the parlor doorway. "Or perhaps, I'd better stay at home and take care of him myself," she added, in a tone of superlative irony, as suggesting an alternative not only utterly absurd and inadmissible, but actually appalling, — as if she had proposed to take off her head, instead of her bonnet, and sacrifice that to the temporary amusement of her child, and the relief of Glory.

Poor Glory, meekly murmuring that it was only to give back some money the girl had dropped, slid past her mistress submissively, like a sentry caught off his post and warned of mortal punishment, and shouldered arms once more; that is, picked up the baby, who, as if taking the cue from his mother, and made conscious of his grievance, had at this moment begun to **cry.**

Mrs. Grubbling, notwithstanding her shaken confidence, put on her gloves, of which she had been sewing up the tips, just now, by the window, when she witnessed Glory's escapade, and departed, leaving the girl to her "pacifying" office, sufficiently secure that it would be fulfilled.

Glory had a good cry of her own first, and then, "killing two birds with one stone," pacified herself and the baby "all under one."

After this, Katie Ryan never came out at the green gate, of a Sunday on the way to church, or of a week-day to run down the little back street of an errand, but she gave a glance up at the Grubblings' windows; and if she caught sight of Glory's illumined head, nodded her own, with its pretty, dark brown locks, quite pleasant and friendly. And between these chance recognitions of Katie's, and the good apple-woman's occasional sympathy, the world began to brighten a little, even for poor Glory.

Still, good times went on, — grand, wonderful good times, — all around her. And she caught distant glimpses, but "was n't in 'em."

One day, as she hurried home from the grocer's with half-a-dozen eggs and two lemons, Katie ran out from the gate, and met her half way down Budd Street.

"I 've been watchin' for ye," said she. "I seen ye go out of an errand, an' I 've been lookin' for ye back. There 's to be a grand party at our house to-morrow night, an' I thought may be ye 'd like to get lave, an' run over to take a peep at it. Put on yer best frock, and make yer hair tidy, an' I 'll see to yer gettin' a good chance."

Poor Glory colored up, as Mrs. Grubbling might have done if the President's wife had bidden her. Not so, either. With a glow of feeling, and an oppression of gratitude, and a humility of delight, that Mrs. Grubbling, under any circumstances whatever, could have known nothing about.

"If I only can," she managed to utter, "and, anyhow, I'm sure I'm thankful to ye a thousand times."

And that night she sat up in her little attic room, after everybody else was in bed, mending, in a poor fashion, a rent in the faded "best frock," and sewing a bit of cotton lace in the neck thereof that she had picked out of the rag-bag, and surreptitiously washed and ironed.

Next morning, she went about her homely tasks with an alacrity that Mrs. Grubbling, knowing nothing of the hope that had been let in upon her dreariness, attributed wholly to the salutary effect of a "good scolding" she had administered the day before. The work she got out of the girl that Thursday forenoon! Never once did Glory leave her scrubbing, or her dusting, or her stove-polishing, to glance from the windows into the street, though the market-boys, and the waiters, and the confectioners' parcels were going in at the Pembertons' gate, and the man from the green-house, even, drove his cart up, filled with beautiful plants for the staircase.

She waited, as in our toils we wait for Heaven, — trusting to the joy that was to come.

After dinner, she spoke, with fear and trembling. Her lips turned quite white with anxiety as she stood before Mrs. Grubbling with the baby in her arms.

The lady had been far from unobservant, on her own part, all the day, of what was going on upon her richer neighbor's premises. Her spirit was not attuned to gentle charity just then. Her mood was not that of gracious compliance. Let us be pitiful to her, also. She, too, saw "good times" going on, and felt, bitterly, that she "wasn't in 'em."

"Please, mum," says Glory, tremulously, "Katie Ryan asked me over for a little while to-night to look at the party."

Mrs. Grubbling actually felt a jealousy, as if her poor, untutored handmaid were taking precedence of herself.

"What party?" she snapped, — nothing else occurring to her, in the sudden shock, to say.

"At the Pembertons', mum. I thought you knew about it."

"And what if I do? Maybe I 'm going, myself."

Glory opened her eyes wide in mingled consternation and surprise.

"I did n't think you was, mum, But if you is —"

"You 're willing, I suppose," retorted her mistress, laughing, in a bitter way. "I 'm very much obliged. But I 'm going out to-night, anyhow, whether it 's there or not, and you can't be spared. Besides, you need n't think you 're going to begin with going out evenings yet awhile. At your age! A pretty thing! There, — go along, and don 't bother me."

Glory went along; and only the baby — of mortal listeners — heard the suffering cry that went up from her poor, pinched, and chilled, and disappointed heart.

"Oh, baby, baby! it was *too* good a time! I'd ought to a knowed I could n't be in it!"

Mr. and Mrs. Grubbling did go out that night. Whether it was a sudden thought, suggested by Glory's application, or a previous resolve adopted by the mistress that she might be out of the way of the tantalizing merriment opposite, I will not undertake to say. It is sufficient that there was a benefit play at one of the secondary theatres, and that Mrs. Grubbling there forgot her jealousies, and the pangs, so far as she had at all understood them, of Glory McWhirk.

So safe as she felt, having bidden her stay, that Glory would be faithful at her post, and " mind" her children well!

Only a stone's throw from those brightly-lighted windows of the Pembertons'. Their superfluous radiance pouring out lavishly across the narrow street, searched even through the dim panes behind which Glory sat, resting her tired arms, after tucking away their ordinary burden in his crib, and answering Herbert's wearisome questions, who from his trundle-bed kept asking, ceaselessly, —

"What are they doing now? Can't you see, Glory?"

"Hush, hush!" said Glory, breathlessly, as a burst of brilliant melody floated over to her ear. "They're making music now. Don't you hear?"

"No. How can I, with my head in the pillow? I'm coming there to sit with you, Glory." And the boy scrambled from his bed to the window.

"No, no! you'll ketch cold. Besides, you'd oughter go to sleep. Well, — only for a little bit of a minute, then," as Herbert persisted, and climbing upon her lap, flattened his face against the window-pane, to look as closely as might be at the show.

Glory gathered up her skirt about his shoulders and held him for awhile, begging him uneasily, over and over, to "be a good boy, and go back to bed." No; he would n't be a good boy, and he would n't go back to bed, till the music paused. Then, by dint of promising that if it began again she would open the window a "teenty little crack," so that he might hear it better, she coaxed him to the point of yielding, and tucked him, chilly, yet half unwilling, in the trundle.

Back again, to look and listen. And, oh, wonderful and unexpected fortune! A beneficent hand has drawn up the white linen shade at one of the back parlor windows to slide the sash a little from the top. It was Katie, whom her young mistress, standing with her partner at that corner of the room, had called in from the hall to do it.

"No, no," whispered the young lady, hastily, as her companion moved to render her the service she desired, "let Katie come in. She'll get such a good look down the room at the dancers." There was no abated admiration in the young man's eye, as he turned back to her side, and allowed her kindly intention to be fulfilled.

Did Katie surmise, in her turn, with the freemasonry of her class, how it was with her humble friend over the way,— that she couldn't get let out for the evening, and that she would be sure to be looking and listening from her old post opposite? However it was, the linen shade was not lowered again, and there between the lace and crimson curtains stood revealed the graceful young figure of Edith Pemberton, in her floating ball robes, with the wreath of morning-glories in her hair.

"Oh, my sakes and sorrows! Aint she just like a princess? Aint it a splendid time? And I come so near to be in it! But I aint; and I s'pose I shan't ever get a chance again. Maybe Katie'd get me over of a common work-day though, sometime, to help her a bit or so. Wouldn't I be glad to?"

"Oh, for gracious, child! Don't ever come here again You'll catch your death. You'll have the croup and whooping-cough, and everything to-morrow." This to Herbert, who had of course tumbled out of bed again at Glory's first rapturous exclamation.

"No, I won't!" cried the boy, rebelliously; "I'll stay as long as I like. And I'll tell my ma how you was a wantin' to go away and be the Pembertons' girl. Won't she lamm you when she hears that?"

"You can tell wicked lies if you want to, Master Herbert; but you know I never said such a word, nor ever thought of it. Of course I could n't if I wanted to ever so bad."

"Could n't live there? I guess not. Think they'd have a girl like you? What a lookin' you'd be, a-comin' to the front door answerin' the bell!"

"Now, Master Herbert," implored Glory, magnanimously ignoring the personal taunt, and intent only on the health and safety of the malicious little scapegrace, who I believe would rather have caught a horrible cold than not, if only Glory might bear the blame, and he be kept in from school and have the monopoly of her services to "keep him pacified" — "do just go back to bed with you, like a good boy, and I'll make a tent over the baby, and open a teenty crack of the windy. The music's beginnin' again."

Here the door bell rang suddenly and sharply, and Master Herbert fancying, as did Glory, that it was his mother come back, scrambled into his bed again and covered himself up, while the girl ran down to answer the summons.

It was Katie Ryan, with cakes and sweetmeats in her hands.

"I've jist rin in to fetch ye these. Miss Edith gave 'em me, so ye need n't be feared. I knows ye 're sich an honest one. An' it's a tearin' shame, if ever there was, that ye could n't come over for a bit of diversion. Why don't ye quit this?"

"Oh, hush!" whispered Glory, with a gesture up the

staircase, where she had just left the little pitcher with tearfully long ears. "And thank you kindly, over and over, I'm sure. It's real good o' you to think o' me so — oh!" And Glory couldn't say anything more for a quick little sob that came in her throat, and caught the last word up into a spasm.

"Pooh! it's just nothing at all. I'd do something better nor that if I had the chance; an' I'd advise ye to get out o' this if ye can. Good-bye. I've set the parlor windy open, an' the shade's up. I knew it would jist be a convenience."

Katie skipped over the street, that was scarcely more than a gutter, and disappeared through the green gate.

Glory ran up the back stairs to the top of the house, and hid away the sweet things in her own room to "make a party" with next day. And then she went down and tented over the crib with an old woolen shawl, and set a high-backed rocking-chair to keep the draft from Herbert, and opened the window "a teenty crack," according to promise. In five minutes the slight freshening of the air and the soothing of the music had sent the boy to sleep, and watchful Glory closed the window and set things in their ordinary arrangement once more.

Next morning Herbert made hoarse complaint, and was kept in from school.

"What did you let him do, Glory, to catch such a cold?" asked Mrs. Grubbling, who assumed for granted, whatever was amiss, that Glory must have done, or let be done, or left undone something.

"Nothing, mum, only he would get out of bed to hear the music," replied the girl.

"Well, you opened the window, you know you did, and

Katie Ryan came over and kept the front door open. And you said how you wished you could go over there and do their chores. I told you I'd tell."

"It's wicked lies, mum," burst out Glory, indignant "I never said no such thing."

"Do you dare to tell him he lies, right before my face, you good-for-nothing girl?" shrieked the exasperated mother. "Where do you expect to go to?"

"I don't expect to go nowheres, mum; and I wouldn't say it was lies if he didn't tell what wasn't true."

"How should such a thing come into his head if you didn't say it? Who do you suppose I'd believe first?"

"There's many things comes into his head," answered Glory, stoutly and simply, "and I think you'd oughter believe me first, when I never told you a lie in my life, and you did ketch Master Herbert fibbing, jist the other day, but."

Somehow, Glory had grown strangely bold in her own behalf since she had come to feel there was a bit of sympathy somewhere for her in the world.

"I know now where he learns it," retorted the mistress, with persistent and angry injustice.

Glory's face blazed up, and she took an involuntary step to the woman's side at the stinging and warrantless accusation.

"You don't mean that, mum, and you'd oughter take it back," said she, excited beyond all fear and habit of submission.

Mrs. Grubbling raised her hand, passionately, and struck the girl upon the cheek.

"I mean *that*, then, for your impudence! Don't answer me up again!"

"No, mum," said Glory, in a low, strange tone; quite white now, except where the vindictive fingers had left their crimson streaks. And she went off out of the room without another word.

Over the knife-board she revolved her wrongs, and sharpened at length the keen edge of desperate resolution.

"Please, mum," said she, in the old form of address, but with quite a new manner, that, in the little dependant of less than fifteen, startled the hard mistress, as she recognized it, "I aint noways bound to you, am I?"

She propounded her question, stopping short in her return toward the china-closet through the sitting-room, and confronting the enemy with both hands full of knives and forks that bristled out before her like a concentrated charge of bayonets.

"Bound? What do you mean?" parried Mrs. Grubbling, dimly foreshadowing to herself what it would be if Glory should break loose, and go.

"To stay, mum, and you to keep me, till I'm growed up," answered Glory, briefly.

"There's no binding about it," replied the mistress. "Of course I wouldn't be held to anything of that sort. I shan't keep you any longer than you behave yourself."

"Then if you please, mum, I think I'll go," said Glory. And she burst into a passion of tears, which she wiped first with the back of one hand, and then with the other, — the bright steel blades and tines flashing up and down dangerously about her head, like lightnings about a rain cloud.

"Humph! Where?" asked Mrs. Grubbling, sarcastically.

"I don't know, yet," said Glory, the sarcasm drying her tears, as she moved on to the closet and deposited her knives and forks in the tray. "I 'spose I can go to a office."

"**And** where'll you get your meals and your lodgings till you find a place?" The cat thought she had her paw on the mouse, now, and could play with her as securely and cruelly as she pleased.

"If you go away at all," continued **Mrs. Grubbling, with** what she deemed a finishing stroke of policy, "you go straight off. I'll have no dancing back and forth to offices from here."

"Do you mean right off, this minute?" asked Glory, **aghast.**

"**Yes, just** that. Pack up and go, or else let me hear no more about it."

The next thing in Glory's programme of duty was to lay the table for dinner. But she went out of the room, **and** slowly off, up stairs.

Pretty soon she came down again, with her eyes very swelled and tearful, and her shabby shawl and bonnet on.

"I'm going, mum," said she, as **one** resolved to face calmly whatever might befall. "**I did** n't mean it to be sudden, **but it are**. And I would n't **never a** gone, if I'd a **thought anybody cared** for me the leastest bit that ever **was**. I would n't mind bein' worked and put upon, and not havin' any good times; but when people hates me, and goes to say I does n't tell the truth,"— here Glory broke down, and the tears poured over her stained cheeks again, and she essayed once more instinctively to dry them, which reminded her that her hands again were full.

"It's some goodies — from the party, mum," — she struggled to say between short breaths and sobs, "that Katie Ryan give me, — an' I kept — to make a party — for the children, with — to-day, mum, — when the chores **was** done, — and I'll leave 'em — for 'em, — if you please."

Glory laid her coals of fire upon the table as she spoke. Master Herbert eyed them, as one utterly unconscious of a scorch.

"I 'spose I might come back and get my bundle," said Glory, standing still in the hope of one last kindly or relenting word.

"Oh, yes, if you get a place," said her mistress, dryly, affecting to treat the whole affair as a childish, though unwonted burst of petulance; and making sure that a few hours would see Glory back, subdued, discouraged, penitent, and ready to bear the double task of to-morrow that should make up for the rebellion and lost time of to-day.

But Glory, not daring, unbidden, even to kiss the baby, went steadily and sorrowfully out into the street, and drew the door behind her, that shut with a catch-lock, and fastened her out into the wide world.

Not stopping to think, she hurried on, up Budd and down Branch Street, and across the green common-path to the apple-stand and Bridget Foye.

"I've done it! I've gone! And I don't know what to do, nor where to go to!"

"Arrah, poor little rid hin! So, ye 've found yer schissors, have ye, an' let yersel' loose out o' the bag? Well, it 's I that is glad, though I would n't pit ye up till it," says Bridget Foye, washing her hands in innocency.

Poor little red hen. She had cut a hole, and jumped out of the bag, to be sure; but here she was, "all alone by nerself" once more, and the foxes — Want and Cruelty — ravening after her all through the great, dreary wood!

This day, at least, passed comfortably enough, however, although with an undertone of sadness, — in the sunshine, by Bridget's apple-stand, watching the gay passers-by, and shaping some humble hopes and plans for the future. For dinner, she shared Mrs. Foye's plain bread and cheese, and made a dessert of an apple and a handful of peanuts. At night Bridget took her home and gave her shelter, and the next day she started her off with a " God-bless-ye and good-luck-till-ye," in the charge of an older girl who lodged in the same building, and who was also " out after a place."

CHAPTER VI.

AUNT HENDERSON'S GIRL-HUNT.

> "Black spirits and white,
> Red spirits and gray;
> Mingle, mingle, mingle,
> You that mingle may."
>
> MACBETH.

It was a small, close, dark room, — Mrs. Griggs's Intelligence Office, — a little counter and show-case dividing off its farther end, making a sanctum for Mrs. Griggs, who combined a little of the tape-and-button business with her more lucrative occupation, and who sat here in immovable and rheumatic ponderosity, dependent for whatever involved locomotion on the rather alarming alacrity of an impish-looking grand-daughter who, just at the moment whereof I write, is tearing in at the street door, and elbowing her way through the throng of applicants for places and servants, quite regardless of the expression of horror and astonishment she has called forth on the face of a severe-looking, elderly lady, who, by her impetuous onset, has been rudely thrust back into the very arms of a fat, unsavory cook with whom she had a minute before been quite unwillingly set to confer by the high-priestess of the place, and who had almost equally relieved and exasperated her, by remarking, as she glanced over her respectable but somewhat unstylish figure and dress, that she "guessed it would n't be worth while to talk about it, for she had never lived with any but fust-class ladies, and her wages was three-and-a-half."

Aunt Henderson grasped Faith's hand as if she felt she had brought her into a danger, and held her close to her side while she paused a moment to observe, with the strange fascination of repulsion, the manifestation of a phase of human life and the working of a vocation so utterly and astoundingly novel to herself.

"Well, Melindy," said Mrs. Griggs, salutatorily.

"Well, grandma," answered the girl, with a pert air of show-off and consequence, "I found the place, and I found the lady. Aint I been quick?"

"Yes. What did she say?"

"Said the girl left last Saturday. Aint had anybody sence. Wants you to send her a first-rate one, right off, straight. Has Care'*line* been here after me?"

"No. Did you get the money?"

"She never said a word about it. Guess she forgot the month was out."

"Did n't you ask her?"

"Me? No. I did the arrant, and stood and looked at her, — jest as pious — ! And when she did n't say nothin', I come away."

"Winny M'Goverin," said Mrs. Griggs, "that place 'll suit you. Leastways, it must, for another month. You 'd better go right round there."

"Where is it?" asked the fat cook, indifferently, over Miss Henderson's shoulder.

"Up in Mount Pleasant Street, Number 53. First-class place, and plenty of privileges. Margaret McKay," she continued, to another, who stood with a waiting expression beside the counter, "you're too hard to please. Here's one more place," — handing her a card with address, — "and if you don't take that, I won't do nothing more for you, if you *air* Scotch and a Protestant! Mary McGinnis, it's no use your talking to that lady from the country. She can't spare you to come down but twice or so a year."

"Lord!" ejaculated Mary McGinnis, "I would n't live a whole year with no lady that ever was, let alone the country!"

"Come out, Faith!" said Miss Henderson, in a deep, ineffable tone of disgust, drawing her niece to the door, just in time to escape a second charge of Miss Melindy's, who was dashing in that direction again, to "look down street after Care*'line*."

"If *that*'s a genteel West End Intelligence Office," cried Aunt Faith, as she touched the sidewalk, "let's go down town and try some of the common ones."

A large hall, — where the candidates were ranged on settees under order and restraint, and the superintendent, or directress, occupied a desk placed upon a platform near the entrance, — was the next scene whereon Miss Henderson and Faith Gartney entered. Things looked clean and respectable. System obtained here. Aunt Faith felt encouraged. But she made no haste to utter her business. Tall, self-possessed, and dignified, she stood a few paces inside the door, and looked down the apartment, surveying coolly the faces there, and analyzing, by a shrewd mental process, their indications.

Her niece had stopped a moment on the landing outside to fasten her boot-lace.

Miss Henderson did not wear hoops. Also, the streets

being sloppy, she had tucked up her plain, gray merino dress over a quilted black alpaca petticoat. Her boots were splashed, and her black silk bonnet was covered with a large gray barege veil, tied down over it to protect it from the dripping roofs. Judging merely by exterior, one unskilled in countenance would hardly take her at a glance, indeed, for a "fust-class" lady.

The directress — a busy woman, with only half a glance to spare for any one — moved toward her.

"Take a seat, if you please. What kind of a place do you want?"

Aunt Faith turned full face upon her, with a look that was prepared to be overwhelming, if it met impertinence.

"I'm looking for a place, ma'am, where I can find a respectable girl."

Her firm, emphatic utterance was heard to the farthest end of the hall.

The girls tittered.

Aunt Faith sent her keen eyes quickly over the benches.

Faith Gartney came in at this moment, and walked up quietly to Miss Henderson's side. There was visibly a new impression made, and the tittering ceased. Especially as the directress also enforced order with a look and word of authority.

"I beg pardon, ma'am. I see. But we have so many in, and I did n't fairly look. General housework?"

"Yes; general and particular — both. Whatever I set her to do."

The directress turned toward the throng of faces whose fire of eyes was now all concentrated on the unflinching countenance of Miss Henderson.

"Ellen Mahoney!"

A stout, well-looking damsel, with an expression that seemed to say she answered to her name, but was nevertheless persuaded of the utter uselessness of the movement, half rose from her seat.

"You need n't call up that girl," said Aunt Faith, decidedly; "I don't want her."

Ellen Mahoney had giggled among the loudest.

"She knows what she *does* want!" whispered a decent-appearing young woman to a girl at her side with an eager face looking out from a friz of short curly hair, "and that's more than half of 'em do. She's a real sensible woman, and the young one's just a picture to look at. I 'd try for it myself, only I 'm half engaged to the one that had me up a minute ago."

"Country, did you say, ma'am? or city?" asked the directress once more of Miss Henderson.

"I did n't say. It's country, though, — twenty miles out."

"What wages?"

"I 'll find the girl first, and settle that afterwards."

"Anybody to do general housework in the country, twenty miles out?"

The prevailing expression of the assemblage changed. There was a settling down into seats, a withdrawing of earnest and curious glances, and a resumption of knitting and needlework.

One pair of eyes, however, looked on, even more eagerly than before. One young girl, — she with the short curly hair, — who had been gazing at the pretty face of Faith since she came in as if it had been a vision, and who had n't seen the country, and had hardly heard it named, for six years and more last gone of her young life, and could with difficulty conceive that there should be any straight or easily traversed path out of these interminable city walls into the breadth and beauty, that came to her as a far-off recollection in her dreams of delight, — caught her breath, convulsively, at the word.

"I wish I dar'st! I've a great mind!" whispered she to her tidy companion.

While she hesitated, a slatternly young woman, a few seats further forward, moved, with a "don't care" sort of look, to answer the summons.

"Oh, dear!" sighed the first, quite sure of her own wish now that she perceived herself anticipated, "I'd ought to a done it!"

"I don't think she would take a young girl like you," replied her friend.

"That's the way it always is!" exclaimed the disappointed voice, in forgetfulness and excitement uttering itself aloud. "Plenty of good times going, but they all go right by. I aint never in any of 'em!"

"Glory McWhirk!" chided the directress from her desk, "be quiet! Remember the rules, or leave the room."

"Call that red-headed girl to me," said Miss Henderson, turning square round from the dirty figure that was presenting itself before her, and addressing the desk. "She looks clean and bright," she added, aside, to Faith, as Glory timidly yet hastily answered a signal and approached. "And poor. And longing for a chance. I'll have her."

A girl with a bonnet full of braids and roses, and a look of general knowingness, started up close at Miss Henderson's side, and interposed, while Glory was yet on her way.

"Did you say twenty miles, mum? How often could I come to town?"

"You have n't been asked to go *out* of town, that I know of," replied Miss Henderson, frigidly, abashing the office-*habitué*, who had not been used to find her catechism cut to summarily short, and moving aside to speak with Glory.

"What was it I heard you say just now?"

"I did n't mean to speak out so, mum. It was only what I mostly thinks. That there's always lots of good times in the world, only I aint never in 'em."

"And you thought it would be good times, did you, to go off twenty miles into the country, to live alone with an old woman like me?"

Miss Henderson's tone softened kindly to the rough, uncouth girl, and encouraged her to confidence.

"Well, you see, mum, I should like so to go where things is green and pleasant. I lived in the country once,— ever so long ago,— when I was a little girl."

Miss Henderson could not help a smile that was half amused, and wholly pitiful, as she looked in the face of this creature of fourteen, so strange and earnest, with its outline of fuzzy, cropped hair, and heard her talk of "ever so long ago."

"There's only just the Common here, you know, mum. And that's when all the chores is done. And you can't go on the grass, either."

"Are you strong?"

"Yes'm. I aint never sick."

"And willing to work?"

"Yes'm. Jest as much as I know how."

"And want to learn more?"

"Yes'm. I don't know as I'd know enough hardly, to begin, though."

"Can you wash dishes? And sweep? And set table?"

To each of these queries Glory successively interposed an affirmative monosyllable, adding, gratuitously, at the close, "And tend baby, too, real good." Her eyes filled, as she thought of the Grubbling baby with the love that always grows for that whereto one has sacrificed one's self.

"You won't have any babies to tend. Time enough for that when you've learnt plenty of other things. Who do you belong to?"

"I don't belong to anybody, mum. Father, and mother, and grandmother is all dead. I've done the chores and tended baby up at Mrs. Grubbling's ever since. That's in Budd Street. I'm staying now in High Street, with Mrs. Foye. Number fifteen."

"I'll come after you to-morrow. Have your things ready to go right off."

"I'm *so* glad you took her, auntie," said Faith, as they went out. "She looks as if she had n't been well treated. Think of her wanting so to go into the country! I should like to do something for her, myself."

"That's my business," answered Aunt Faith, curtly, but not crossly. "You'll find somebody to do for, if you look out. If your mother's willing, though, you might mend up one of your old school dresses for her. 'T is n't likely she's got anything to begin with." And so saying, Aunt Faith turned precipitately into a dry-goods store, where she bought a large plaid woolen shawl, and twelve yards of dark calico. Coming out, she darted as suddenly, and apparently unpremeditatedly, across the street into a milliner's shop, and ordered home a brown rough-and-ready straw bonnet, and four yards of ribbon to match.

"And that you can put on, too," she said to Faith.

That evening, Faith was even unwontedly cheery and

busy, taking a burned half-breadth out of a dark cashmere dress, darning it at the armhole, and pinning the plain ribbon over the brown straw bonnet.

At the same time, Glory, all unconscious of the great things preparing for her, went up across the city to Budd Street, with a mingled heaviness and gladness at her heart, and, after a kindly farewell interview with good-natured Katie Ryan at the Pembertons'· green gate, rang, with a half guilty feeling at her own independence, at the Grubblings' door. "Bubby" opened it.

"Why, ma!" he shouted up the staircase, "it's Glory come back!"

"I've come to get my bundle," said the girl.

Mrs. Grubbling had advanced to the stair-head, somewhat briskly, with the wakeful baby in her arms. Two days' "tending" had greatly mollified her sentiments toward the offending Glory.

"And she's come to get her bundle," added the young usher, from below.

Mrs. Grubbling retreated into her chamber, and shut herself and the baby in.

Poor Glory crept up stairs to her little attic, like a housebreaker.

Coming down again, she set her bundle on the stairs, and knocked.

"What is it?" was the ungracious response.

"Please, mum, mightn't I say good-bye to the baby?"

The latch had slipped, and the door was already slightly ajar. Baby heard the accustomed voice, and struggled in his mother's arms.

"A pretty time to come disturbing him to do it!" grumbled she. Nevertheless, she set the baby on the floor, who tottled out, and was seized by Glory, standing there in the dark entry, and pressed close in her poor, long-wearied, faithful arms.

"Oh, baby, baby! I'm in it now! And I don't know rightly whether it's a good time or not!"

CHAPTER VII.

CARES; AND WHAT CAME OF THEM.

> "To speed to-day, to be put back to-morrow;
> To feed on hope, to pine with feare and sorrow;
> . . . .
> To fret thy soul with crosses and with cares;
> To eate thy heart through comfortlesse despaires"
> SPENSER

Two years and more had passed since the New Year's dance at the Rushleighs'.

The crisis of '57 and '58 was approaching its culmination. The great earthquake that for months had been making itself heard afar off by its portentous rumbling was heaving to the final crash. Already the weaker houses had fallen and were forgotten. The statelier edifices were tottering and crumbling on every side. Men saw great cracks and fissures opening at their feet, and hardly dared move to the right hand or to the left. All through the great city, when the pavements were still at night, and the watchmen paced their quiet rounds, who might count the chambers where lay sleepless heads, revolving feverishly the ways and means for the morrow? Ah! God only knows the life that wakes and struggles when the outer, daily, noisy life of a great metropolis is laid asleep!

When a great financial trouble sweeps down upon a people, there are three general classes who receive and feel it, each in its own peculiar way.

There are the great capitalists, — the enormously rich, — who, unless a tremendous combination of adversities shall utterly ruin here and there one, grow the richer yet for the calamities of their neighbors. There are also the very poor, who have nothing to lose but their daily labor and their daily bread, — who may suffer and starve; but who, if by any little saving of a better time they can manage just to buy bread, shall be precisely where they were, practically, when the storm shall have blown over. Between these lies the great middle class, — among whom, as on the middle ground, the world's great battle is continually waging, — of persons who are neither rich nor poor; who have neither secured fortunes to fall back upon, nor yet the independence of their hands to turn to, when business and its income fail. This is the class that suffers most. Most keenly in apprehension, in mortification, in after privation.

Of this class was the Gartney family.

Mr. Gartney was growing pale and thin. No wonder; with sleepless nights, and harassed days, and forgotten, or unrelished meals. His wife watched him and waited for him, and contrived special comforts for him, and listened to his confidences, and turned in her brain numberless plans and possibilities within her limited sphere of action.

This is what women do when the world " on 'change " is seething, and tossing, and agonizing in the clutch of a great commercial crisis.

Faith felt that there was a cloud upon the house, and knew that it had to do with money. So she hid her own little wants as long as she could, wore her old ribbons, mended last year's discarded gloves, and yearned vaguely and helplessly to do something, — some great thing if she only could, that might remedy or help.

Once, she thought she would learn Stenography. She had heard somebody speak one day of the great pay a lady short-hand-writer had received at Washington, for some Congressional reports. Why should n't she learn how to do it, and perhaps, some time or other, if the terrible worst should ever come to the worst, make known her secret resource, and earn enough for all the family?

Something like this, — some "high and holy work of love,"—she longed to do. Longed almost,—if she were once prepared and certain of herself, — for even misfortune that should justify and make practicable her generous purpose.

She got an elementary book, and set to work, by herself. She toiled wearily, every day, at such times as she could command, for nearly a month; despairing at every step, yet persevering; for, beside the grand dream for the future, there was a present fascination in the queer little scrawls and dots, the mystic keys to such voluminous meaning, that held her interested, of itself.

Well, and how did it all end?

She did n't master the short-hand art, of course. Everybody knows that is a work for patient years. It cannot be known how long she might have gone on with the attempt, if her mother had not come to her one day with some parcels of cut-out cotton cloth.

"Faithie, dear," said she, deprecatingly, "I don't like to put such work upon you while you go to school; but you have a good deal of leisure time, after all; and I ought not to afford to have Miss McElroy this spring. Can't you make up some of these with me before the summer?"

They were articles of clothing for Faith, herself. She felt the present duty upon her; and how could she rebel? Yet what was to become of the great scheme and the heroic future? She could n't help thinking — if her mother had only known how this leisure of hers was really being used, would she have brought her all this cotton to stitch?

What then? Could she never do anything better than this? Meantime, the stitching must be done.

By-and-by would come vacation, and in the following spring, at furthest, she would leave school, and then — she would see. She would write a book, may be. Why not? And secretly dispose of it, for a large sum, to some self-regardless publisher. Should there never be another Fanny Burney? Not a novel, though, or any grown-up book, at first; but a juvenile, at least, she could surely venture on. Look at all the Cousin Maries, and Aunt Fannies, and Sister Alices, whose productions piled the booksellers' counters during the holiday sales, and found their way, sooner or later, into all the nurseries, and children's bookcases! And think of all the stories she had invented to amuse Hendie with! Better than some of these printed ones, she was quite sure, if only she could set them down just as she had spoken them under the inspiration of Hendie's eager eyes and ready glee.

She made two or three beginnings, during the summer holidays, but always came to some sort of a "sticking-place," which could n't be hobbled over in print as in verbal relation. All the links must be apparent, and everything be made to hold well together. She would n't have known what they were, if you had asked her, — but the "unities" troubled her. And then the labor loomed up so large before her! She counted the lines in a page of a book of the ordinary juvenile size, and the number of letters in a line, and found out the wonderful compression of which manuscript is capable. And there must be two hundred pages, at least, to make a book of tolerable size.

She remembered how her elder brother, now away off in San Francisco, had told her once, when she was a very little girl, that he was going to make her a baby-house. Such a wonderful baby-house as it was to be! It should have three stories, and the proper number of furnished rooms in each, and doll inhabitants, likewise, of marvellous wiry mechanism, that should move and walk about. (Long before the Peripatetikos, or whatever they call the wind-up walking dolls, were thought of by any older brain, mind you!) And how all he ever did about it, when urged to execution, was to take his little hatchet out into the woodshed and chop away upon a shapeless log! Always making a visionary beginning, — always unfolding fascinating plans, — believing in them devoutly, and never getting really and fairly into the work! Ah, how we all build, and build, and make such feeble actual strokes toward completion!

So Faithie's brain-puppets waited in limbo, and could not by any sorcery of hers be evoked from shade into life and action.

There seemed to be nothing in the world that she could do. She could not give her time to charity, and go about among the poor. She had nothing to help them with. Her father gave, already, to ceaseless applications, more than he could positively spare. So every now and then she relinquished in discouragement her aspirations, and fell into the ordinary channel again, and lived on, from day to day, as other girls did, getting what pleasure she could; hampered continually, however, with the old, inevitable tether, of "can't afford."

"If something only would happen!" If some new circumstance would creep into her life, and open the way for a more real living!

Do you think girls of seventeen don't have thoughts and longings like these? I tell you they do; and it isn't that they want to have anybody else meet with misfortune, or die, that romantic combinations may thereby result to them; or that they are in haste to enact the every-day romance, — to secure a lover, — get married, — and set up a life of their own; it is that the ordinary marked-out bound of civilized young-lady existence is so utterly inadequate to the fresh, vigorous, expanding nature, with its noble hopes, and its apprehension of limitless possibilities.

Something did happen.

Winter came on again. After a twelvemonth of struggle and pain such as none but a harassed man of business can ever know or imagine, Mr. Gartney found himself "out of the wood," and safe, as it were, in open country once more; but stripped, and torn, and bruised, and weary, and seeing no path before him over the wide, waste moor.

He had survived the shock, — his last note was taken up, — he had **labored through, — and** that was all. He was like a man from off a wreck, who **has** brought away nothing **but his** life.

He came home one morning from New York, whither he **had** been to attend a meeting of creditors of a failed firm, and went straight to his chamber with a raging headache.

The next day, the physician's chaise was at the door, and on the landing, where Mrs. Gartney stood, pale and anxious, gazing into **his** face for **a word,** after the visit to the sick room was over, **Dr. Gracie drew on** his gloves, and said to **her,** with one **foot on the stair,** — "Symptoms of typhoid. **Keep** him absolutely quiet."

CHAPTER VIII.

A NICHE IN LIFE, AND A WOMAN TO FILL IT.

"A Traveller between Life and Death."
WORDSWORTH.

MISS SAMPSON was at home this evening. It was not what one would have pictured to one's self as a scene of home comfort or enjoyment; but Miss Sampson was at home. In her little room of fourteen feet square, up a dismal flight of stairs, sitting, in the light of a single lamp, by her air-tight stove, whereon a cup of tea was keeping warm; that, and the open newspaper on the little table in the corner, being the only things in any way cheery about her.

Not even a cat or a canary-bird had she for companionship. There was no cozy arrangement for daily feminine employment; no work-basket, or litter of spools and tapes; nothing to indicate what might be her daily way of going on. On the broad ledges of the windows, where any other woman would have had a plant or two, there was no array of geraniums or verbenas — not even a seedling orange-tree or a monthly-rose. But in one of them lay a plaid shawl and a carpet-bag, and in the other that peculiar and nearly obsolete piece of feminine property, a paper bandbox, tied about with tape.

— Packed up for a journey?

Reader, Miss Sampson was *always* packed up. She was that much-enduring, all-foregoing creature, a professional nurse.

There would have been no one to feed a cat, or a canary-bird, or to water a rose-bush, if she had had one. Her home was no more to her than his station at the corner of the street is to the handcart-man or the hackney-coachman. It was only the place where she might receive orders; whence she might go forth to the toilsomeness and gloom of one sick-room after another, returning between each sally and the next to her cheerless post of waiting, — keeping her strength for others, and living no life of her own. She dwelt, as it were, in the dim and desolate border-land that lies between the stirring world and the unconscious grave; now going down into the verge of the infinite gloom with one who must pass beyond it, and now upholding and helping one who struggles back to the light of earth; but never tarrying long herself among the living and the strong.

There was nothing in Miss Sampson's outer woman that would give you, at first glance, an idea of her real energy and peculiar force of character. She was a tall and slender figure, with no superfluous weight of flesh; and her long, thin arms seemed to have grown long and wiry with lifting, and easing, and winding about the poor wrecks of mortality that had lost their own vigor, and were fain to beg a portion of hers. Her face was thin and rigid, too, — moulded to no mere graces of expression, — but with a strong outline, and a habitual compression about the mouth that told you, when you had once learned somewhat of its meaning, of the firm will that would go straight forward to its object, and do, without parade or delay, whatever there might be to be done. Decision, determination, **judgment**, and readiness were all in that habitual look of a face on which little else had been called out for years. But you would not so have read it at first sight. You would almost inevitably have called her a "scrawny, sour-looking old maid."

A creaking, deliberate, weighty step was heard upon the stair, and then a knock of decision at Miss Sampson's door.

"Come in!"

And as she spoke, Miss Sampson took her cup and saucer in her hand. That was to be kept waiting no longer for whatever visitor it might chance to be. She was composedly taking her first sip as Doctor Gracie entered.

"Don't move, Miss Sampson; don't let me interrupt."

"I don't mean to!" answered the nurse, laconically "What sends you here?"

"A new patient."

"Humph! Not one of the last sort, I hope. You know my kind, and 't aint any use talking up about any others. Any old woman can make gruel, and feed a baby with catnip tea. Don't offer me any more such work as that! If it's work that *is* work, speak out! — I'm always ready."

"It's work that nobody else can do for me. A critical case of typhoid, and nobody in the house that understands such illness. I've promised to bring you to-night."

"You knew I was back, then?"

"I knew you would be. I only sent you at the pinch. I warned them you'd go as soon as things were tolerably comfortable."

"Of course I would. What business should I have where there was nothing wanted of me but to go to bed at nine o'clock, and sleep till daylight? That aint the sort of corner I was cut out to fill."

7

"Well, drink your tea, and put on your bonnet. There's a carriage at the door."

"Man? or woman?" asked Miss Sampson, setting down her empty cup on the now cooling stove.

"A man, — Mr. Henderson Gartney, Hickory Street."

"Out of his head?"

"Yes, — and getting more so. Family all frightened to death."

"Keep 'em out of my way, then, and let me have him to myself. One crazy patient is enough, at a time, for any one pair of hands. I'm ready."

The plaid shawl and bonnet were on, and Miss Sampson had her bandbox in her hand. The doctor took up the carpet-bag.

In fifteen minutes more, they were in Hickory Street; and the nurse was speedily installed, or rather installed herself, in her office. Dr. Gracie hastened away to another patient, promising to call again at bedtime.

"Now, ma'am," said Miss Sampson to Mrs. Gartney, who, after taking her first to the bedside of the patient, had withdrawn with her to the little dressing-room adjoining, and given her a *résumé* of the treatment thus far followed, with the doctor's last directions to herself, — "you just go down stairs to your supper. I know, by your looks, you aint had a mouthful to-day. That's no way to help take care of sick folks."

Mrs. Gartney smiled a little, feebly; and an expression of almost childlike rest and relief came over her face. She felt herself in strong hands.

"And you?" she asked. "Shall I send you something here?"

"I've drunk a cup of tea, before I started. f I see my

way clear, I'll run down for a bite after you get through. I don't want any special providings. I take my nibbles anyhow, as I go along. You need n't mind, more 'n as if I was n't here. I shall find my way all over the house, and pick up what's necessary. Now, you go."

"Only tell me how he seems to you," questioned Mrs. Gartney, lingering anxiously.

"Well, — not so terrible sick. Just barely bad enough to keep me here. I don't take any easy cases."

The odd, abrupt manner and speech comforted, while they somewhat astonished Mrs. Gartney. Only that she felt sure Dr. Gracie would have brought her no one but the very person who ought to be here, she would have hardly known what to think of this rough-spoken, unceremonious woman.

"Leave the bread and butter and cold chicken on the table," said she to her parlor maid afterward, when the tea-things were about to be removed; "and keep the chocolate hot, down stairs. Faithie, — sit here; and if Miss Sampson comes down by-and-by, see that she is made comfortable."

It was ten o'clock when Miss Sampson came down, and then it was with Dr. Gracie, who had just made his last visit for the night.

"Cheer up, little lady!" said the doctor, meeting Faith's anxious, inquiring glance that sped so quickly and eagerly from one face to the other. "Not so bad, by any means, as we might be. The only difficulty will be to keep Nurse Sampson here. She won't stay a minute, if we begin to get better too fast. Yes — I will take a bit of chicken, I think; and — what have you there that's hot?" as the maid came in with the chocolate pot, in answer to Faith's ring of the bell. "Ah, yes! Chocolate! I missed my tea, somehow, to-night." The "somehow" had been in his kindly quest of the best nurse in Mishaumok for his long-time friend and patient.

"Sit down, Miss Sampson. Save muscle, when you can. Let me help you to a scrap of cold chicken. What? Drumstick! Miss Faithie, — here is a woman who makes it a principle to go through the world, choosing drumsticks! She's a study; and I set you to finding her out."

So the doctor chatted on, for the ten minutes of his further stay, and then took leave, ordering Faith off to bed, as he departed.

Last night, as he had told Miss Sampson, the family had been "frightened to death." He had found Faith sitting on the front stairs, at midnight, when he came in at a sudden summons, severer symptoms having declared themselves in the sick man. She was pale and shivering, and caught him nervously by both hands, as he ascended.

"Oh, doctor!"

"And oh, Miss Faithie! This is no place for you. You ought to be in bed."

"But I can't. Mother is all alone, except Mahala. And I don't dare stay up there, either. What *shall* we do?"

For all answer, the doctor had just taken her in his arms, and carried her down to the sofa in the hall, where he laid her, and covered her over with his great-coat. There she staid, passively, till he came back. And then he told her, kindly and gravely, that if she could be *quite* quiet, and firm, she might go and lie on the sofa in her mother's dressing-room for the remainder of the night, to be at hand for any needed service. To-morrow he would see that they were otherwise provided.

And so, to-night, here was Miss Sampson eating her drumstick.

Faith watched the hard lines of her face as she did so, and wondered what, and how much Dr. Gracie had meant by "setting her to find her out."

"I'm afraid you haven't had a very nice supper," said she, timidly. "Do you like that best?"

"Somebody must always eat drumsticks," was the concise reply.

And so, presently, without any farther advance toward acquaintance, they went up stairs: and the house, under the new, energetic rule, soon subsided into quiet for the night.

CHAPTER IX.

LIFE OR DEATH?

"With God the Lord belong the issues from death."— Ps. 68; 18.

The nursery was a corner room, opening both into Faith's and her mother's. Hendie and Mahala Harris had been removed up stairs, and the apartment was left at Miss Sampson's disposal. Mrs. Gartney's bed had been made up in the little dressing-room at the head of the front entry, so that she and the nurse had the sick-room between them.

Faith came down the two steps that led from her room into the nursery, the next night at bedtime, as Miss Sampson entered from her father's chamber to put on her night wrapper and make ready for her watch.

"How is he, nurse? He will get well, won't he? What does the doctor say?"

"Nothing," said Miss Sampson, shortly. "He don't know, and he don't pretend to. And that's just what proves he's good for something. He aint one of the sort that comes into a sick-room as if the Almighty had made him a kind of special delegit, and left the whole concern to him. He knows there's a solemner dealing there than his, whether it's for life or death."

"But he can't help *thinking*," said Faith, tremblingly. "And I wish I knew. What do *you*—?" But Faith paused, for she was afraid, after all, to finish the question, and to hear it answered.

"I don't think. I just keep doing. That's my part. Folks that think too much of what's a-coming, most likely won't attend to what there is."

Faith was finding out,—a little of Miss Sampson, and a good deal of herself. Had she not thought too much of what might be coming? Had she not missed, perhaps, some of her own work, when that work was easier than now? And how presumptuously she had wished for "something to happen!" Was God punishing her for that?

"You just keep still, and patient,—and wait," said Miss Sampson, noting the wistful look of pain. "That's your work, and after all, maybe it's the hardest kind. And I can't take it off folks' shoulders," added she to herself in an under-voice; "so I need n't set up for the *very* toughest jobs, to be sure."

"I'll try," answered Faith, submissively, with quivering lip, "only if there *should* be anything that I could do,— to sit up, or anything,—you'll let me, won't you?"

"Of course I will," replied the nurse, cheerily. "I shan't be squeamish about asking when there's anything I really want done."

Faith moved toward the door that opened to her father's room. It was ajar. She pushed it gently open, and paused. "I may go in, may n't I, nurse, just for a good-night look?"

The sick man heard her voice, though he did not catch her words.

"Come in, Faithie," said he, with one of his half-gleams of consciousness, "I'll see you, daughter, as long as I live."

Faith's heart nearly broke at that, and **she came, tearfully and silently,** to the bed side, **and laid** her little, cool **hand on her** father's fevered one, and looked down on his face, worn, and suffering, **and flushed,**— and thought within herself,— it was **a prayer and vow** unspoken,— "Oh, if God will only let him **live,** I will *find* something that **I can do for him!**"

And then she lifted the linen cloth that was laid over his forehead, and dipped it afresh in the bowl of ice-water beside the bed, and put it gently back, and just kissed his hair softly, and went out into her own room.

Three nights— three days— more, the fever raged. And on the fourth night after, Faith and her mother knew, by the scrupulous care with which the doctor gave minute directions for the few hours to come, and the resolute way in which Miss Sampson declared that "whoever else had a mind to watch, she should sit up till morning this time," that the critical point was reached; that these dark, silent moments that **would flit by so fast, were** to spell, as they passed by, the sentence of life **or** death.

And so the midnight settled down upon **the** street and **city,** crowded full of human thought, and hope, and fear, **but whose** vital centre to them was all in that one, dim chamber.

Faith would not be put by. Her mother sat on one side the bed, while the nurse busied herself noiselessly, or waited, motionless, upon the other. Down by the fireside, on a low stool, with her head on the cushion of an easy-chair, leaned the young girl,— her heart full, and every nerve strained with emotion **and** suspense.

She will never know, precisely, how those hours went on. **She** can remember the low breathing **from the** bed, and the now and then half-distinct utterance, as the brain wandered still in a dreamy, feverish maze; and she never will forget the precise color and pattern of the calico wrapper that Nurse Sampson wore; but she can recollect nothing else of it all, except that, after a time, longer or shorter, she glanced up, fearfully, as a strange hush seemed to have come over the room, and met a look and gesture of the nurse that warned her down again, for her life.

And then, other hours, or minutes, she knows not which, went by.

And then, a stir, — a feeble word, — a whisper from Nurse Sampson, — a low "Thank God!" from her mother.

The crisis was passed. Henderson Gartney lived.

CHAPTER X.

ROUGH ENDS.

> "So others shall
> Take patience, labor, to their heart and hand,
> From thy hand and thy heart, and thy brave cheer,
> And God's grace fructify through thee to all."
>
> Mrs. Browning.

"M. S. What does that stand for?" said little Hendie, reading the white letters painted on the black leather bottom of nurse's carpet-bag. He got back, now, often, in the daytime, to his old nursery quarters, where his father liked to hear his chatter and play, for a short time together, — though he still slept, with Mahala, up stairs. "Does that mean 'Miss Sampson?'"

Faith glanced up from her stocking-mending, with a little fun and a little curiosity in her eyes. She, too, had noted the initials with a sort of wondering thought whether they could possibly mean anything else. Whether the stiff, dry, uncompromising woman whom she daily saw going methodically through a round of hard and wearing duty, could have ever had a Christian name to go by; could ever have been a little Mary or Margaret. It seemed as if she must have come into the world tall, and straight, and pinched, and resolute, and gone to nursing sick people forthwith.

That she could ever have lived a child life, with nothing to do but play, — that was a thing hardly to be believed.

"What does 'M.' stand for?" repeated Hendie.

The nurse was "setting to rights" about the room. She turned round at the question, from hanging a towel straight over the stand, and looked a little amazed, as if she had almost forgotten, herself. But it came out, with a quick opening and shutting of the thin lips, like the snipping of a pair of scissors, — "Mehitable."

That was not so wonderful. Faith could believe that. But she knew it could never have been anything shorter or softer.

Faith had been greatly drawn to this odd, efficient woman. Beside that her skilful, untiring nursing had, humanly, been the means of saving her father's life, which alone had warmed her with an earnest gratitude that was restless to prove itself, and that welled up in every glance and tone she gave Miss Sampson, there were a certain respect and interest that could not withhold themselves from one who so evidently worked on with a great motive that dignified her smallest acts. In whom self-abnegation was the underlying principle of all daily doing.

Miss Sampson had staid on at the Gartneys', notwithstanding the doctor's prediction, and her usual habit. And, in truth, her patient did not "get well *too* fast." She was needed now as really as ever, though the immediate danger which had summoned her was past, and the fever had gone. The months of overstrained effort and anxiety that had culminated in its violent attack were telling upon him now, in the scarcely less perilous prostration that followed. And Mrs. Gartney had quite given out since the excessive tension of nerve and feeling had relaxed. She was almost ill enough to be regularly nursed herself. She alternated between her bed in the dressing-room and an easy-chair opposite her husband's, at his fireside. Miss Sampson knew when she was really wanted, whether the emergency were more or less obvious. She knew the mischief of a change of hands at such a time. And so she staid on, though she did sleep comfortably of a night, and had many an hour of rest in the daytime, when Faith would come into the nursery with a book, or her work-basket, and constitute herself her companion.

Miss Sampson was to her like a book to be read, whereof she turned but a leaf or so at a time, as she had accidental opportunity, yet whose every page rendered up a deep, strong, — above all, a most sound and healthy meaning.

She turned over a leaf, one day, in this wise.

"Miss Sampson, how came you, at first, to be a sicknurse?"

The shadow of some old struggle seemed to come over Miss Sampson's face, as she answered, briefly, —

"I wanted to find the very toughest sort of a job to do."

Faith looked up, surprised.

"But I heard you tell my father that you had been nursing more than twenty years. You must have been quite a young woman when you began. I wonder — " and here Faith checked herself, lest her wondering should seem to verge upon impertinence.

"You wonder why I was n't like most other young women, I suppose. Why I did n't get married, perhaps, and have folks of my own to take care of? Well, I did n't; and the Lord gave me a pretty plain indication that He had n't laid out that kind of a life for me. So then I just looked round to find out what better He had for me to do. And I hit on the very work I wanted. A trade that it took all the old Sampson grit to follow. I made up my mind, as the doctor says, that *somebody* in the world had got to choose drumsticks, and I might as well take hold of one."

"But don't you ever get tired of it all, and long for something to rest or amuse you?"

"Amuse! I couldn't be amused, child. I've been in too much awful earnest ever to be much amused again. No, I want to die in the harness. It's hard work I want. I couldn't have been tied down to a common, easy sort of life. I want something to fight and grapple with; and I'm thankful there's been a way opened for me to do good according to my nature. If I hadn't had sickness and death to battle against, I should have got into human quarrels, maybe, just for the sake of feeling ferocious."

"And you always take the very worst and hardest cases. Doctor Gracie says."

"What's the use of taking a tough job if you don't face the toughest part of it? I don't want the comfortable end of the business. *Somebody*'s got to nurse small pox, and yellow fever, and raving-distracted people; and I *know* the Lord made me fit to do just that very work. There aint many that He *does* make for it, but I'm one. And if I shirked, there'd be a stitch dropped."

"Yellow fever! where have you nursed that?"

"Do you suppose I didn't go to Norfolk? I've nursed it, and I've *had* it, and nursed it again. I've been in the cholera hospitals, too. I'm seasoned to most everything."

"Do you think everybody ought to take the hardest thing they can find, to do?"

"Do you think everybody ought to eat drumsticks? We'd have to kill an unreasonable lot of fowls to let 'em! No,

The Lord portions out breast and wings, as well as legs. If He puts anything into your plate, take it."

Doctor Gracie always had a word for the nurse, when he came; and, to do her justice, it was seldom but she had a word to give him back.

"Well, Miss Sampson," said he gayly, one bright morning, you're as fresh as the day. What pulls down other folks seems to set you up. I declare you're as blooming as — twenty-five.

"You — fib — like — sixty! It's no such thing! And if it was, I'd ought to be ashamed of it."

"Prodigious! as your namesake, the Dominie, would say. Don't tell me a woman is ever ashamed of looking young, or handsome!"

"Now, look here, Doctor!" said Miss Sampson, with her firmest intonation, setting down a pitcher she had just brought in, and facing round to do battle, — "I never was handsome; and I thank the Lord He's given me enough to do in the world to wear off my young looks long ago! And any woman ought to be ashamed that gets to be thirty and upwards, to say nothing of forty-five, and keeps her baby face on! It's a sign she aint been of much account, anyhow."

"Oh, but there are always differences and exceptions," persisted the doctor, who liked nothing better than to draw Miss Sampson out. "There are some faces that take till thirty, at least, to bring out all their possibilities of good looks, and wear on, then, till fifty. I've seen 'em. And the owners were no drones or do-nothings, either. What do you say to that?"

"I say there's two ways of growing old. And growing old aint always growing ugly. Some folks grow old from the inside, **out**; and some from the outside, **in**. There's old furniture, and there's growing trees!"

"**And** the trunk that is **roughest** below **may branch out** greenest a-top!" said the doctor.

But the conversation had got as nearly into poetry as was possible with practical Miss Sampson, and she broke it off, or brought it down, by saying, as she handed Mr. Gartney his port-wine tonic, —

"It's lucky we touched on bark, **sir, or you** might n't **have** got your strengthener to-day!"

The talk Faith heard now and then, in her walks from home, or when some of "the girls" came in and called her down into the parlor, — about pretty looks, and becoming dresses, and who danced with who at the "German" last night, and what a scrape Loolie Lloyd had got into with mixing **up** and misdating her engagements at the **class**, and the last new roll for the hair, — used to seem rather trivial and aimless to her in these days!

Occasionally, when Mr. Gartney had what nurse called **a** "good" day, he would begin to ask for some of his books and papers, with a thought toward business; and then Miss Sampson would display her carpet-bag, and make a show of picking **up** things to **put** in it; "For," said she, "when you get at **your** business, it 'll be high **time for** me to go about mine."

"But only for half-an-hour, nurse! I'll give **you that** much leave of absence, and then we'll have things back again as they were before."

"I guess you will! And *further* than they were before. No, Mr. Gartney, you've got to behave. I *won't* have **them** vicious-looking accounts about, and it don't signify."

"If it don't, why not?" But it ended in the accounts and the carpet-bag disappearing together.

Until one morning, some three weeks from the beginning of Mr. Gartney's illness, when, after a few days' letting alone the whole subject, he suddenly appealed to the doctor.

"Doctor," said he, as that gentleman entered, "I must have Braybrook up here this afternoon. I dropped things just where I stood, you know. It's time to take an observation."

The doctor looked at his patient gravely. Apparently, he saw that he must yield a point for the present.

"What *must* be, must, I suppose," he said. But he added this, which startled Mrs. Gartney as she heard it, and set her husband into an uneasy thinking, for an hour after Doctor Gracie had gone.

"Can't you be content with simply picking up things, and putting them by, for this year? What I ought to tell you to do would be to send business to the right about, and go off for an entire rest and change, for three months, at least."

"You don't know what you're talking about, doctor!"

"Perhaps not, on one side of the subject. I feel pretty certain on the other, however."

Mr. Gartney did not send for Braybrook that afternoon. The next morning however he came, and the tabooed books and papers were got out.

In another day or two, Miss Sampson *did* pack her carpet-bag, and go back to her air-tight stove and solitary cups of tea. Her occupation in Hickory Street was gone.

Was this all the Gartneys were ever to have in common with her? Were the lives that had touched, — had coincided for a little length, and gone together through a deep experience, — to separate and be nothing to each other henceforth, among all the tangle and criss-cross of human destiny and purpose? He who brings together and divides, and never without a meaning, knows. The lives *had* touched, — had qualified each other.

8*

CHAPTER XL.

CROSS CORNERS.

"O thou that pinest in the imprisonment of the Actual, and criest bitterly to the Gods for a kingdom, wherein to rule and create, know this of a truth, the thing thou seekest is already with thee, 'here or nowhere,' couldst thou only see!"— CARLYLE.

"It is of no use to talk about it," said Mr Gartney, wearily. "If I live, — as long as I live, — I must do business. How else are you to get along?"

"How shall we get along if you do *not* live?" asked his wife, in a low, anxious tone.

"My life's insured," was all Mr. Gartney's answer, after a minute's pause.

"Father!" cried Faith, distressfully.

Faith had been taken more and more into counsel and confidence with her parents since the time of the illness that had brought them all so close together. And more and more helpful she had grown, both in word and doing, since she had learned to look daily for the daily work set before her, and to perform it conscientiously, even although it consisted only of little things. She still remembered with enthusiasm Nurse Sampson and the "drumsticks," and managed to pick up now and then one for herself. Small disagreeabilities, to be sure, they were, that she could find to take upon herself; but she was learning to scorn the "comforts

ble end of a business." She had taken in a lesson, — rather God had sent her one, — by the way, that was to fit her for future greater doing. Meantime she began to see, indistinctly, before her, the vision of a work that must be done by some one, and the duty of it pressed hourly closer home to herself. Her father's health had never been fully reestablished. He had begun to use his strength before, and faster than, it came. There was danger, — it needed no Doctor Gracie, even, to tell them so, — of grave disease, if this went on. And still, whenever urged, his answer was the same. "What would become of his family without his business?"

Faith turned these things over and over in her mind.

"Father," said she, after a while, — the conversation having been dropped at the old conclusion, and nobody appearing to have anything more to say, — "I don't know anything about business; but I wish you 'd tell me how much money you 've got!"

Her father laughed; a sad sort of laugh though, that was not so much amusement as tenderness and pity. Then, as if the whole thing were a mere joke, yet with a shade upon his face that betrayed there was far too much truth under the jest, after all, he took out his portmonnaie and told her to look and see.

"You know I don't mean that, father! How much in the bank, and everywhere?"

"Precious little in the bank, now, Faithie. Enough to keep house with for a year, nearly, perhaps. But if I were to take it and go off and spend it in travelling, you can understand that the housekeeping would fall short, can't you?"

Faith looked horrified. She was bringing down her vague ideas of money that came from somewhere, through her father's pocket, as water comes from Lake Kinsittewink by the turning of a faucet, to the narrow point of actuality.

"But that is n't all, I know! I've heard you talk about railroad dividends, and such things."

"Oh! what does the Western Road pay this time?" asked his wife.

"I've had to sell out my stock there," replied Mr. Gartney, with a sigh.

"And where's the money, father?" asked Faith, not curious, but bold with her good intent.

"Gone to pay debts, child," was the answer.

Mrs. Gartney said nothing, but she looked very grave. Her husband surmised, perhaps, that she would go on to imagine worse than had really happened, and so added, presently, —

"I hav n't been obliged to sell *all* my railroad stocks, wifey. I held on to some. There's the New York Central all safe; and the Michigan Central, too. That would n't have sold so well, to be sure, just when I was wanting the money; but things are looking better, now."

"Father," said Faithie, with her most coaxing little smile, "please just take this bit of paper and pencil, and set down these stocks and things, will you?"

The little smile worked its way; and half in idleness, half in acquiescence, Mr. Gartney took the pencil and noted down a short list of items.

"It's very little, Faith, you see." They ran thus:

New York Central Railroad . 20 shares
Michigan Central " . . 15 "
Kinnicutt Branch " . . 10 "
Mishaumok Insurance Co. . . 15 "
Merchants Bank . . . 30 "

"How much are the shares worth, father?" asked persistent Faith.

"Well — at this moment — so — and so —" noting down against each the cash valuation.

"And now, father, please put down how much you get a year in dividends."

"Not always the same, little busybody."

Nevertheless he noted down the average sums. And the total was between six and seven hundred dollars.

"But that is 'nt all. You've got other things. Why, there's the house at Cross Corners."

"Yes, but I can't let it, you know."

"What used you to get for it?"

"Two hundred and fifty. For house and land."

"And you own this house, too, father?"

"Yes. This is your mother's."

"How much rent would this bring?"

Mr. Gartney turned round and looked at his daughter. He began to see there was a meaning in her questions. And as he caught her eye, he read, or discerned without fully reading, a certain eager kindling there.

"Why, what has come over you, Faithie, to set you catechising so?"

Faith laughed.

"Just answer this, please, and I won't ask a single question more to-night."

"About the rent? Why, this house ought to bring six hundred, certainly. And now, if the court will permit, I'll read the news."

Mr. Gartney took up the evening paper, and Faith sat thinking.

When she went up to her own room, she carried thither the bit of paper, with its calculation.

About a week after this, in the latter half of one of those spring days that come with a warm breath to tell that summer is glowing somewhere, and that her face is northward, Aunt Faith Henderson came out upon the low, vine-latticed stoop of her house in Kinnicutt. There is a story to tell of that house, innocent of paint, that has darkened and darkened in the suns and rains, and yet stood solidly, with infrequent repairs of shingle and clapboard, for more than two hundred years. But it cannot be told at this moment, for I must tell you of another thing — Aunt Henderson's surprise.

She stood at the westerly end of this porch, looking down and off toward the sunset, that rolled its golden waves over the low, distant hills, till they seemed to fill up the broad meadow-space that intervened with a molten glory, sublimating overhead into a glittering mist that melted out at last into the pure depth of blue.

Aunt Henderson's thoughts had wandered off as far, or farther, seemingly, than her eyes.

Up the little foot-path from the road, — across the bit of greensward that lay between it and the stoop, — came a quick, noiseless step, and there was a touch, presently, on the old lady's arm.

Faith Gartney stood beside her, in trim straw bonnet and shawl, with a black leather bag upon her arm.

"Auntie! I've come to make you a tiny little visit! Till day after to-morrow."

Aunt Henderson wheeled round suddenly at the touch, — set her shoulders back against the house, which fortunately stood in the way, or she might have described such an arc of a circle as is included between two radii at right angles to each other and five feet six-and-a-half inches in length; brought her thoughts home again from their far outstretch.

and concentrated them as best she might on the pretty figure immediately before her.

"Faith Gartney! However came you here? And in such a fashion, too, without a word of warning, like — an angel from heaven!" Concluding her sentence with a simile somewhat unexpected to herself, growing out of those mingled impressions of the resplendent sky and Faithie's fair, smiling face.

"I came up in the cars, auntie! I felt just like it! Will you keep me?"

"Glory! Glory McWhirk!" Like the good Vicar of Wakefield, Aunt Henderson liked often to give the whole name; and calling, she disappeared round the corner of the stoop, without ever a word of more assured welcome.

"Put on the teapot again, and make a slice of toast." The good lady's voice, going on with farther directions, was lost in the intricate threading of the inner maze of the singular old dwelling, and Faith followed her as far as the first apartment, where she set down her bag and removed her bonnet.

It was a quaint, dim room, overbrowed and gloomed by the roofed projection of the stoop; low-ceiled, high-wainscoted and panelled. All in oak, of the natural color, deepened and glossed by time and wear. The heavy beams that supported the floor above were undisguised, and left the ceiling in panels also, as it were, between. In these highest places, a man six feet tall could hardly have stood without bending. He certainly would not, whether he could or no. Even Aunt Faith, with her five feet, six-and-a-half, dropped a little of her dignity, habitually, when she entered. But then, as she said, "A hen always bobs her head when she comes in at a barn-door." Between the windows stood an old, old-fashioned secretary, that filled up from floor to ceiling; and over the fireplace a mirror of equally antique date tilted **forward from the** wall. Opposite the secretary, a plain mahogany table; and eight high-backed, claw-footed chairs ranged stiffly around **the room.**

Aunt Henderson was proud of her old **ways, her old furniture,** and her house, that was older than **all.**

Some far back ancestor and early settler had built it, — **the beginning of it,** — before Kinnicutt had even become a town; and — rare exception to the changes elsewhere — generation after generation of the same name and line had inhabited it until now. Aunt Faith, exultingly, told each curious visitor that it had been built precisely two hundred and ten years. Out in the back kitchen, or lean-to, was hung to a rafter the identical gun with which the "old settler" had ranged the forest that stretched then from the **very door;** and higher up, across **a** frame contrived for **it, was the** "wooden saddle" fabricated for the back of the placid, slow-moving ox, **in** the time when **horses were as yet rare in the** new country, and used with **pillions, to transport I can't** definitely say **how** many of the **family to** "meeting."

Between these, — the best room **and the** out-kitchen, — **the** labyrinth **of** sitting-room, bedrooms, kitchen proper, milk-room and pantry, partitioned off, or added on, many of them since the primary date of the main structure, would defy the pencil of modern architect, and must be left in their dim confusion to the imagination.

In **one of** these irregularly clustered apartments that opened out **on** different aspects, unexpectedly, from their conglomerant **centre, Faith sat, some** fifteen minutes after **her entrance into the house, at a little round table between two corner windows that looked northwest and southwest,** and together **took in the full radiance of the evening sky.**

Opposite sat her aunt, taking care of her as regarded tea, toast, and plain country loaf-cake, and watching somewhat curiously, also, her face.

Faith's face had changed a little since Aunt Henderson had seen her last. It was not the careless girl's face she had known. There was a thought in it now. A thought that seemed to go quite out from, and forget the self from which it came.

Aunt Henderson wondered greatly what sudden whim or inward purpose had brought her grand-niece hither.

When Faith absolutely declined any more tea or cake, Miss Henderson's tap on the table-leaf brought in Glory McWhirk.

A tall, well-grown girl of eighteen was Glory, now, — quite another Glory than had lightened, long ago, the dull little house in Budd Street, and filled it with her bright, untutored dreams. The luminous tresses had had their way since then; that is, with certain comfortable bounds prescribed; and rippled themselves backward from a clear, contented face, into the net that held them tidily, but had its — meshes — full to do it, after a style of their own, that in these later days Fashion and Art have striven hopelessly to achieve with crimping-pins and — 'rats!'"

I said Glory's face was contented, yet it was not with the utter content of a little soul that looks not beyond the moment. There was a yearning and a dreaminess deep in her eyes, when you looked far enough to find it, that told, even yet, of unfulfilment; of something unconsciously waited for still, and sure to come. It was one of those faces that, find them where you may, carry God's prophecy in them.

Faith looked up, and remembered the poor office-girl of

three years since, half clad and hopeless, with a secret amaze at what "Aunt Faith had made of her."

"You may give me some water, Glory," said Miss Henderson.

Glory brought the pitcher, and poured into the tumbler, and gazed at Faith's pretty face, and the dark-brown glossy rolls that framed it, until the water fairly ran over upon the table.

"There! there! Why, Glory, what are you thinking of?" cried Miss Henderson.

Glory was thinking her old thoughts,— wakened always by all that was beautiful and *beyond*.

She came suddenly to herself, however, and darted off, with her face as bright a crimson as her hair was golden; flashing up so, as she did most easily, into as veritable a Glory as ever was. Never had baby been more aptly or prophetically named.

Coming back, towel in hand, to stop the freshet she had set flowing, she dared not give another glance across the table; but went busily and deftly to work, clearing it of all that should be cleared, that she might make her shy way off again before she should be betrayed into other unwonted blundering.

"And now, Faith Gartney, tell me all about it! What sent you here?"

"Nothing. Nobody. I came, aunt. I wanted to see the place, and you."

The rough eyebrows were bent keenly across the table.

"Hum!" breathed Aunt Henderson, a little doubtful, and very much puzzled.

Then Faith asked the news in Kinnicutt, and told of home matters, what people usually tell, and consider that they have given account of themselves. Aunt Henderson's questions were few. She cared little for outside commonplace, and there was small interior sympathy between her ideas and those that governed the usual course of affairs in Hickory Street. Fond of her nephew and his family, after her fashion, notwithstanding Faith's old rebellion, and all other differences, she certainly was; but they went their way, and she hers. She felt pretty sure theirs would sooner or later come to a turning; and when that should happen, whether she should meet them round the corner, or not, would depend. Her path would need to bend a little, and theirs to make a pretty sharp angle, first.

But here was Faith cutting across lots to come to her! Aunt Henderson put away her loaf-cake in the cupboard, set back her chair against the wall in its invariable position of disuse, and departed to the milk-room and kitchen for her evening duty and oversight.

Glory's hands were busy in the bread-bowl, and her brain kneading its secret thoughts that no one knew or intermeddled with.

Faith sat at the open window of the little tea-room, and watched the young moon's golden horn go down behind the earth-rim among the purple, like a flamy flower bud floating over, and so lost.

And the three lives gathered in to themselves, separately, whatsoever the hour brought to each.

At nine o'clock Aunt Faith came in, took down the great leather-bound Bible from the corner shelf, and laid it on the table. Glory appeared, and seated herself beside the door.

For a few moments, the three lives met in the One Great Life that overarches and includes humanity. Miss Henderson read from the sixth chapter of St. John.

They were fed with the five thousand.

CHAPTER XII.

A RECONNOISSANCE.

'Then said his Lordship, 'Well, God mend all!' 'Nay, Donald, we must help Him to mend it,' said the other."—Quoted by CARLYLE.

"Oh, leave these jargons, and go your way straight to God's work in simplicity and singleness of heart!"—MISS NIGHTINGALE.

"AUNTIE," said Faith, next morning, when, after some exploring, she had discovered Miss Henderson in a little room, the very counterpart of the one she had had her tea in the night before, only that this opened to the southeast, and hailed the morning sun as that had taken in its setting,—"Auntie, will you go over with me to the Cross Corners house, after breakfast? It's empty, isn't it?"

"Yes, it's empty. But it's no great show of a house. What do you want to see it for?"

"Why, it used to be so pretty, there. I'd like just to go into it. Have you heard of anybody wanting it yet?"

"No; and I guess nobody's likely to, for one while. Folks don't make many changes, out here."

"What a bright little breakfast-room this is, auntie! And how grand you are to have a room for every meal!"

"It aint for the grandeur of it. But I always did like to follow the sun round. For the most part of the year, at any rate. And this is just as near the kitchen as the other

Besides, I kind of hate to shut up any of the rooms, altogether. They were all wanted, once; and now I'm all alone in 'em."

For Miss Henderson, this was a great opening of the heart. But she did n't go on to say that the little west room had been her young brother's, who long ago, when he was just ready for his Master's work in this world, had been called up higher; and that her evening rest was sweeter, and her evening reading holier for being holden there; or that here, in the sunny morning hours, her life seemed almost to roll back its load of many years, and to set her down beside her mother's knee, and beneath her mother's gentle tutelage, once more; that on the little "light-stand" in the corner by the fireplace stood the self-same basket that had been her mother's then, — just where she had kept it, too, when it was running over with little frocks and stockings that were always waiting finishing or mending, — and now held only the plain gray knitting-work and the bit of sewing that Aunt Faith might have in hand.

A small, square table stood now in the middle of the floor, with a fresh brown linen breakfast-cloth upon it; and Glory, neat and fresh, also, with her brown spotted calico dress and apron of the same, came in smiling like a very goddess of peace and plenty, with the steaming coffee-pot in one hand, and the plate of fine, white rolls in the other. The yellow print of butter and some rounds from a brown loaf were already on the table. Glory brought in, presently, the last addition to the meal, — six eggs, laid yesterday, the water of their boiling just dried off, and modestly took her own seat at the lower end of the board.

Aunt Faith, living alone, kept to the kindly old country fashion of admitting her handmaid to the table with herself.

"Why not?" she would say. "In the first place, why should we keep the table about, half an hour longer than we need? And I suppose hot cakes and coffee are as much nicer than cold, for one body as another. Then where's the sense? We take Bible-meat together. Must we be more dainty about 'meat that perisheth?'" So her argument climbed up from its lower reason to its climax.

Glory had little of the Irish now about her but her name. And all that she retained visibly of the Roman faith she had been born to, was her little rosary of colored shells, strung as beads, that had been blessed by the Pope.

Miss Henderson had trained and fed her in her own ways, and with such food as she partook herself, physically and spiritually. Glory sat, every Sunday, in the corner pew of the village church, by her mistress's side. And this church-going being nearly all that she had ever had, she took in the nutriment that was given her, to a soul that recognized it, and never troubled itself with questions as to one truth differing from another, or no. Indeed, no single form or theory could have contained the "credo" of her simple, yet complex, thought. The old Catholic reverence clung about her still, that had come with her all the way from her infancy, when her mother and grandmother had taught her the prayers of their Church; and across the long interval of ignorance and neglect flung a sort of cathedral light over what she felt was holy now.

Rescued from her dim and servile city life, — brought out into the light and beauty she had mutely longed for, — feeling care and kindliness about her for the long-time harshness and oppression she had borne, — she was like a spirit newly entered into heaven, that needs no priestly ministration any more. Every breath drew in a life and teaching purer than human words.

And then the words she *did* hear were Divine. Miss Henderson did no preaching, — scarcely any lip-teaching, however brief. She broke the bread of life God gave her, as she cut her daily loaf and shared it, — letting each soul, God helping, digest it for itself.

Glory got hold of some old theology, too, that she could but fragmentarily understand; but that mingled itself, — as all we gather does mingle, not uselessly, — with her growth. She found old books among Miss Henderson's stores, that she read and mused on. She trembled at the warnings, and reposed in the holy comforts of Doddridge's "Rise and Progress," and Baxter's "Saint's Rest." She travelled to the Holy City, above all, with Bunyan's Pilgrim. And then, Sunday after Sunday, she heard the simple Christian preaching of an old and simple Christian man. Not terrible, — but earnest; not mystical, — but high; not lax, — but liberal; and this fused and tempered all.

So "things had happened" for Glory. So God had cared for this, his child. So, according to His own Will, — not any human plan or forcing, — she grew.

Aunt Faith washed up the breakfast cups, dusted and "set to rights" in the rooms where, to the young Faith's eyes, there seemed such order already as could not be righted, made up a nice little pudding for dinner, and then, taking down her shawl and silk hood, and putting on her overshoes, announced herself ready for Cross Corners.

"Though it's all cross corners to me, child, sure enough. I suppose it's none of my business, but I can't think what you're up to."

"Not up to any great height, yet, auntie. But I'm growing," said Faith, merrily, and with meaning somewhat beyond the letter.

They went out at the back door, which opened on a little foot-path down the sudden green slope behind, and stretched across the field, diagonally, to a bar-place and stile at the opposite corner. Here the roads from five different directions met and crossed, which gave the locality its name.

Opposite the stile at which they came out, across the shady lane that wound down from the Old Road whereon Miss Henderson's mansion faced, a gateway in a white paling that ran round and fenced in a grassy door-yard, overhung with pendent branches of elms and stouter canopy of chestnuts, let them in upon the little "Cross Corners Farm."

The house stood but a few paces back, the long, sweeping tips of the elm-boughs kissing its roof; and behind it swelled a ridge of land so wooded over with miscellaneous growth of tree and shrub, that it was like the entrance to a forest. The uprising of the ground filled in with its dark coloring, and gave an effect of density, beside cutting off all view between or beyond the trees; so that, although a few moments' walk would carry one over and through it all into the cleared and cultivated fields beyond, the illusion was utter, and very charming.

Faith felt it so, even in this early spring-time, before the grass was fully green, or the branches draped in all their summer breadth and beauty.

"Oh, Aunt Faith! It's just as lovely as ever! I remember that path up the hill, among the trees, so well! When I was a little bit of a girl, and nurse and I came out to stay with you. I had my "fairy house" there. I'd like to go over this minute, only that we shan't have time. How shall we get in? Where is the key?"

"It's in my pocket. But it mystifies me, what you want there."

"I want to look out of all the windows, auntie, to begin with."

Aunt Faith's mystification was not lessened.

The front door opened on a small, square hall, with doors to right and left. Opposite, went up the narrow staircase. Narrow, and steep, but straight; lighted by a window from the landing at its head; and railed at either side above, to give passage to the chambers at the front.

The room on the left, spite of the bare floor and fireless hearth, was warm with the spring sunshine that came pouring in at the south windows. Beyond this, embracing the corner of the house rectangularly, projected an equally sunny and cheery kitchen; at the right of which, communicating with both apartments, was divided off a tiny tea-and-breakfast-room. So Faith mentally decided it, though it had very likely been a bedroom. This looked northerly, however, and would seem pleasanter, doubtless, in July; though the high ridge that trended north and easterly behind, sheltered the whole house in comparative comfort, even from December gales.

From the entrance hall at the right opened a room larger than either of the others, — so large that the floor above afforded two bedrooms over it, — and having, beside its windows south and east, a door in the farther corner beyond the chimney, that gave out directly upon the grassy slope, and looked up the path among the trees that crossed the ridge.

Faith drew the bolt and opened it, expecting to find a closet or a passage somewhither. She fairly started back with surprise and delight. And then seated herself plump upon the threshold, with her feet on the flat flag-stone before it, and went into a midsummer dream.

"Oh, auntie!" she cried, at her waking, presently, "was ever anything so perfect? To think of being let out so! Right from a regular, proper parlor, into the woods!"

"Do you mean to go up stairs?" inquired Miss Henderson, with a vague amaze in her look that seemed to question whether her niece had not possibly been "let out" from her "regular and proper" wits!

Whereupon Faith scrambled up from her seat upon the sill, and hurried off to investigate and explore above.

Miss Henderson closed the door, pushed the bolt, and followed quietly after.

It was a funny little pantomime that Faith enacted then, for the further bewilderment of the staid old lady.

Darting from one chamber to another, with an inexplicable look of business and consideration in her face, that contrasted comically with her quick movements and her general air of glee, she would take her stand in the middle of each one in turn, and wheeling round to get a swift panoramic view of outlook and capabilities, would end by a succession of mysterious and apparently satisfied little nods, as if at each pause some point of plan or arrangement had settled itself in her mind.

"Aunt Faith!" cried she, suddenly, as she came out upon the landing when she had peeped into the last corner, and found Miss Henderson on the point of making her descent, — "what sort of a thing do you think it would be for us to come here and live?"

Aunt Faith sat down now as suddenly, in her turn, on the stair-head. Recovering, so, from her momentary and utter astonishment, and taking in, during that instant of repose, the full drift of the question propounded, she rose from her involuntarily assumed position, and continued her way down,—answering, without so much as turning her head.—"It would be just the most sensible thing that Henderson Gartney ever did in his life!"

What made Faithie a bit sober, all at once, when the key was turned, and they passed on, out under the elms, into the lane again?

Did you ever project a very wise and important scheme, that involved a little self-sacrifice, which, by a determined looking at the bright side of the subject, you had managed tolerably to ignore; and then, by the instant and unhesitating acquiescence of some one to whose judgment you submitted it, find yourself suddenly wheeled about in your own mind to the stand-point whence you discerned only the difficulty again?

"There's one thing, Aunt Faith," said she, as they slowly walked up the field-path; "I could n't go to school any more."

Faith had discontinued her regular attendance since the recommencement for the year, but had gone in for a few hours on "French and German days."

"There's another thing," said Aunt Faith. "I don't believe your father can afford to send you any more. You're eighteen, aint you?"

"I shall be, this summer."

"Time for you to leave off school. Bring your books and things along with you. You'll have chance enough to study."

Faith had n't thought much of herself before. But when she found her aunt did n't apparently think of her at all, she began to realize keenly all that she must silently give up.

"But it's a good deal of help, auntie, to study with

other people. And then — we shouldn't have any society out here. I don't mean for the sake of parties, and going about. But for the improvement of it. I shouldn't like to be shut out from cultivated people."

"Faith Gartney!" exclaimed Miss Henderson, facing about in the narrow footway, "don't you go to being fine and transcendental! If there's one word I despise more than another, in the way folks use it now-a-days, — it's 'Culture!' As if God didn't know how to make souls grow! You just take root where He puts you, and go to work, and live! He'll take care of the cultivating! If He means you to turn out a rose, or an oak-tree, you'll come to it. And pig-weed's pig-weed, no matter where it starts up!"

"Aunt Faith!" replied the child, humbly and earnestly, "I believe that's true! And I believe I want the country to grow in! But the thing will be," she added, a little doubtfully, "to persuade father."

"Don't he want to come, then? Whose plan is it, pray?" asked Miss Henderson, stopping short again, just as she had resumed her walk, in a fresh surprise.

"Nobody's but mine, yet, auntie! I haven't asked him, but I thought I'd come and look."

Miss Henderson took her by the arm, and looked steadfastly in her dark, earnest eyes.

"You're something, sure enough!" said she, with a sharp tenderness.

Faith didn't know precisely what she meant, except that she seemed to mean approval. And at the one word of appreciation, all difficulty and self-sacrifice vanished out of her sight, and everything brightened to her thought, again, till her thought brightened out into a smile.

"What a sky-full of lovely white clouds!" she said, looking up to the pure, fleecy folds that were flitting over the blue. "We can't see that in Mishaumok!"

"She's just heavenly!" said Glory to herself, standing t the back door, and gazing with a rapturous admiration t Faith's upturned face. "And the dinner's all ready, and I'm thankful, and more, that the custard's baked so beautiful!"

CHAPTER XIII.

DEVELOPMENT.

"Sits the wind in that corner?"
MUCH ADO ABOUT NOTHING.

"For courage mounteth with occasion."
KING JOHN.

THE lassitude that comes with spring had told upon Mr. Gartney. He had dyspepsia, too; and now and then came home early from the counting-room with a headache that sent him to his bed. Dr. Gracie dropped in, friendly-wise, of an evening, — said little that was strictly professional, — but held his hand a second longer, perhaps, than he would have done for a mere greeting, and looked rather scrutinizingly at him when Mr. Gartney's eyes were turned another way. Frequently he made some slight suggestion of a journey, or other summer change.

"You must urge it, if you can, Mrs. Gartney," he said, privately, to the wife. "I don't quite like his looks. Get him away from business, at *almost any* sacrifice," he came to add, at last.

"At *every* sacrifice?" asked Mrs. Gartney, anxious and perplexed. "Business is nearly all, you know."

"Life is more, — reason is more," answered the doctor, gravely.

And the wife went about her daily task with a secret heaviness at her heart.

"Father," said Faith, one evening, after she had read to him the paper while he lay resting upon the sofa, "if you had money enough to live on, how long would it take you to wind up your business?"

"It's pretty nearly wound up now! But what's the use of asking such a question?" answered her father, turning his head away, somewhat fretfully.

"Because," said Faith, timidly, "I've got a little plan in my head, if you'll only listen to it."

A pause. Faith hardly knew whether to venture on, or not.

Presently the head came round again, and the eyes met hers, with a look that was a little surprised, yet wistful and kindly, also.

"Well, Faithie, I'll listen. What is it?"

And then Faith spoke it all out, at once.

"That you should give up all your business, father, and let this house, and go to Cross Corners, and live at the farm."

Mr. Gartney started to his elbow. But a sudden pain that leaped in his temples sent him back again. For a minute or so, he did not speak at all. Then he said, —

"Do you know what you are talking of, daughter?"

"Yes, father; I've been thinking it over a good while, — since the night we wrote down these things."

And she drew from her pocket the memorandum of stocks and dividends.

"You see you have six hundred and fifty dollars a year from these, and this house would be six hundred more, and mother says she can manage on that, in the country, if I will help her."

A simple wording of a simple conclusion. But it told a great deal.

Mr. Gartney shaded his eyes with his hand. Not wholly, perhaps, to shield them from the light.

"You're a good girl, Faithie," said he, presently; and there was assuredly a little tremble in his voice.

"And so, you and your mother have talked it over, together?"

"Yes; often, lately. And she said I had better ask you myself, if I wished it. She is perfectly willing. She thinks it would be good."

"Faithie," said her father, "you make me feel, more than ever, how much I *ought* to do for you!"

"You ought to get well and strong, father, — that is all!" replied Faith, with a quiver in her own voice, this time.

Mr. Gartney sighed.

"I'm no more than a mere useless block of wood!" said he, despondingly.

"We shall just have to set you up, and make an idol of you, then!" cried Faith, cheerily, with tears on her eyelashes, that she winked off, and forbade to be followed.

There had been a ring at the bell while they were speaking; and now Mrs. Gartney entered, followed by Dr. Gracie.

"Well, Miss Faith," said the doctor, after the usual greetings, and a prolonged look at Mr. Gartney's flushed face, and an injunction to him, as he was rising, to keep quiet, — "what have you done to your father, to-night?"

"I've been reading the paper," answered Faith, quietly, "and talking a little."

"Mother!" said Mr. Gartney, catching his wife's hand,

as she came round to find a seat near him, "are you really in the plot, too?"

"I'm glad there *is* a plot," said the doctor, quickly, glancing round with a keen inquiry. "It's time!"

"Wait till you hear it," said Mr. Gartney. "Are you in a hurry to lose your patient?"

"Depends upon *how!*" replied the doctor, touching the truth in a jest.

"This is how. Here's a little jade who has the conceit and audacity to propose to me to wind up my business, (as if she understood the whole process!) and let my house, and go to my farm at Cross Corners. What do you think of that?"

"I think it would be the most sensible thing you ever did in your life!"

"Just exactly what Aunt Henderson said!" cried Faith, exultant.

"Aunt Faith, too! The conspiracy thickens! How long has all this been discussing?" continued Mr. Gartney, fairly roused, and springing, despite the doctor's request, to a sitting position, throwing off, as he did so, the Affghan Faith had laid over his feet.

"There hasn't been much discussion," said Faith. "Only when I went out to Kinnicutt I got auntie to show me the house; and I asked her how she thought it would be if we were to do such a thing, and she said just what Dr. Gracie has said now. And, father," — she continued, — "you *don't* know how beautiful it is there!"

"So you really want to go? and it isn't drumsticks?" queried the doctor, turning round to Faith.

"Some drumsticks are very nice," said Faith.

"Gartney!" said Dr. Gracie, "you'd better mind what this girl of yours says. She's worth attending to."

10*

The wedge had been entered, and Faith's hand had driven it.

The plan was taken into consideration. Of course, such a change could not be made without some pondering; but when almost the continual thought of a family is concentrated upon a single subject, a good deal of pondering and deciding can be done in three weeks. At the end of that time an advertisement appeared in the leading Mishaumok papers, offering the house in Hickory Street to be let; and Mrs. Gartney and Faith were busy packing boxes to go to Kinnicutt.

Only a passing shade had been flung on the project which seemed to brighten into sunshine, otherwise, the more they looked at it, when Mrs. Gartney suddenly said, after a long "talking over," the second evening after the proposal had been first broached, —

"But what will Saidie say?"

Now Saidie, — whom before it has been unnecessary to mention, — was Faith's elder sister, travelling at this moment in Europe, with a wealthy elder sister of Mrs. Gartney.

"I never thought of Saidie," cried Faith.

Saidie was pretty sure not to like Kinnicutt. A young lady, educated at a fashionable New York school, — petted by an aunt who found nobody else to pet, and who had money enough to have petted a whole asylum of orphans, — who had shone in London and Paris for two seasons past, — was not exceedingly likely to discover all the possible delights that Faith had done, under the elms and chestnuts at Cross Corners.

But, after all, this could make no practical difference.

"She would n't like Hickory Street any better," said

Faith, "if we could n't have parties or new furniture any more. And she 's only a visitor, at the best. Aunt Etherege will be sure to have her in New York, or travelling about, ten months out of twelve. She can come to us in June and October. I guess she 'll like strawberries and cream, and — whatever comes at the other season, besides red leaves."

Now this was kind, sisterly consideration of Faith, however little so it seems, set down. It was very certain that no more acceptable provision could be made for Saidie Gartney in the family plan, than to leave her out, except where the strawberries and cream were concerned. In return, she wrote gay, entertaining letters home to her mother and young sister, and sent pretty French, or Florentine, or Roman ornaments for them to wear. Some persons are content to go through life with such exchange of sympathies as this.

By-and-by, Faith being in her own room, took out from her letter-box the last missive from abroad. There was something in this which vexed Faith, and yet stirred her a little, obscurely, aside from the mere vexation.

All things are fair in love, war, and — story-books! So, though she would never have shown the words to you or me, we will peep over her shoulder, and share them, "*en rapport*."

"And Paul Rushleigh, it seems, is as much as ever in Hickory Street! Well — my little Faithie might make a far worse '*parti*' than that! Tell papa I think he may be satisfied there!"

Faith would have cut off her little finger, rather than have had her father dream that such a thing had been put into her head! But unfortunately it was there, now, and could not be helped. She could only,—sitting there in her chamber window with the blood tingling to the hair upon her temples, as if from every neighboring window of the clustering houses about her, eyes could overlook and read what she was reading now,— " wish that Saidie would not write such things as that!" And then wonder how she or her mother could possibly have said so much about their young visitor as to have brought so unreserved a deduction upon her from across the Atlantic.

For all that, it was one pleasant thing Faith would have to lose in leaving Mishaumok. It was very agreeable to have him dropping in, with his gay college gossip; and to dance the "German" with the nicest partner in the Monday class; and to carry the flowers he so often sent her. Had she done things greater than she knew in shutting her eyes resolutely to all her city associations and enjoyments, and urging, for her father's sake, this exodus into the desert?

Only that means were actually wanting to continue on as they were, and that health must at any rate be first striven for as a condition to the future enlargement of means, her father and mother, in their thought for what their child hardly considered for herself, would surely have been more difficult to persuade. They hoped that a summer's rest might enable Mr. Gartney to undertake again some sort of lucrative business, after business should have revived from its present prostration; and that a year or two, perhaps, of economizing in the country, might make it possible for them to return, if they chose, to the house in Hickory Street.

There were leave-takings to be gone through,—questions to be answered, and reasons to be given; for Mrs. Gartney.

the polite wishes of her visiting friends that "Mr. Gartney's health might allow them to return to the city in the winter," with the wonder, unexpressed, whether this were to be a final break-down of the family, or not; and for Faith, the horror and extravagant lamentations of her young *coterie*, at her coming occultation — or setting, rather, out of their sky.

Paul Rushleigh demanded eagerly if there were n't any sober old minister out there, with whom he might be rusticated for his next college prank, which he would contrive with nice adaptation for the express purpose.

Everybody promised to come as far as Kinnicutt "sometime" to see them; the good-byes were all said at last; the city cook had departed, and a woman had been taken in her place who "had no objections to the country;" and on one of the last bright days of May they skimmed, steam-sped, over the intervening country between the brick-and-stone-encrusted hills of Mishaumok and the fair meadow reaches of Kinnicutt; and so disappeared out of the places that had known them so long, and could yet, alas! do so exceedingly well without them.

By the first of June nobody in the great city remembered, or remembered very seriously to regard, the little gap that had been made in its midst.

Do the cloven waters stand a-gape for the little dipper-full of drops that may be drawn out from among them?

CHAPTER XIV.

A DRIVE WITH THE DOCTOR.

"And what is so rare as a day in June?
 Then, if ever, come perfect days;
 Then heaven tries the earth if it be in tune,
 And over it softly her warm ear lays."
LOWELL.

"All lives have their prose translation as well as their ideal meaning."
CHARLES AUCHESTER.

But Kinnicutt opened wider to receive them than Mishaumok had to let them go.

If Mr. Gartney's invalidism had to be pleaded to get away with dignity, it was even more needed to shield with anything of quietness their entrance into the new sphere they had chosen.

It is astonishing how wide the circuit of neighborhood is in and around a centre of bucolic life. The embrace widens with the horizon. Where brick walls shut away the vision, the thickness of a brick shuts out all knowledge. But with the sweep of the far hills, and the up-arching blue, comes a human relationship that takes in all the hills include — all that the blue looks down upon. It is everybody's business to find out everybody, and to know just how everybody is "getting along."

"Faith, with her young adaptability, found great fund

or entertainment in the new social developments that unfolded themselves at Cross Corners.

All sorts of quaint vehicles drove up under the elms in the afternoon visiting hours, day after day, — hitched horses, and unladed passengers. Both doctors and their wives came promptly, of course; the "old doctor" from the village, and the "young doctor" from "over at Lakeside." Quiet Mrs. Holland walked in at the twilight, by herself, one day, to explain that her husband, the minister, was too unwell to visit, and to say her pleasant, unpretentious words of welcome. Square Leatherbee's daughters made themselves fine in lilac silks and green Estella shawls, to offer acquaintance to the new "city people." Aunt Faith came over, once or twice a week, at times when "nobody else would be round under foot," and always with some dainty offering from dairy, garden, or kitchen. At other hours, Glory was fain to seize all opportunity of errands that Miss Henderson could not do, and irradiate the kitchen, lingeringly, until she herself might be more ecstatically irradiated with a glance and smile from Miss Faith, who found and came to understand that whatever might chance to bring her over, her aunt's handmaid would never willingly depart without a return message, or an inquiry whether "there was any message to send, if she pleased?" It was never "any matter about the basket," and — "oh, dear! she did n't wait to be thanked, no more would Miss Henderson;" but what she did wait for hardly appeared, save as a quick kindliness might divine it, seeing that she had no sooner got her thanks and her basket from Faith's own hand and lip, than she was off, shy and happy, and 'glorified up to the topmost wave of her golden locks.

There was need enough of Aunt Faith's ministrations

during these first, few, unsettled weeks. The young woman who "had no objections to the country," objected no more to these pleasant country fashions of neighborly kindness. She had reason. Aunt Faith's "thirds bread," or crisp "vanity cakes," or "velvet creams," were no sooner disposed of than there surely came a starvation interval of sour biscuits, heavy gingerbread, and tough pie-crust, and dinners feebly cooked, with no attempt at desserts, at all.

This was gloomy. This was the first trial of their country life. Plainly, this cook was no cook, neither could she easily be replaced with a better. Mr. Gartney's dyspepsia must be considered. Kinnicutt air and June sunshine would not do all the curative work. The healthy appetite they stimulated must be wholesomely supplied.

Faith took to the kitchen. To Glory's mute and rapturous delight, she began to come almost daily up the field-path, in her pretty round hat and morning wrapper, to waylay her aunt in the tidy kitchen at the early hour when her cookery was sure to be going on, to ask questions and investigate, and "help a little," and then to go home and repeat the operation as nearly as she could for their somewhat later dinner.

"Miss McGonegal seems to be improving," observed Mr. Gartney, complacently, one day, as he partook of a simple, but favorite pudding, nicely flavored and compounded; "or is this a charity of Aunt Henderson's?"

"No," replied his wife, "it is home-manufacture,"—and she glanced at Faith without dropping her tone to a period. Faith shook her head, and the sentence hung in the air, unfinished.

Mrs. Gartney had not been strong, for years. Moreover, she had not a genius for cooking. That is a real gift, as much as a genius for poetry or painting. Faith was finding out, suddenly, that she had it. But she was quite willing that her father should rest in the satisfactory belief that Miss McGonegal, in whom it never, by any possibility, could be developed, was improving; and that the good things that found their way to his table had a paid and permanent origin. He was more comfortable so, she thought. Meanwhile, they would inquire if the region round about Kinnicutt might be expected to afford a substitute.

Dr. Wasgatt's wife told Mrs. Gartney of a young American woman who was staying in the "factory village" beyond Lakeside, and who had asked her husband if he knew of any place where she could "hire out." Doctor Wasgatt would be very glad to take her or Miss Faith over there, of a morning, to see if she would answer.

Faith was very glad to go.

Doctor Wasgatt was the "old doctor." A benign man, as old doctors,—when they don't grow contrariwise, and become unspeakably gruff and crusty,—are apt to be. A benign old doctor, a docile old horse, an old-fashioned two-wheeled chaise that springs to the motion like a bough at a bird-flitting, and an indescribable June morning wherein to drive four miles and back,—well! Faith couldn't help exulting in her heart that they wanted a cook.

It took them a long while to accomplish the four miles, though. It was lucky the first dish of strawberries was ready in the ice, for dinner, and that the roast lamb of yesterday was to be eaten cold to-day, and that Mahala had promised to see that Norah didn't overboil the peas. Faith was free, so, to enjoy to the full all the enchantment and novelty of her drive, and not to care a bit if she shouldn't get home till sunset.

Doctor Wasgatt had half-a-dozen patients to see between Cross Corners and the factory village. Half-a-dozen, that is, that he had known of, and set out with intent to see; and half-a-dozen more, or thereabouts, to whom he was summoned by waylayment. A woman standing at the window of one house upon the road, holding a pillow by the end between her teeth, and preparing to shake it into its case, spied his chaise with the eye she had kept outward for the purpose all the morning, and, dropping her extraordinary mouthful, as the raven did who sang, of old, to the fox, hailed him with outstretched head and sudden cry. And then, with the overzeal some women have who never know when a thing is accomplished, she distrusted the force of a single shot across his bows, and seeing that he appeared about to pass the gate, — which was really that he might only place his horse and his companion under the shade of the butternuts beyond, — leaned half her person from the window and fluttered the pillow-case at arm's length at him, as a signal to lay to. Which, at the moment, he did; leaving Faith, not unwilling, under the flickering shade of the tall trees; breathing in, with all June balms whereof the air was full, the spicy smell of a chip-yard round the corner, where the scraps of pine lay fervid and fragrant under the summer sun.

There was neither sight, nor sound, nor odor, this perfect day, but seemed an addition of delight. People were picturesque, even though they held feather-pillows between their teeth, and screamed frantically from chamber windows. The joyous and bounteous air found no utterance so discordant that it could not take into its clear, mellow sweep, and soften into harmony. The crow that flew over the young cornfields, — the farmer hallooing to his cattle, — the creak of wagons, — all, as really as the bird-twitterings that rained, pure musical, from every bough, — made up a summer melody together. Faith could n't be left suddenly anywhere, to wait while Doctor Wasgatt dispensed pills, and drops, and powders, where it was n't an ecstasy to be.

At another farm-house dooryard, an urchin had had an hour's swing on the otherwise forbidden gate, that he might, by that means, be at hand to "stop the doctor." It is greatly to be feared that "grandma'am's bad night" had hardly been deplored with a due sympathy, meanwhile.

There were scarcely any other patients, in truth, to-day, among them all, than the old, who were "kinder pulled down by the warm spell," or babies, who must cut teeth, and consequently worry, though the earth they had scarcely looked upon was rioting in all this growing joy, cutting, painless, quick, green blades of life everywhere, and so smiling but the more widely; and two or three consumptive invalids, who must soon shut their weary eyes upon the summer, let her lavish herself gloriously as she might. What others, truly, could be ill in June?

The way was very lovely toward Lakeside, and across to Factory Village. It crossed the capricious windings of Wachaug two or three times within the distance, and then bore round the Pond Road, which kept its old traditional cognomen, though the new neighborhood that had grown up at its farther bend had got a modern name, and the beautiful pond itself had come to be known with a legitimate dignity as Lake Wachaug.

Graceful birches, with a spring, and a joyous, whispered secret in every glossy leaf, leaned over the road toward the water; and close down to its ripples grew wild shrubs and flowers, and lush grass, and lady-bracken, while out over the still depths rested green lily-pads, like floating thrones waiting the fair water-queens who, a few weeks hence, should rise to claim them. Back, behind the birches, reached the fringe of woodland that melted away, presently in the sunny pastures, and held in bush and branch hundreds of little mother-birds, brooding in a still rapture, like separate embodied pulses of the Universal Love, over a coming life and joy.

Life and joy were everywhere. A thrill came up from the warm earth, where insect and root were stirring at its every pore, and the whole air was tremulous with a gentle breath and motion. The sunlight danced and shimmered downward through the sky, as with the very overcharge of vitality it came to bring. Faith's heart danced and glowed within her. She had thought, many a time before, that she was getting somewhat of the joy of the country, when, after dinner and business were over, she had come out from Mishaumok, in proper fashionable toilette, with her father and mother, for an afternoon airing in the city environs. But here, in the old doctor's "one-hoss shay," and with her round straw hat and chintz wrapper on, she was finding out what a rapturously different thing it is to go out into the bountiful morning, and identify one's self therewith.

She had almost forgotten that she had any other errand when they turned away from the lake, and took a little side road that wound off from it, and struck the river again, and brought them at last to the Wachaug Mills and the little factory settlement around them.

"This is Mrs. Pranker's," said the doctor, stopping at the third door in a block of factory houses, "and it's a sister-in-law of hers who wants to 'hire out.' I've a patient in the next row, and if you like, I'll leave you here a few minutes."

Faith's foot was instantly on the chaise-step, and she sprang to the ground with only an acknowledging touch of the good doctor's hand, upheld to aid her.

A white-haired boy of three, making gravel puddings in a scolloped tin dish at the door, scrambled up as she approached, upset his pudding, and sidled up the steps in a scared fashion, with a finger in his mouth, and his round gray eyes sending apprehensive peeps at her through the linty locks.

"Well, tow-head!" ejaculated an energetic female voice within, to an accompaniment of swashing water, and a scrape of a bucket along the floor; "what's wanting now? Can't you stay put, nohow?"

An unintelligible jargon of baby chatter followed, which seemed, however, to have conveyed an idea to the mother's mind, for she appeared immediately in the passage, drying her wet arms upon her apron.

"Mrs. Pranker?" asked Faith.

"That's my name," replied the woman, as who should say, peremptorily, "what then?"

"I was told — my mother heard — that a sister of yours was looking for a place."

"She haint done much about *lookin'*," was the reply, "but she was sayin' she did n't know but what she 'd hire out for a spell, if anybody wanted her. She's in the keepin'-room. You can come in and speak to her, if you're a mind to. The kitchen floor's wet. I'm jest a washin' of it. — You little sperrit!" This to the child, who was amusing himself with the floor-cloth which he had fished out of the bucket, and held up, dripping, letting a stream of dirty water run down the front of his red calico frock. "If children aint the biggest torments! Talk about Job! His wife had to have more patience than he did, I'll be bound! And patience aint any use, either! The more you have, the more you're took advantage of! I declare and testify, it makes me as cross as sin, jest to think how good-natured I be!" And with this, she snatched the cloth from the boy's hands, shook first him and then his frock, to get rid, in so far as a shake might accomplish it, of original depravity and sandy soapsuds, and carried him, vociferant, to the door, where she set him down to the consolation of gravel-pudding again.

Meanwhile Faith crossed the sloppy kitchen, on tiptoe, toward an open door, that revealed a room within.

Here a very fat young woman, with a rather pleasant face, was seated, sewing, in a rocking-chair, her elbows resting on the arms thereof, and her work held up, so, before her, while her feet, visible below the hem of her dress at a rather wide interval from each other, were keeping up, by a slight, regular rebound from the floor, an easy motion that seemed not at all to interfere with her use of the needle.

She did not rise, or move, at Faith's entrance, otherwise than to look up, composedly, and let fall her arms along those of the chair, retaining the needle in one hand and her work in the other.

"I came to see," said Faith, — obliged to say something to explain her presence, but secretly appalled at the magnitude of the subject she had to deal with, — "if you wanted a place in a family."

"Take a seat," said the young woman.

Faith availed herself of one, and, doubtful precisely what to say next, waited for indications from the other party.

"Well — I *was* calc'latin' to hire out this summer, but I aint very partic'ler about it, neither."

She made little scratches, indifferently, on the end of the chair-arm, with the point of her needle, as she spoke, and rubbed them out with the moist finger-tip from which she had slipped her thimble.

"Can you cook?"

"Most kinds. I can't do much fancy cookin'. Guess I can make bread, — all sorts, — and roast, and bile, and see to common fixin's, though, as well as the next one!"

"We like plain country cooking," said Faith, thinking of Aunt Henderson's delicious, though simple, preparations. "And I suppose you can make new things if you have direction."

"Well — I'm pretty good at workin' out a resate, too. But then, I aint anyways partic'ler 'bout hirin' out, as I said afore."

Faith judged rightly that this was a salvo put in for pride. The Yankee girl would not appear anxious for a servile situation. All the while the conversation went on, she sat tilting herself gently back and forth in the rocking-chair, with a lazy touching of her toes to the floor. Her very *vis inertiæ* would not let her stop.

Faith's only question, now, was with herself, — how she should get away again. She had no idea that this huge, indolent creature would be at all suitable as their servant. And then, her utter want of manners!

"I'll tell my mother what you say," said she, rising. "I only came to inquire."

"What's your mother's name, and where d' ye live?"

"We live at Kinnicutt Cross Corners. My mother is Mrs. Henderson Gartney."

"'M!"

Faith turned toward the kitchen.

"Look here!" called the stout young woman **after her**; you may jest say **if** she wants me she can send for **me**. I don't mind if I try it a spell."

"I did n't ask *your* name," remarked Faith, **pausing on** the threshold and waiting for enlightenment.

"Oh! my name's Mis' Battis!"

Faith escaped over the wet floor, sprang past the white-haired child at the door-step, and was just in time to be put into the chaise by Doctor Wasgatt, who drove up as she came out. She did not dare trust her voice to speak within hearing of the house; but when they had come round the mills again, into the secluded river road, she startled its quietness and the doctor's composure, with a laugh that rang out clear and overflowing like the very soul of fun.

"So that's all you've got out of your visit?" asked the doctor, guessing easily at some ludicrous **conjuncture**.

"Yes, that is all," said Faith. "But it's a great deal!" And she laughed again, — such a merry little waterfall of a laugh as chimed in wonderfully with all the broad, bright cheer of the summer day, and made a fitting music there, between the woods and river.

When she reached home, Mrs. Gartney met her at the door.

"Well, Faithie," she cried, somewhat eagerly, "what have you found?"

Faith's eyes danced with merriment.

"I don't know, mother! A — hippopotamus, **I think!**"

"**Won't she do?** What do you mean?"

"Why she's as big! **I can't** tell you how big! And she sat in a rocking-chair and rocked all the time, — and she says her name is Miss Battis!"

Mrs. Gartney looked rather perplexed than amused.

"But, Faith! — I can't think how she knew, — she must have been listening, — Norah has been so horribly angry! And she's up stairs packing her things to go right off. How *can* we be left without a cook?"

"It seems Miss McGonegal means to demonstrate that we can! Perhaps — the hippopotamus *might* be trained to domestic service! She said you could send if you wanted her. And she knows about plain country cooking."

"I don't see anything else to do. Norah won't even stay till morning. And there isn't a bit of bread in the house. I can't send this afternoon, though, for your father has driven over to Sedgely about some celery and tomato plants, and won't be home till tea-time."

"I'll make some cream biscuits like aunt Faith's. And I'll go out into the garden and find Luther. If he can't carry us through the Reformation, somehow, he does n't deserve his name."

Luther was found — thought Jerry Blanchard would n't "value lettin' him have his old horse and shay for an hour." and he would n't "be mor'n that goin'." He could "fetch her, easy enough, if that was all."

Mis' Battis came.

She entered Mrs. Gartney's presence with calm *nonchalance*, and "flumped" incontinently into the easiest and nearest chair.

Mrs. Gartney began with the common preliminary — the name. Mis' Battis introduced herself as before.

"But your first name?" proceeded the lady.

"My first name was Parthenia Pranker. I'm a relic."

Mrs. Gartney experienced an internal convulsion, but retained her outward composure.

"I suppose you would quite as lief be called Parthenia?"

"Ruther," replied the relict, laconically.

And **Mrs. Parthenia** Battis was forthwith installed, — *pro tem.*, — in the Cross Corners kitchen.

"She's got considerable gumption," was the opinion Luther volunteered, of his own previous knowledge, — for Mrs. Battis was an old schoolmate and neighbor, — "but she's powerful slow."

CHAPTER XV

NEW DUTIES.

"Whatsoever thy hand findeth to do, do it with thy might."—Ecc. 9: 10.

> "A servant with this clause
> Makes drudgery divine;—
> Who sweeps a room as for Thy laws,
> Makes that and the action fine."
>   GEORGE HERBERT.

MIS' BATTIS'S "gumption" was a relief,—conjoined, even, as it was, to a mighty *inertia*,—after the experience of Norah McGonegal's utter incapacity; and her admission, *pro tempore*, came to be tacitly looked upon as a permanent adoption, for want of a better alternative. She continued to seat herself, unabashed, whenever opportunity offered, in the presence of the family; and invariably did so, when Mrs. Gartney either sent for, or came to her, to give orders. Dishcloth, or rolling-pin, or bread-knife, or poker, or whatever other utensil in hand,—down she would plump the instant active operations, if hers might ever be so denominated, were suspended, by having her attention demanded otherwise. She always spoke of Mr. Gartney as "he," addressed her mistress as Miss Gartney, and ignored all prefix to the gentle name of Faith. The first of these habits was simply borne with, in consideration of inalienable laws.

Heavy bodies have a right to gravitate; and power of resistance can only be expected in inverse proportion to the force of attraction. For the matter of appellations, Mrs. Gartney at last remedied the pronominal difficulty by invariably applying all remarks bearing no other indication, to that other "he" of the household — Luther. Her own claim to the matronly title she gave up all hope of establishing; for if the "relic'" abbreviated her own wifely distinction, how should she be expected to dignify other people?

As to Faith, her mother ventured one day, sensitively and timidly, to speak directly to the point.

"My daughter has always been accustomed to be called *Miss* Faith," she said, gently, in reply to an observation of Parthenia's, in which the ungarnished name had twice been used. "It isn't a *very* important matter, — still, it would be pleasanter to us, and I dare say you won't mind trying to remember it?"

"'M!" Mis' Battis's invariable intonation in response to the suggestion of any new idea was somewhat prolonged. "No, — I aint partic'ler. Faith aint a long name, and 't won't be much trouble to put a handle on, if that's what you want. It's English-fashion, aint it?"

Parthenia's coolness enabled Mrs. Gartney to assert, somewhat more confidently, her own dignity.

"It is a fashion of respect and courtesy, everywhere, I believe."

"'M!" re-ejaculated the relict.

Thereafter, Faith was "Miss," with a slight pressure of emphasis upon the handle.

"Mamma!" cried Hendie, impetuously, one day, as he rushed in from a walk with his attendant, "I *hate* Mahala

Harris! I wish you'd let me dress myself, and go to walk alone, and send her off to Jericho!"

"Whereabouts do you suppose Jericho to be?" asked Faith, laughing.

"I don't know. It's where she keeps wishing I was, when she's cross, and I want anything. I wish she was there!—and I mean to ask papa to send her!"

"Go and take your hat off, Hendie, and have your hair brushed, and your hands washed, and then come back in a nice quiet little temper, and we'll talk about it," said Mrs. Gartney.

"I think," said Faith to her mother, as the boy was heard mounting the stairs to the nursery, right foot foremost all the way, "that Mahala doesn't manage Hendie as she ought. She keeps him in a fret. I hear them in the morning while I am dressing. She seems to talk to him in a taunting sort of way; and he gets so angry, sometimes! I'm afraid she's spoiling his temper."

"What can we do?" exclaimed Mrs. Gartney, worriedly. "These changes are dreadful. We might get some one worse. And then we can't afford to pay extravagantly. Mahala has been content to take less wages, and I think she means to be faithful. Perhaps if I make her understand how important it is, she will try a different manner."

"Only it might be too late to do much good, if Hendie has really got to dislike her. And — besides — I've been thinking, — only, you will say I'm so full of projects — "

But what the project was, Mrs. Gartney did not hear at once, for just then Hendie's voice was heard again at the head of the stairs.

"I tell you, mother said I might! I'm going — down — in a nice — little temper — to ask her — to send you — to

Jericho!" Left foot foremost, a drop between each few syllables, he came stumping, defiantly, down the stairs, and appeared with all his eager story in his eyes.

"She plagues me, mamma! She tells me to see who'll get dressed first; and if *she* does, she says, —

"'The first's the best,
   The second's the same;
   The last's the worst
   Of all the game!'

And if *I* get dressed first, — all but the buttoning, you know, — she says, —

"'The last's the best,
   The second's the same;
   The first's the worst
   Of all the game!'

And then she keeps telling me that 'her little sister never behaved like me.' I asked her where her little sister was, and she said she'd gone over Jordan. I'm glad of it! I wish Makala would go too!"

Mrs. Gartney smiled, and Faith could not help laughing outright.

Hendie burst into a passion of tears.

"Everybody keeps plaguing me! It's too bad!" he cried, with tumultuous sobs.

Faith checked her laughter instantly. She took the indignant little fellow on her lap, in despite of some slight, implacable struggle on his part, and kissed his pouting lips.

"No, indeed, Hendie! We wouldn't plague you for all the world! And you don't know what I've got for you, just as soon as you're ready for it!"

Hendie took his little knuckles out of his eyes, and

looked up, inquiringly, holding his hands upraised, meantime, on either side his tearful face, as quite ready to begin crying again, in case the proffered diversion should not prove satisfactory.

"A bunch of great red cherries, as big as your two hands!"

The hands went alternately to the eyes again, and streaked away the tears for clearer seeing.

"Where?"

"I'll get them, if you're good. And then you can go out in the front yard, and eat them, so that you can drop the stones on the grass."

Hendie was soon established on a flat stone under the old chestnut-trees, in a happy temporary oblivion of Mahala's injustice, and her little sister's unendurable perfections.

"I'll tell you, mamma. I've been thinking we need not keep Mahala, if you don't wish. She has been so used to do nothing but run round after Hendie, that, really, she isn't much good about the house; and I'll take Hendie's trundle-bed into my room, and there'll be one less chamber to take care of; and you know we always dust and arrange down here."

"Yes,— but the sweeping, Faithie! And the washing! Parthenia never would get through with it all."

"Well, somebody might come and help wash. And I guess I can sweep."

"But I can't bear to put you to such work, darling! You need your time for other things."

"I have ever so much time, mother! And, besides, as Aunt Faith says, I don't believe it makes so very much matter *what* we do. I was talking to her, the other day, about doing coarse work, and living a narrow, common kind of life, and what do you think she said?"

"I can't tell, of course. Something blunt and original."

"We were out in the garden. She pointed to some plants that were coming up from seeds, that had just two tough, clumsy, coarse leaves. 'What do you call them?' said auntie. 'Cotyledons, are n't they?' said I. 'I don't know what they are in botany,' said she; 'but I know the use of 'em. They 'll last awhile, and help feed up what's growing inside and underneath, and by-and-by they 'll drop off, when they 're done with, and you 'll see what's been coming of it. Folks can't live the best right out at first, any more than plants can. I guess we all want some kind of — cotyledons.'"

Mrs. Gartney's eyes shone with affection, and something that affection called there, as she looked upon her daughter.

"I guess the cotyledons won't hinder your growing," said she.

And so, in a few days after, Mahala was dismissed, and Faith took upon herself new duties.

It was a bright, happy face that glanced hither and thither, about the house, those fair summer mornings; and it was n't the hands alone that were busy, as under their dexterous and delicate touch all things arranged themselves in attractive and graceful order. Thought straightened and cleared itself, as furniture and books were dusted and set right; and while the carpet brightened under the broom, something else brightened and strengthened, also, within.

It is so true, what the author of "Euthanasy" tells us, that exercise of limb and muscle develops not only themselves, but what is in us as we work.

"Every stroke of the hammer upon the anvil hardens

a little what is at the time the temper of the smith's mind."

"The toil of the ploughman furrows the ground, and so it does his brow with wrinkles, visibly; and invisibly, but quite as certainly, it furrows the current of feeling, common with him at his work, into an almost unchangeable channel."

Faith's life-purpose deepened as she did each daily task. She had hold, already of the "high and holy work of love" that had been prophesied.

"I am sure of one thing, mother," said she, gayly; "if I don't learn much that is new, I am bringing old knowledge into play. It's the same thing, taken hold of at different ends. I've learned to draw straight lines, and shade pictures; and so there is n't any difficulty in sweeping a carpet clean, or setting chairs straight. I never shall wonder again that a woman who never heard of a right angle can't lay a table even."

CHAPTER XVI.

"BLESSED BE YE, POOR."

And so we yearn, and so we sigh,
 And reach for more than we can see;
And, witless of our folded wings,
 Walk Paradise, unconsciously.

OCTOBER came, and brought small **dividends**. The expenses upon the farm had necessarily been considerable, also, to put things in "good running order." Mr. Gartney's health, though greatly improved, was not yet so confidently to be relied on, as to make it advisable for him to think of any change, as yet, with a view to business. Indeed, there was little opportunity for business, to tempt him. Everything was flat. The exhaustion of the great financial struggle it had passed through lay, like a paralysis, upon the community. There was neither confidence nor credit. Without actual capital, nothing could be done. Mr. Gartney must wait. But when a man finds himself, at five-and-forty years of age, out of business, with broken health, and in disastrous times, there is little likelihood of his launching successfully ever again into any large mercantile life. Mrs. Gartney and Faith felt, though they talked of waiting, that the prospect really before them was that of a careful, obscure life, upon a very limited income. The house in Mishaumok had stood vacant all the summer

There was hope, of course, of letting it now, as the winter season came on, but rents were falling, and people were timid and discouraged. Nobody made any sort of move who could help it.

October was beautiful at Kinnicutt. And Faith, when she looked out over the glory of woods and sky, and felt the joy of the sunshine, as the hem of summer's departing robe overswept the bright frost-broideries of autumn, making such a palpable blessedness abroad — felt rich with the great wealth of the world, and forgot about economies and privations. She was so glad they had come here with their altered plans, and had not struggled shabbily and drearily on in Mishaumok!

It was only when some chance bit of news from the city, or a girlish, gossipy note from some school-friend found its way to Cross Corners, that she felt, a little keenly, her denials, — realized how the world she had lived in all her life was going on without her, and how here, environed with the beauty of all earth and heaven, she was yet so nearly shut out from congenial human companionship. There were so many things she had hoped to learn, and to do, and to enjoy, that now must be only dreams! So many things she felt herself fitted for, that now might never come in her way! What a strange thing was life! A longing — a reaching — an imagining — a hoping, — was it ever a substantial grasping? Were we just put here to catch a glimpse of things that *might* be, and to turn away from all, knowing that it *may* not be, for us?

It was the old plaint that Glory made, in her dark days of childhood, — this feeling of despondency and loss that assailed Faith now and then, — "such lots of good times in the world, and she not in 'em!"

Mrs. Etherege and Saidie were coming home. Gertrude Rushleigh, Saidie's old intimate, was to be married on the twenty-eighth, and had fixed her wedding thus for the very last of the month, that Miss Gartney might arrive to keep her promise of long time, by officiating as bridesmaid.

The family eclipse would not overshadow Saidie. She had made her place in the world now, and with her aunt's aid and countenance, would keep it. It was quite different with Faith, — disappearing, as she had done, from notice, before ever actually "coming out."

"It was a thousand pities," Aunt Etherege said, when she and Saidie discussed with Mrs. Gartney, at Cross Corners, the family affairs. "And things just as they were, too! Why, another year might have settled matters for her, so that this need never have happened! At any rate, the child shouldn't be moped up here, all winter!"

Mrs. Etherege had engaged rooms, on her arrival, at the Mishaumok House; and it seemed to be taken for granted by her, and by Saidie as well, that this coming home was, as Faith had long ago prophesied, a mere visit; that Miss Gartney would, of course, spend the greater part of the winter with her aunt; and that lady extended also an invitation to Mishaumok for a month — including the wedding festivities at the Rushleighs' — to Faith.

Faith shook her head. She "knew she couldn't be spared so long." Secretly, she doubted whether it would be a good plan to go back and get a peep at things that might send her home discontented and unhappy.

But her mother reasoned, or felt impulse, otherwise. Faithie must go. "The child mustn't be moped up." She would get on, somehow, without her. Mothers always can. So Faith, by a compromise, went for a fortnight. She couldn't quite resist her newly-returned sister.

Besides, a pressing personal invitation had come from Margaret Rushleigh to Faith herself, with a little private announcement at the end, that "Paul was refractory, and utterly refused to act as fourth groomsman, unless Faith Gartney were got to come and stand with him."

Faith tore off the postscript, and might have lit it at her cheeks, but dropped it, of habit, into the fire; and then the note was at the disposal of the family.

It was a whirl of wonderful excitement to Faith — that fortnight! So many people to see, so much to hear, and in the midst of all, the gorgeous wedding festival!

What wonder if a little dream flitted through her head, as she stood there, in the marriage group, at Paul Rushleigh's side, and looked about her on the magnificent fashion wherein the affection of new relatives and old friends had made itself tangible; and heard the kindly words of the elder Mr. Rushleigh to Kate Livingston, who stood with his son Philip, and whose bridal, it was well known, was to come next? Jewels, and silver, and gold, are such flashing, concrete evidences of love! And the courtly condescension of an old and world-honored man to the young girl whom his son has chosen, is such a winning and distinguishing thing!

Paul Rushleigh had finished his college course, and was to go abroad this winter — between the weddings, as he said — for his brother Philip's was to take place in the coming spring. After that, — things were not quite settled, but something was to be arranged for him meanwhile, — he would have to begin his work in the world; and then — he supposed it would be time for him to find a helpmeet. Marrying was like dying, he believed; when a family once began to go off there was soon an end of it!

Blushes were the livery of the evening, and Faith's deeper glow at this audacious rattle passed **unheeded**, except, perhaps, as it might be somewhat wilfully interpreted.

There **were** two **or** three parties made for **the newly-married** couple in the week that followed. The week **after,** Paul Rushleigh, with the bride and groom, was to sail **for** Europe. At each of these brilliant entertainments he constituted himself, as in duty bound, Faith's knight and sworn attendant; and a superb bouquet for each occasion, the result of the ransack of successive greenhouses, came punctually, from him, to her door. For years afterward, — perhaps for all her life, — Faith could n't smell heliotrope, **and** geranium and orange flowers, without floating back, momentarily, into the dream of those few, enchanted days!

She staid **in** Mishaumok a little beyond the limit she had fixed for herself, to go, with the others, on board the steamer at the time of her sailing, and see the gay party off. **Paul** Rushleigh had more significant words, and another **gift of** flowers as a farewell.

When she carried these last **to** her own room, to put them **in** water, on her return, something she had not noticed before glittered among **their stems**. It was a delicate little ring, of twisted gold, with a forget-me-not in turquoise and enamel upon the top.

Faith was half-pleased, half-frightened, and wholly ashamed.

Paul Rushleigh was miles out on the Atlantic. There was no help for it, she thought. **It** had been cunningly done.

And so, **in the short November days,** she went back to Kinnicutt.

The east parlor had to be shut up now, for the winter. The family gathering-place was the sunny little sitting-room; and with closed doors and doubled windows, they began, for the first time, to find that they were really living in a little bit of a house.

It was very pretty, though, with the rich carpet and the crimson curtains that had come from Hickory Street, replacing the white muslin draperies and straw matting of the summer; and the books and vases, and statuettes and pictures, gathered into so small space, seemed to fill the room with luxury and beauty.

Faith nestled her little work-stand into a nook between the windows. Hendie's blocks and picture books were stowed in a corner cupboard. Mr. Gartney's newspapers and pamphlets, as they came, found room in a deep drawer below; and so, through the wintry drifts and gales, they were "close hauled" and comfortable.

Faith was happy; yet she thought, now and then, when the whistling wind broke the stillness of the dark evenings, of light and music elsewhere; and how, a year ago, there had always been the chance of a visitor or two to drop in, and while away the hours. Nobody rang the bell or lifted the old-fashioned knocker, here at Cross Corners.

By day, even, it was scarcely different. Kinnicutt was hibernating. Each household had drawn into its shell. And the huge drifts, lying defiant against the fences in the short, ineffectual winter sunlight, held out little hope of reanimation. Aunt Faith, in her pumpkin hood, and Rob Roy cloak, and carpet moccasins, came over once in two or three days, and even occasionally staid to tea, and helped make up a rubber of whist for Mr. Gartney's amusement; but, beyond this, they had no social excitement.

January brought a thaw; and, still further to break the monotony, there arose a stir and an anxiety in the parish.

Good Mr. Holland, its minister of thirty years, whose health had been failing for many months, was at last compelled to relinquish the duties of his pulpit for a time; and a supply was sought with the ultimate probability of a succession. A new minister came to preach, who was to fill the pastor's place for the ensuing three months. On his first Sunday among them, Faith heard a wonderful sermon.

I indicate thus, not the oratory, nor the rhetoric; but the *sermon*, of which these were the mere vehicle, — the word of truth itself, — which was spoken, seemingly, to her very thought.

So also, as certainly, to the long life-thought of one other. Glory McWhirk sat in Miss Henderson's corner pew, and drank it in, as a soul athirst.

A man of middle age, one might have said, at first sight, — there was, here and there, a silver gleam in the dark hair and beard; yet a fire and earnestness of youth in the deep, beautiful eye, and a look in the face as of life's first flush and glow not lost, but rather merged in broader light, still climbing to its culmination, belied these tokens, and made it as if a white frost had fallen in June, — rising up before the crowded village congregation, looked round upon the upturned faces, as One had looked before who brought the bread of Life to men's eager asking; and uttered the self-same simple words.

It was a certain pause and emphasis he made, — a slight new rendering of punctuation, — that sent home the force of those words to the people who heard them, as if it had been for the first time, and fresh from the lips of the Great Teacher.

"Blessed are the poor: *in spirit:* for theirs is the kingdom of heaven."

"Herein Christ spoke, not to a class, only, but to the world! A world of souls, wrestling with the poverty of life!

"In that whole assemblage — that great concourse — that had thronged from cities and villages to hear His words upon the mountain-side, — was there, think you, *one satisfied nature?*

"Friends — are *ye* satisfied?

. . . .

"Or, does every life come to know, at first or at last, how something, — a hope, or a possibility, or the fulfilment of a purpose, — has got dropped out of it, or has even never entered, so that an emptiness yawns, craving, therein, forever?

"How many souls hunger till they are past their appetite! Go on, — down through the years, — needy and waiting, and never find or grasp that which a sure instinct tells them they were made for?

"This, this is the poverty of life! These are the poor, to whom God's Gospel was preached in Christ! And to these denied and waiting ones the first words of Christ's preaching — as I read them — were spoken in blessing.

"Because, elsewhere, he blesses the meek; elsewhere and presently, he tells us how the lowly in spirit shall inherit the earth; so, when I open to this, his earliest uttered benediction upon our race, I read it with an interpretation that includes all humanity.

"'Blessed, in spirit, are the poor. Theirs is the kingdom of heaven.'

. . . .

"They, only, who go without, know, truly, what it is to have. The light, and the music, and the splendor, and the feasting, are greater to the beggar who peeps in from the street, than to him who sits at the revel. It is the naked and the hungry who can tell you best the good of food and raiment. So we live in a paradox. We feel, keenest, the joy we never come to.

.   .   .   .   .   .

"Ye who have missed out of your actual living the answer to your soul's passionate asking, — ye whom something afar off, that ought to be your very own, passes by like a mirage, who see, away off upon the distant horizon, like dwellers in a wintry Arctic, a sun circling over happier zones, that never comes nigh your zenith, — see here! where the unsetting Sun of the Kingdom sends down its full and glorious rays into the secret cold and ache within you!

.   .   .   .   .   .

"Outside may be cold and darkness. Your hands may stretch into an unresponsive void. Yet in your spirits are ye blessed. There find ye, wide open, the door into the Kingdom! As out of a dream, paths impossible to sense and every day show plain and sudden transit into distant places, — so from your shut souls widens out an entrance-way into God's everlasting Joy!

.   .   .   .   .   .

"Yours is the Kingdom! Because earth is so little, the world that lies in and about this visible that we call earth becomes so much!

"What is this Kingdom of Heaven? 'It is within you.' It is that which you hold, and live in spiritually; the *real*, of which all earthly, outward being and having are but the show. It is the region wherein little children "do always behold the Face of my Father which is in Heaven." It is where we are when we shut our eyes and pray in the words that Christ taught us.

* * * * * * * *

"There are souls who do not need to live out, coarsely, in detail. Their inward conception transcends the visible form. Count it an assurance of more vital good, when God denies you.

* * * * * * * *

"All that in any life you know of or can imagine that seems to you lovely, and to be longed for, is yours already, in that very longing. You take its essence, so, into your souls. And you hold it as God's promise for the great time to come. So you have His seal upon your foreheads. So He calls you, and shall lead you, into the place He has prepared for you from the foundation of the world. There is no joy, — there is no beauty, — there is no glory of living or of acting, — no supreme moment you can picture in your dreams, that is not in your life, as God sees it, — stirring in the intuition you have of it now, — waiting for you in the glorious fulfilment that shall be There!

* * * * * * * *

"What matters, then, where your feet stand, or wherewith your hands are busy? So that it is the spot where God has put you, and the work He has given you to do? Your real life is within, — hid in God with Christ, — ripening, and strengthening, and waiting, as through the long, geologic ages of night and incompleteness waited the germs of all that was to unfold into this actual, green, and bounteous earth!

* * * * * * * *

"Take in to yourselves, then, fearlessly, all life whereto your own life, by any far or secret sympathy, touches, —

for it is yours! Rejoice with that which **doth** rejoice, and weep with all that **weeps!**

"Your **body can only traverse minute spaces of a tiny globe: the** minutes of your breathing, mortal life **can only** give you time for puny and unfinished action; — **but the** soul of all that is broad and beautiful, noble and great, **may** be none the less nourishing within you, feeding itself **on all the** life that is living, or has **been** living, or shall **be** lived!

. . . .

"The narrower your **daily round, the wider.** maybe, the outreach. Isolated **upon a barren** mountain-peak, **you** may take in river and lake, — **forest,** field, and **valley.** A hundred **gardens and harvests lift** their **bloom and fulness** to **your single eye.**

"There **is a sunlight that contracts the vision; there is a** starlight that **enlarges it to take in infinite space.**

> "God sets some souls in shade, alone.
> They have no daylight of their own.
> Only in lives of happier ones
> They see the shine of distant suns.
>
> "God knows. Content thee with thy night.
> Thy greater heaven hath grander light.
> To day is close. The hours are small.
> Thou sitst afar, and hast them all.
>
> "Lose the less joy that doth but blind;
> Reach forth a larger bliss to find.
> To-day is brief: the inclusive spheres
> Rain raptures of a thousand years."

Faith could not tell what hymn was sung, or what were **the words of the prayer that followed the sermon.** There was a music **and an uplifting in her own soul** that made them needless, but for the pause they gave **her.**

She hardly knew that a notice was read as the people rose before the benediction, when the minister gave out, as requested, that "the Village Dorcas Society would meet on Wednesday of the coming week, at Mrs. Parley Gimp's."

She was made aware that it had fallen upon her ears, though heard unconsciously, when Serena Gimp caught her by the sleeve in the church porch.

"Aint it awful," said she, with a simper and a flutter of importance, "to have your name called right out so in the pulpit? I declare, if it had n't been for seeing the new minister, I would n't have come to meeting, I dreaded it so! Aint he handsome? He 's old, though — thirty-five! He 's broken-hearted, too! Somebody died, or something else, that he was going to be married to, ever so many years ago; and they say he has n't hardly spoken to a lady since. That 's so romantic! I don't wonder he preaches such low-spirited kind of sermons. Only I wish they war n't quite so. I suppose it 's beautiful, and heavenly-minded, and all that; but yet I 'd rather hear something a little kind of cheerful. Don't you think so? But the poetry was elegant — war n't it? I guess it 's original, too. They say he puts things in the 'Mishaumok Monthly.' — Come Wednesday, won't you? We shall depend, you know."

To Miss Gimp, the one salient point, amid the solemnities of the day, had been that pulpit notice. She had put new strings to her bonnet for the occasion. Mrs. Gimp, being more immediately and personally affected, had modestly remained away from church.

Faith got away, she hardly knew how. Her mind misgave her afterward that it had been by a precipitate and positive promise to attend the meeting of the Village Dorcas Society.

Glory McWhirk went straight through the village, home; and out to her little room in the sunny side of the low, sloping roof. This was her winter nook. She had a shadier one, looking the other way, for summer.

Does it seem unlikely that this untaught girl should have taken in the meaning of the words that had burned upon her ear to-day? The speaker's diction may have been beyond her, here and there; it might be impossible for her now to gather up in her memory any portion of the precise form in which the glorious truth had come to her; that mattered not. It needs not a critical interpretation of language to apprehend a thought whose rudiment has been lying in the soul before. The little seed underneath the earth can no further analyze the sunbeam than to snatch from it the mysterious vivification it was waiting for. This it does, surely.

"I wonder if it's all true!" she cried, silently, in her soul, while she stood for a minute with bonnet and shawl still on, and grasping still in her fingers what she had held there all the morning — her Testament and Sunday-school question-book, and folded pocket-handkerchief, — looking out from her little window, dreamily, over the dazzle of the snow, even as her half-blinded thought peered out from its own narrowness into the infinite splendor of the promise of God, — "I wonder if God will ever make me beautiful! I wonder if I shall ever have a real, great joyfulness, that isn't a make-believe!"

Glory called her fancies so. They followed her still. She lived yet in an ideal world. The real world, — that is, the best good of it, — had not come close enough to her, even in this, her widely amended condition, to displace the other. Remember, — this child of eighteen had missed her childhood; had known neither father nor mother, sister nor brother.

Don't think her simple, in the pitiful meaning of the word; but she still enacted, in the midst of her plain, daily life, wonderful dreams that nobody could have ever suspected; and here, in her solitary chamber, called up at will creatures of imagination who were to her what human creatures, alas! had never been. Above all, she had a sister here, to whom she told all her secrets. This sister's name was Leonora.

CHAPTER XVII.

FROST-WONDERS.

"No hammers fell, no ponderous axes rung;
Like some tall palm, the mystic fabric sprung.
Majestic silence!" HEBER.

THE thaw continued till the snow was nearly gone. Only the great drifts against the fences, and the white folds in the rifts of distant hill-sides lingered to tell what had been. Then came a day of warm rain, that washed away the last fragment of earth's cast-off vesture, and bathed her pure for the new adornment that was to be laid upon her. At night, the weather cooled, and the rain changed to a fine, slow mist, congealing as it fell.

Faith stood next morning by a small round table in the sitting-room window, and leaned lovingly over her jonquils and hyacinths that were coming into bloom. A tall stem that had been opening day by day, successively, bright bits of golden blossom, stood erect in a small stateliness, with its last wee flower unfolded, and seemed to have taken a new attitude and expression, since yesterday, of satisfied and proud accomplishment. It was so pert, so dainty, so prim, that Faith laughed in the six saucy little faces that looked out at her from its slender culm. Then she drew the curtain-cord to let in the first sunbeam that should slant from the south upon her bulbs. She had somehow hurried from her room, forgetting to throw up her window at the moment of her leaving, as it was her habit to do. She knew the sunbeams were coming, though, for they were bright from the east upon the linen shades. So her first fair glimpse of the day was at raising the white curtain slowly over its roller, like the uplifting of a drapery from before a scene.

She gave a little cry of rapturous astonishment. It was a diamond morning!

Away off, up the lane, and over the meadows, every tree and bush was hung with twinkling gems that the slight wind swayed against each other with tiny crashes of faint music, and the sun was just touching with a level splendor.

Every spire and thorn stood stiff with crystal armor; the stones and fences and tree-boles were veneered with glass. The tiniest twig was visible in separate light. The gorgeous tracery of the boughs seemed to open interminable vistas of resplendent intricacy. The field whose green summer plenitude gave but one soft sensation to the eye, was a wilderness now, where every glistening grass-blade insisted on its individuality. The earth widened out — was magnified. The unmeasured blue above seemed to dwindle in the presence of all the myriad growths it overarched.

After that first, quick cry, Faith stood mute with ecstasy.

"Mother!" said she, breathlessly, at last, as Mrs. Gartney entered, "look there! have you seen it? Just imagine what the woods must be this morning! How can we think of buckwheats?"

Sounds and odors betrayed that Mis' Battis and breakfast were in the little room adjoining.

"There is a thought of something akin to them, is n't

there, under all this splendor? Men must live, and grass and grain must grow."

Mr. Gartney said this, as he came up behind wife and daughter, and laid a hand on a shoulder of each.

"I know one thing, though," said Faith. "I'll eat the buckwheats, as a vulgar necessity, and then I'll go over the brook and up in the woods behind the Pasture Rocks. It'll last, wont it?"

"Not many hours, with this spring balm in the air," replied her father. "You must make haste. By noon, it will be all a drizzle."

"Will it be quite safe for her to go alone?" asked Mrs. Gartney.

"I'll ask Aunt Faith to let me have Glory. She showed me the walk last summer. It is fair she should see this, now."

So the morning odds and ends were done up quickly at Cross Corners and at the Old House, and then Faith and Glory set forth together, — the latter in as sublime a rapture as could consist with mortal cohesion.

The common road-side was an enchanted path. The glittering rime transfigured the very cart-ruts into bars of silver; and every coarse weed was a fretwork of beauty.

"Bells on their toes" they had, this morning, assuredly; each footfall made a music on the sod.

And the fringes up and down the brook-side! In and out the arches of his rare "ice-palace," leaped the frost-defying current, dashing new jewels right and left, like a king scattering largess as he rides along!

Over the slippery bridge, — out across a stretch of open meadow, and then along a track that skirted the border of a sparse growth of trees, projecting itself like a promontory upon the level land, — round its abrupt angle into a sweep of meadow again, on whose farther verge rose the Pasture Rocks. This was their way.

Behind these rocks swelled up gently a slope, half pasture, half woodland, — neither open ground nor forest; but, although clear enough for comfortable walking, studded pretty closely with trees that often interlaced their branches overhead, and made great, pillared aisles, among whose shade, in summer, wound delicious little foot-paths that all came out together, midway up, into — what you shall be told of presently.

Around the borders of the meadows they had crossed, grew luxuriant elms, that made, with their low, sweeping boughs, festoons, and bowers, and far-off mounds of light.

Here, among and beyond the rocks, were oaks, and pines, and savins, — each needle-like leaf a shimmering lance, — each clustering branch a spray of gems, — and the stout, spreading limbs of the oaks delineating themselves against the sky above in Gothic frost-work.

Great icicles hung from points of craggy stone, and dropped, crashing in the stillness, from tips of branches that overhung them as they went. This, with now and then a chick-a-dee's note, was all the winter music of the woods. But the grandeur of that silence! The awe of standing there, with the flashing groins of those wild and mighty arches overhead, and the low wind whispering through, like an awaking organ, and the sunlight coming down out of the blue above, and penetrating in broad gleams, like a living Presence!

One chant reiterated itself in Faith's soul, as she gazed and listened. "The Lord is in His Holy Temple; let all the earth keep silence before Him!"

As for Glory, she walked on, in a hushed joy, as if an angel led her.

Suddenly, — before they thought it could be so near, — they came up and out into a broader opening. Between two rocks that made, as it were, a gate-way, and around whose bases were grouped sentinel evergreens, they came into this wider space, floored with flat rock, the surface of a hidden ledge, carpeted with crisp mosses in the summer, whose every cup and hollow held a jewel now, — and enclosed with lofty oaks and pines, while, straight beyond, where the woods shut in again far closer than below, rose a bold crag, over whose brow hung pendent birches that in their icy robing drooped like glittering wings of cherubim above an altar.

All around and underneath, this strange magnificence. Overhead, the everlasting Blue, that roofed it in with sapphire. In front, the rough, gigantic shrine.

"It is like a cathedral!" said Faith, solemnly and low.

"See!" whispered Glory, catching her companion hastily by the arm, — "there is the minister!"

A little way beyond them, at the right, out from among the clumps of evergreen where some other of the little wood-walks opened, a figure advanced without perceiving them. It was Roger Armstrong, the new minister. He held his hat in his hand. He walked, uncovered, as he would have done into a church, into this forest temple, where God's finger had just been writing on the walls.

When he turned, slowly, his eye fell on the other two who stood there. It lighted up with a quick joy of sympathy. He came forward. Faith bowed. Glory stood back, shyly. Neither party seemed astonished at the meeting. It was so plain *why* they came, that if they had wondered at all, it would have been that the whole village should not be pouring out hither, also.

Mr. Armstrong led them to the centre of the rocky space. "This is the best point," said he. And then was silent. There was no need of words. A greatness of thought made itself felt from one to the other, without expression.

Only, between still pauses, words came that almost spoke themselves.

"'Eye hath not seen, nor hath it entered into the heart of man to conceive, that which God hath prepared for them that love him.' What a commentary upon His promise is a glory like this!"

"'And they shall all shine like the sun in the kingdom of my Father!'"

Faith stood by the minister's side, and glanced, when he spoke, from the wonderful beauty before her to a face whose look interpreted it all. There was something in the very presence of this man that drew others who approached him into the felt presence of God. Because he stood therein in the spirit. These are the true apostles whom Christ sends forth.

Glory could have sobbed with an oppression of reverence, enthusiasm, and joy.

"It is only a glimpse," said Mr. Armstrong, by-and-by. "It is going, already."

A drip — drip — was beginning to be heard in the woods.

"You ought to get away from under the trees before the thaw comes fully on," continued he. "A branch breaks, now and then, and the ice will be falling constantly, when it once begins to loosen. I can show you a more open way than the one you came by, I think."

And he gave his arm to Faith over the slope that even

now was growing wet and slippery in the sun. Faith touched it with a reverence, and dropped it again, modestly, when they reached a safer foothold.

Glory kept behind. Mr. Armstrong turned now and then, with a kindly word, and a thought for her safety. Once he took her hand, and helped her down a sudden descent in the path, where the water had run over and made a smooth, dangerous glare.

"I shall call soon to see your father and mother, Miss Gartney," said he, when they reached the road again beyond the brook, and their ways home lay in different directions. "This meeting, to-day, has given me pleasure."

"How?" Faith wondered silently, as she kept on to the Cross Corners. She had hardly spoken a word. But, then, she might have remembered that the minister's own words had been few, yet her very speechlessness before him had come from the deep pleasure that his presence had given to her. The recognition of souls cares little for words. Faith's soul had been in her face to-day, as Roger Armstrong had seen it each Sunday, also, in the sweet, listening look she uplifted before him in the church. He bent towards this young, pure life, with a joy in its gentle purity; the joy of an elder over a younger angel in the school of God.

And Glory? she laid up in her own heart a beautiful remembrance of something she had never known before. Of a near approach to something great and high, yet gentle and beneficent. Of a kindly, helping touch, a gracious smile, a glance that spoke straight to the mute aspiration within her.

The minister had not failed, through all her humbleness and shyness, to read some syllables of that large, unuttered life of hers that lay beneath. He whose labor it is to save souls, learns always the insight that discerns souls.

"I have seen the Winter!" cried Faith, glowing and joyous, as she came in from her walk.

"It has been a beautiful time!" said Glory to her shadow-sister, when she went to hang away hood and shawl. "It has been a beautiful time, — and I've been really in it, — partly!"

CHAPTER XVIII.

OUT IN THE SNOW.

"Sydneian showers
Of sweet discourse, whose powers
Can crown old winter's head with flowers."
CRASHAW.

WINTER had not exhausted her repertory, however. She had more wonders to unfold.

There came a long snow-storm.

Steadily, patiently, persistently, the tiny flakes came down out of a great, gray, inexhaustible gloom above, and fell, each to its appointed place, rounding up and out, everywhere, the marvellous sculpture that is builded, not chiselled, and transforming common things into shapes of dreamy grace and splendor. Stilly and surely, — all day, all night, almost all day again, — the work of atoms went on mightily; till the clouds, like artists falling back before their finished work, parted, and let in the sun to look on what they had achieved. Then fell an afternoon effulgence over all. Peaks and mounds and drifts glanced in a rosy light. The great trees held their branches in a breathless quietness, lest their perfect draperies should be disturbed. There was a strange hush in nature. The world was muffled. All the indefinite stir that tells us in the stillest of other scenes, that a deep, palpitating life goes on under whatever look of **rest the earth assumes,** was covered and soundless now. It was a pause of pure completeness.

"Faithie," said her father, coming in, wrapped up in furs, from a visit to the stable, "put your comfortables on, and we'll go and see the snow. We'll make tracks, literally, for the hills. There isn't a road fairly broken between here and Grover's Peak. The snow lies beautifully, though; and there isn't a breath of wind. It will be a sight to see."

Faith brought, quickly, sontag, jacket, and cloak, — hood **and veil, and** long, warm snow-boots, and in ten minutes **was ready, as** she averred, for a sledge ride to Hudson's Bay.

Luther drove the sleigh close to the kitchen door, that Faith might not have to cross the yard to reach it, and she stepped directly from the threshold into the warm nest of buffalo-robes; **while** Mis' **Battis put** a great stone jug of **hot water in beside her** feet, asserting that it was "a real comfortin' **thing on a sleigh-ride,** and that they need n't **be** afraid of its **leakin', for the cork was druv in** as tight as **an eye-tooth!"**

So, **out** by **the** barn, into the road, and away from the village toward the hills, they went, with the glee of resonant bells and excited expectation.

A mile, **or** somewhat more, along the Sedgely turnpike, **took** them into a bit of woods that skirted the road on either side, for a considerable distance. **Away in, under the trees,** the stillness and **the** whiteness and the wonderful multiplication of snow-shapes were like enchantment. Each **bush** had an attitude and drapery and expression of its own, as if some **weird** life had suddenly been spell-bound in these depths. **Cherubs,** and **old** women, and tall statue-shapes **like** images of gods, hovered, and bent, and stood majestic, **in a** motionless poise. **Over all, the** bent boughs made marble and silver arches in shadow and light, and, far down between, the vistas lengthened endlessly, still crowded with mystic figures, haunting the long galleries with their awful beauty.

They went on, penetrating a lifeless silence; their horse's feet making the first prints since early morning in the unbroken smoothness of the way, and the only sound the gentle tinkle of their own bells, as they moved pleasantly, but not fleetly, along.

So, up the ascent, where the land lay higher, toward the hills.

"I feel," said Faith, "as if I had been hurried through the Louvre, or the Vatican, or both, and had n't half seen anything. Was there ever anything so strange and beautiful?"

"We shall find more Louvres presently," said her father. "We 'll keep the road round Grover's Peak, and turn off, as we come back, down Garland Lane."

"That lovely, wild, shady road we took last summer so often, where the grape-vines grow so, all over the trees?"

"Exactly," replied Mr. Gartney. "But you must n't scream if we thump about a little, in the drifts up there. It's pretty rough, at the best of times, and the snow will have filled in the narrow spaces between the rocks and ridges, like a freshet. Shall you be afraid?"

"Afraid! Oh, no, indeed! It's glorious! I think I should like to go everywhere!"

"There is a good deal of everywhere in every little distance," said Mr. Gartney. "People get into cars, and go whizzing across whole States, often, before they stop to thoroughly enjoy something that is very like what they might have found within ten miles of home. For my part, I like microscopic journeying."

"Leaving 'no stone unturned.' So do I," said Faith. "We don't half know the journey between Kinnicutt and Sedgely yet, I think. And then, too, they're multiplied, over and over, by all the different seasons, and by different sorts of weather. Oh, we shan't use them up, in a long while!"

Saidie Gartney had not felt, perhaps, in all her European travel, the sense of inexhaustible pleasure that Faith had when she said this.

Down under Grover's Peak, with the river on one side, and the white-robed cedar thickets rising on the other, — with the low afternoon sun glinting across from the frosted roofs of the red mill-buildings and barns and farm-houses to the rocky slope of the Peak, where pines and cedars and hemlocks stood, like sheeted sentinels, and from every crevice sprang a sturdy shrub in grotesque disguise, like a gnome guarding or indicating treasure, — they seemed to go, as Faith said, "right into a fairy tale;" the wild forms and aspects of nature blending so with the signs of simple, human life. She could fancy a bold peasant, coming up from the little settlement beneath to his wood-piles on the steep hill-side, encountering strange adventures there among the crags; and that the sprite-like apparitions gleaming out so in the twilight of the place, watched and presided, elfishly, over the mortal haps below. Certain physical aspects transport us, mysteriously, into certain mental atmospheres. She got a flavor of Grimm and Andersen, here, under Grover's Peak.

Then they came round and up again, over a southerly ridge, by beautiful Garland Lane, that she knew only in its summer look, when the wild grape festooned itself wantonly from branch to branch, and sometimes, even, from side to side; and so gave the narrow forest-road its name.

Quite into fairy-land they had come now, in truth; as if, skirting the dark peak that shut it off from ordinary espial, they had lighted on a by-path that led them covertly in. Trailing and climbing vines wore their draperies lightly, delicate shrubs bowed like veiled shapes in groups around the bases of tall tree-trunks, and slight-stemmed birches quivered under their canopies of snow. Little birds hopped in and out under the pure, still shelter, and left their tiny tracks, like magical hieroglyphs, in the else untrodden paths.

"Lean this way, Faith, and keep steady!" cried Mr. Gartney, as the horse plunged breast-high into a drift, and the sleigh careened toward the side Faith was on. It was a sharp strain, but they ploughed their way through, and came upon a level again. This by-street was literally unbroken. No one had traversed it since the beginning of the storm. The drifts had had it all their own way there, and it involved no little adventurousness and risk, as Mr. Gartney began to see, to pioneer a passage through. But the spirit of adventure was upon them both. On all, I should say; for the strong horse plunged forward, from drift to drift, as though he delighted in the encounter. Moreover, to turn was impossible.

Faith laughed, and gave little shrieks, alternately, as they rose triumphantly from deep, "slumpy" hollows, or pitched headlong into others again. Thus, struggling, enjoying,—just frightened enough, now and then, to keep up the excitement,—they came upon the summit of the ridge. Now their way lay downward. This began to look really almost perilous. With careful guiding, however, and skilful balancing, — tipping, creaking, sinking, emerging, — they kept on slowly, about half the distance down the descent.

The sagacious horse grew warier at every step. He seemed to understand the difficulty and the danger. Lifting his fore feet high, one after the other, with tremendous strides, he would reach them on, and plant them deep in the uncertain drifts, and then, with a strain and a tug, bring hinder feet and all his burden after.

In the intervals of immediate excitement and anxiety, Faith took in the wonderful, almost mountainous aspect of the snow-piled group of hills they were among. It was wild, dreary, solitary. Not a house was to be seen. There were, in fact, none nearer than the little settlement at Grover's Mills. Down below them wound the level road which they had to regain.

Suddenly, the horse, as men and brutes, however sagacious, sometimes will, made a miscalculation of depth or power, — lost his sure balance, — sunk to his body in the yielding snow, — floundered violently in an endeavor to regain safe footing, — and, snap! crash! was down against the drift at the left, with a broken shaft under him!

Mr. Gartney sprang to his head.

One runner was up, — one down. The sleigh stuck fast at an angle of about thirty degrees. Faith clung to the upper side.

Here was a situation! What was to be done? Twilight coming on, — no help near, — no way of getting anywhere!

"Faith," said Mr. Gartney, "what have you got on your feet?"

"Long, thick snow-boots, father. What can I do?"

"Do you dare to come and try to unfasten these buckles? There is no danger. Major can't stir while I hold him by the head."

Faith jumped out into the snow, and valorously set to work at the buckles. She managed to undo one, and to slip out the fastening of the trace, on one side, where it held to the whiffletree. But the horse was lying so that she could not get at the other.

"I'll come there, father!" she cried, clambering and struggling through the drift till she came to the horse's head. "Can't I hold him while you undo the harness?"

"I don't believe you can, Faithie. He isn't down so flat as to be quite under easy control."

"Not if I sit on his head?" asked Faith, seeing that her father simply pressed with both hands downward upon it.

"That might do," replied her father, laughing. "Only you would get frightened, maybe, and jump up too soon."

"No, I won't," said Faith, quite determined upon heroism. While she spoke, she had picked up the whip, which had fallen close by, doubled back the lash against the handle, and was tying her blue veil to its tip. Then she sat down on the animal's great cheek, which she had never fancied to be half so broad before, and gently patted his nose with one hand, while she upheld her blue flag with the other. Major's big, panting breaths came up, close beside her face. She kept a quick, watchful eye upon the road below.

"He's as quiet as can be, father! It must be what Miss Beecher called the 'chivalry of horses!'"

"It's the chivalry that has to develop under petticoat government!" retorted Mr. Gartney, glancing at the meek nose that projected itself beyond the sweep of crinoline, as he came nearer to unbuckle the saddle-girth.

At this moment Faith's blue flag waved vehemently over

her head. She had caught the jingle of bells, and perceived a sleigh, with a man in it, come out into the crossing at the foot of Garland Lane. The man descried the signal and the disaster, and the sleigh stopped. Alighting, he led his horse to the fence, fastened him there, and turning aside into the steep, narrow, unbroken road, began a vigorous struggle through the drifts to reach the wreck.

Coming nearer, he discerned and recognized Mr. Gartney, who also, at the same moment, was aware of him. It was Mr. Armstrong.

"Keep still a minute longer, Faith," said her father, lifting the remaining shaft against the dasher, and trying to push the sleigh back, away from the animal. But this, alone, he was unable to accomplish. He was forced to await the arrival of his timely helper. So the minister came up, and found Faith still seated on the horse's head.

"Miss Gartney! Let me hold him!" cried he, advancing to relieve her.

"I'm quite comfortable!" laughed Faith. "If you would just help my father, please! I couldn't do that so well."

The sleigh was drawn back by the combined effort of the two gentlemen, and then both came quickly round to Faith.

"Now, Faith, jump!" said her father, placing his hands upon the creature's temple, close beside her, while Mr. Armstrong caught her arms to snatch her safely away. Faith sprang, or was lifted as she sprang, quite to the top of the huge bank of snow under and against which they had, among them, beaten in and trodden down such a hollow, and the instant after, Mr. Gartney releasing Major's head, and uttering a sound of encouragement, the horse raised himself, with a half roll, and a mighty scramble, first to his knees.

and then to his four feet again, and shook his great skin, and all his loosened trappings, with an enormous shudder, to scatter the snow. Then he looked round, with an expression of undeserved discomfiture. He was like a general who has planned well, and fought well, but, by a sheer misfortune, has lost his battle, and stands for the world to look upon him as it may.

Mr. Gartney examined the harness. The broken shaft proved the extent of damage done. This, at the moment, however, was irremediable. He knotted the hanging straps and laid them over the horse's neck. Then he folded a buffalo-skin, and arranged it, as well as he could, above and behind the saddle, which he secured again by its girth.

"Mr. Armstrong," said he, as he completed this disposal of matters, "you came along in good time. I am very much obliged to you. If you will do me the further favor to take my daughter home, I will ride to the nearest house where I can obtain a sleigh, and some one to send back for these traps of mine."

"Miss Gartney," said the minister, in answer, "can you sit a horse's back as well as you did his eyebrow?"

Faith laughed, and reaching her arms to the hands upheld for them, was borne safely from her snowy pinnacle to the buffalo cushion. Her father took the horse by the bit, and Mr. Armstrong kept at his side holding Faith firmly to her seat. In this fashion, grasping the bridle with one hand, and resting the other on Mr. Armstrong's shoulder, she was transported somewhat roughly, but not uncomfortably, to the sleigh at the foot of the hill.

"We were talking about long journeys in small circuits," said Faith, when she was well tucked in, and they had set off easily and with tolerable rapidity on a level and not utterly untracked road. "I think I have been to the Alhambra, and to Rome, and have had a peep into fairy-land, and come back, at last, over the Alps!"

Mr. Armstrong understood her. It is such a comfort to know one's hearer will!

"It has been beautiful," said he. After a little pause,— "I shall begin to expect always to encounter you whenever I get among things wild and wonderful!"

"And yet I have lived all my life, till now, in tame streets," said Faith. "I thought I was getting into tamer places still, when we first came to the country. But I am finding out Kinnicutt. One can't see the whole of anything at once."

"We are small creatures, and can only pick up atoms as we go, whether of things outward or inward. People talk about taking 'comprehensive views;' and they suppose they do it. There is only One who does."

Faith was silent.

"Did it ever occur to you," said Mr. Armstrong, "how little your thought can really grasp at once, even of what you already know? How narrow your mental horizon is?"

Faith looked up with a timid flash of questioning intelligence. Her silence asked him to say more.

"Literally, I mean," continued the minister. "How little we clearly conceive of what we think we have learned longest and best? For instance, Arithmetic. We have what we call a science of numbers, and we talk *about* numbers, and manage them on paper; but how many separate things that numbers stand for, can you think of at once? Suppose they were only apples, lying on a table?"

Faith laughed, and then considered.

"Twenty — five, perhaps," said she.

"Ah, you multiply!" said Mr. Armstrong. "You are thinking of five times five!"

"Yes, I was," she answered, with an amused thoughtfulness. "I must come down to five," said she, frankly, after a pause. "Six are twice three."

"You come down to your five fingers, to speak with the common latitude," said Mr. Armstrong. "That seems to be the foundation and the limit. Yet, there is One who knoweth 'all the cedars of Lebanon,' and the 'cattle upon a thousand hills.' Who notes every sparrow as it falls, and 'numbers the very hairs of our heads.'"

"We do think of large numbers, in the abstract, though," said Faith, after a minute's hushed reception of that last thought.

"Yes, but how?" replied the minister, "I'll tell you how I do it. I wonder if your way is at all like mine. Do you fancy the figures, from one to one hundred, ranged in three sides of a parallelogram, with the tens a little taller than the rest, and the corners turned somewhere about twenty and eighty?"

Faith's face brightened all over with a surprised recognition of something in another that she had imagined all her own.

"That is so strange!" she exclaimed. "But why do you turn those sharp corners? My numbers stand round in a smooth semicircle."

Mr. Armstrong laughed. "The difference of minds," said he. "Yours seems to be spherical, — mine angular."

"Then there are the days, and the months," said Faith.

"Yes," replied Mr. Armstrong. "Really, the days and months are nowhere, except as the globe measures them out in space, and the sunlight scores them between the poles:

but I see them stretching out, before and after, in little oblong mosaics, set in lines, for weeks and years."

"And the Sundays a little longer and wider and whiter than the rest," put in Faith. "And the nights are the broad, black spaces between."

"I think my nights are steps down, from one day to another, and of no perceptible length or color. At least, that is what they used to be when I was a child, and I have never got rid of the old image."

"Then," resumed the minister, "what sort of Geography do we really learn? How much of a notion do we get of Europe and Asia, Africa and America? For me, I've got a little spectrum of an Atlas in my head, and that is all. My idea of the whole globe would n't cover the space we have to traverse between here and Cross Corners. Just look out there to the west," continued he, pointing toward the sunset, "and remember that you only see three or four miles, and then think of all the rest that lies between this and the Hudson, and of New York, and Ohio, and Indiana, and Illinois! We can no more picture the outstretch of the continent, — away out beyond the Green Ridge, and the Catskills, and the Great Lakes, and the Mississippi, and the Rocky Mountains, to the forests of Oregon and the beaches of the Pacific, — than we can take eternity into our thought!"

"Don't it seem strange," said Faith, in a subdued tone, "that it should all have been made for such little lives to be lived in, each in its corner?"

"If it did not thereby prove these little lives to be but the beginning. This great Beyond that we get glimpses of, even upon earth, makes it so sure to us that there must be an Everlasting Life, to match the Infinite Creation God puts us, as He did Moses, into a cleft of the rock, that we may catch a glimmer of His glory as He goes by; and then He tells us that one day we "shall know even as also we are known!"

"And I suppose it ought to make us satisfied to live whatever little life is given us?" said Faith, gently and wistfully.

Mr. Armstrong turned toward her, and looked earnestly into her eyes.

"Has that thought troubled *you*, too? Never let it do so again, my child! Believe that however little of tangible present good you may have, you have the unseen good of heaven, and the promise of all things to come."

"But we do see lives about us in the world that seem to be and to accomplish so much!"

"And so we ask why ours should not be like them? Yes; all souls that aspire, must question that; but the answer comes! I will give you, some day, if you like, the thought that comforted me at a time when that question was a struggle."

"I *should* like!" said Faith, with deeply stirred and grateful emphasis.

Then they drove on in silence, for awhile; and then the minister, pleasantly and easily, brought on a conversation of every-day matters; and so they came to Cross Corners, just as Mrs. Gartney was gazing a little anxiously out of the window, down the road.

"Father is coming," said Faith, reassuringly, the instant the door was opened. "We broke a shaft in getting through a great drift, and he had to go and borrow a sleigh. Mr. Armstrong has been kind enough to bring me home, mother."

Mrs. Gartney urged the minister to come in and join them

at the tea-table; but "it was late in the week, — he had writing to finish at home that evening, — he would very gladly come another time."

"Mother!" cried Faith, presently, moving out of a dream in which she had been sitting before the fire, — "I wonder whether it has been two hours, or two weeks, or two years, since we set off from the kitchen door! I have seen so much, and I have heard so much. I told Mr. Armstrong, after we met him, that I had been through the Alhambra and the Vatican, and into fairy-land, and over the Alps. And after that, mother," she added, low, "I think he almost took me into heaven!"

CHAPTER XIX.

A "LEADING."

"The least flower, with a brimming cup, may stand
And share its dew-drop with another near."
MRS. BROWNING.

GLORY MCWHIRK was waiting up stairs, in Faith's pretty, white, dimity-hung chamber.

These two girls, of such utterly different birth and training, were drawing daily toward each other across the gulf of social circumstance that separated them. They were together in Mr. Armstrong's Bible Class. Sunday after Sunday, they sat side by side, and received the same beautiful interpretation of truth into eager, listening souls. And, as Aunt Henderson said, "when we take our Bible-meat together, why not the meat that perisheth?"

Faith Gartney came to know much of Glory's secret inner nature and wants. And from sitting down together sometimes on a Saturday afternoon in the southwest room at the old house, to look over the lesson for the Sunday, there grew up a little plan of kindliness and benefit between them.

Twice a week, now, Glory came over, and found her seat and her books ready in Miss Faith's pleasant room, and Faith herself waiting to impart to her, or to put her in the way of gathering, those bits of week-day knowledge she had ignorantly hungered for so long.

Glory made quick progress. A good, plain, foundation had been laid during the earlier period of her stay with Miss Henderson, by a regular attendance, half-daily, at the district school. Aunt Faith said "nobody's time belonged to anybody that knew better themselves, until they could read, and write, and figure, and tell which side of the globe they lived on." Then, too, the girl's indiscriminate gleaning from such books as had come in her way, through all these years, assorted itself gradually, now, about new facts, like patchwork that had been laid by in bits, confusedly, but began to be arranged in symmetry, and to grow toward a whole. Or rather, — for knowledge, in its accretion, follows such law, — that which had been held loosely, as particles, in solution, gathered and crystallized, — each atom finding its sure place, and building up forms of light and beauty.

Glory's "good times" had, verily, begun at last.

On this day that she sat waiting, Faith had been called down by her mother to receive some village ladies who had walked over to Cross Corners to pay a visit. Glory had time for two or three chapters of "Ivanhoe," and to tell Hendie, who strayed in, and begged for it, Bridget Foye's old story of the little red hen, while the regular course of topics was gone through below, of the weather, — the new minister, — the last meeting of the Dorcas Society, — the everlasting wants and helplessness of Mrs. Sheffley and her seven children, and whether the society had better do anything more for them, — the trouble in the west district school, and the question "where the Dorcas bag was to go next time."

At last, the voices and footsteps retreated, through the

entry, the door closed somewhat promptly as the last "good-afternoon" was said, and Faith sprang up the narrow staircase.

There were a lesson in Geography, and a bit of Natural Philosophy to be done first, and then followed their Bible talk; for this was Saturday.

Before Glory went it had come to be Faith's practice always to read to her some bit of poetry, — a gem from Tennyson or Mrs. Browning, or a stray poem from a magazine or paper which she had laid by as worthy. This was as we give children a cake or a sugar-plum, at parting, to carry away with them.

"Glory," said she, to-day, "I'm going to let you share a little treasure of mine, — something Mr. Armstrong gave me."

Glory's eyes deepened and glowed.

"It is thoughts," said Faith. "Thoughts in verse. I shall read it to you, because I think it will just answer you, as it did me. Don't you feel, sometimes, like a little brook in a deep wood?"

Glory's gaze never moved from Faith's face. Her poetical instinct seized the image, and the thought of her life applied it.

"All alone, and singing to myself? Yes, I *did*, Miss Faith. But I think it is growing lighter and pleasanter every day. I think I am getting —"

"Stop! stop!" said Faith. "Don't steal the verses before I read them! You're such a queer child, Glory! One never can tell you anything. You have always all but got it, already."

And then Faith gave her pearls; because she knew they would not be trampled under foot, but taken into a heart and held there; and because just such a rapt and reverent ecstasy as her own had been when the minister had given her, in fulfilment of his promise, this thought of his for the comfort that was in it, looked out from the face that was uplifted to hers, radiant with a joy like that of one taken into converse with the angels.

> "Up in the wild, where no one comes to look,
> There lives and sings, a little lonely brook;
> Liveth and singeth in the dreary place,
> Yet creepeth on to where the daylight shines.
>
> "Pure from their heaven, in mountain chalice caught,
> It drinks the rains, as drinks the soul her thought;
> And down dim hollows, where it winds along,
> Bears its life-burden of unlistened song.
>
> "I catch the murmur of its undertone
> That sigheth, ceaselessly, — alone! alone!
> And hear, afar, the Rivers gloriously
> Shout on their paths toward the shining sea!
>
> "The voiceful Rivers, chanting to the sun;
> And wearing names of honor, every one;
> Outreaching wide, and joining hand with hand
> To pour great gifts along the asking land.
>
> "Ah, lonely brook! creep onward through the pines!
> Press through the gloom, to where the daylight shines!
> Sing on among the stones, and secretly
> Feel how the floods are all akin to thee!
>
> "Drink the sweet rain the gentle heaven sendeth;
> Hold thine own path, howeverward it tendeth;
> For, somewhere, underneath the eternal sky,
> Thou, too, shalt find the Rivers, by-and-by!"

Faith's voice trembled with earnestness as she finished. When she looked up from the paper as she refolded it, tears of feeling were running down Glory's cheeks.

"Why, the little brook has overflowed!" cried Faith.

playfully. If she had not found this to say, she would have cried, herself.

"Miss Faith!" said Glory, "I aint sure whether I was meant to tell; but do you know what the minister has asked Miss Henderson? Perhaps she won't; I'm afraid not; it would be *too* good a time! but he wants her to let him come and board with her! Just think what it would be for him to be in the house with us all the time! Why, Miss Faith, it would be just as if one of those great Rivers had come rolling along through the dark woods, right among the little lonely brooks!"

Faith made no answer. She was astonished. Miss Henderson had said nothing of it. She never did make known her subjects of deliberation till the deliberations had become conclusions.

"Why, you don't seem glad!"

"I *am* glad," said Faith, slowly and quietly. She was strangely conscious at the moment that she said so, glad as she would be if Mr. Armstrong were really to come so near, and she might see him daily, of a half-jealousy that Glory should be nearer still.

It was quite true that Mr. Armstrong had this wish. Hitherto, he had been at the house of the elder minister, Mr. Holland. But the three months had expired, — Mr. Holland, convinced by continued weakness and the growing infirmities of his age that his active labors were ended, had offered his resignation of the parochial charge; and this having been accepted, a unanimous invitation had been given to Mr. Armstrong by the people to remain among them as their settled pastor. This he had not yet consented to do. But he had entered upon another engagement of six months, to preach for them. Now he needed a permanent home, which he could not conveniently have at Mr. Holland's.

There was great putting of heads together at the "Dorcas," about it.

Mrs. Gimp "would offer; but then — there was Serena, and folks would talk."

Other families had similar holdbacks, — that is the word, for they were not absolute insuperabilities, — wary mothers were waiting until it should appear positively necessary that *somebody* should waive objection, and take the homeless pastor in; and each watched keenly for the critical moment when it should be just late enough, and not too late, for her to yield.

Meanwhile, Mr. Armstrong quietly left all this seething, and walked off out of the village, one day, to Cross Corners, and asked Miss Henderson if he might have one of her quaint, pleasant, old-fashioned rooms.

Miss Henderson was deliberating.

This very afternoon, she sat in the southwest tea-parlor, with her knitting forgotten in her lap, and her eyes searching the bright western sky, as if for a gleam that should light her to decision.

"It aint that I mind the trouble. And it aint that there is n't house-room. And it aint that I don't like the minister," soliloquized she, after a way she had of talking over matters to herself when she and the old house were left dreaming together. "It's whether it would be respectable common sense. I aint going to take the field with the Gimps and the Leatherbees, nor to have them think it, either. — She's over here almost every blessed day of her life. I might as well try to keep the sunshine out of the old house, as to keep her; and I should be about as likely to

want to do one as the other. **But just** let me take in Mr Armstrong, **and there** 'd be **all the eyes in** the village watching. There could n't so much **as a cat** walk in or out, but **they 'd know it,** somehow. And they 'd be sure to say she was running after the minister."

Miss Henderson's pronouns were not **precise in their** reference. It is n't necessary for soliloquy to be **exact.** She understood herself, and that sufficed.

"It 's being ridiculous would n't be any argument. To **be** sure, he 's old enough to **be** her — uncle!" This was not emphasizing **the** absurdity quite so strongly or so definitely as she intended; but Aunt Faith's climaxes broke **down,** unexpectedly, sometimes, just **as** they culminated, because the honest fact fell short. Her rhetoric might **go** lame; but the truth **came** never halt or maimed from **her** upright handling.

"It would be a disgrace **to** the parish, anyhow," she resumed, "to let those Gimps and Leatherbees get him into their net; **and they** 'll do it if Providence or somebody don't interpose. **I wish I was** sure whether it was a leading **or** not!"

By-and-by, after **a** silent revolving, in which her kindly inclinations toward **the** minister, — her memories of long time, when that young brother wrote his first sermons in the pleasant room she sat in now, — her shrewd reading **of** plans and purposes in others, — her thought for Faith, and her calculations about the white hangings with **the ball and** fringe **trimmings that** must be bleached and put **up** if Mr. Armstrong came, and **how** soon they **could** be ready for him, were curiously mixed **up and** interwoven, — she reverted at last, as she always did, **to that** question of its being a "leading," or not; and, taking down the old Bible from the corner shelf, she laid it with solemnity on the little light-stand at her side, and opened it, as she had known her father do, in the important crises of his life, for an "indication."

The wooden saddle and the gun were not all that had come down to Aunt Faith from the primitive days of the Puritan settlers.

The leaves parted at the story of the Good Samaritan. Bible leaves are apt to part, as the heart opens, in accordance with long habit and holy use.

That evening, while Glory was washing up the tea-things, Aunt Faith put on cloak and hood, and walked over to Cross Corners.

"No — I won't take off my things," she replied to Mrs. Gartney's advance of assistance. "I've just come over to tell you what I'm going to do. I've made up my mind to take the minister to board. And when the washing and ironing's out of the way, next week, I shall fix up a room for him, and he'll come."

"That's a capital plan, Aunt Faith!" said her nephew, with a tone of pleased animation. "Cross Corners will be under obligation to you. Mr. Armstrong is a man whom I greatly respect and admire."

"So do I," said Miss Henderson. "And if I didn't, when a man is beset with thieves all the way from Jerusalem to Jericho, it's time for some kind of a Samaritan to come along!"

Next day, Mis' Battis heard the news, and had her word of comment to offer.

"She's got room enough for him, if that's all; but I wouldn't a believed she'd have let herself be put about and upset so, if it was for John the Baptist! I always thought she was setter 'n an old hen! But then, she's gittin' into years, and it's kinder handy, I s'pose, havin' a minister round the house, sayin' she should be took anyways sudden!"

Village comments it would be needless to attempt to chronicle.

April days began to wear their tearful beauty, and the southwest room at the old house was given up to Mr Armstrong.

CHAPTER XX.

PAUL.

> " Standing, with reluctant feet,
> Where the brook and river meet,
> Womanhood and childhood fleet!"
> LONGFELLOW.

GLORY had not been content with the utmost she could find to do in making the southwest room as clean, and bright, and fresh, and perfect in its appointments as her zealous labor and Miss Henderson's nice, old-fashioned methods and materials afforded possibility for. Twenty times a day, during the few that intervened between its fitting up and Mr. Armstrong's occupation of it, she darted in, to settle a festoon of fringe, or to pick a speck from the carpet, or to move a chair a hair's-breadth this way or that, or to smooth an invisible crease in the counterpane, or, above all, to take a pleased survey of everything once more, and to wonder how the minister would like it.

So well, indeed, he liked it, when he had taken full possession, that he seemed to divine the favorite room must have been relinquished to him, and to scruple at keeping it quite solely to himself.

In the pleasant afternoons, when the spring sun got round to his westerly windows, and away from the southeast apartment, whither Miss Henderson had betaken herself, her knitting-work, and her Bible, and where now the meals were always spread, he would open his door, and let the pleasantness stray out across the passage, and into the keeping-room, and would often take a book, and come in, himself, also, with the sunlight. Then Glory, busy in the kitchen, just beyond, would catch words of conversation, or of reading, or even be called in to hear the latter. And she began to think that there were good times, truly, in this world, and that even she was "in 'em!"

April days, as they lengthened and brightened, brought other things, also, to pass.

The Rushleigh party had returned from Europe.

Faith had a note from Margaret. The second wedding was close at hand, and would she not come down?

But her services as bridesmaid were not needed this time; there was nothing so exceedingly urgent in the invitation,— Faith's intimacy was with the Rushleighs, not the Livingstons,— that she could not escape its acceptance if she desired; and so — there was a great deal to be done in summer preparation, which Mis' Battis, with her deliberate dignity, would never accomplish alone; also, there was the forget-me-not ring lying in her box of ornaments, that gave her a little troubled perplexity as often as she saw it there; and Faith excused herself in a graceful little note, and staid at Cross Corners, helping her mother fold away the crimson curtains, and get up the white muslin ones, make up summer sacks for Hendie, and retouch her own simple wardrobe, which this year could receive little addition.

Kind, sisterly fingers helped Hendie now, in his morning robings; and sweet words and pretty stories replaced the old, taunting rhyme; and there were little, easy, pleasant lessons after the rooms were all made nice for the day; and on Sunday there was a special happy walk up over the Ridge, when Faith simplified for him and made beautiful to his childish comprehension the truth, whatever it might have been, that a stronger soul had fed herself with, a few hours before.

Faith was finding work, daily, at her hand, to do. The lessons with Glory went on; and the Bible-class, — Faith's one great, weekly joy, — to which Mr. Armstrong walked with them, in the bright, balmy, Sunday mornings, giving them beautiful words, or keeping beautiful silence as they went, so that, like the disciples, journeying toward Emmaus, "their hearts burned within them by the way." After the Sunday-school, Glory disappeared into her corner seat in Miss Henderson's pew, and when the service in church was ended, took her quiet and speedy way home, alone, reaching it enough earlier than her mistress to have removed her outside garments, put on a clean calico apron, and begun to dish the simple dinner by the time Miss Henderson and Mr. Armstrong came in.

However joyfully and gratefully she might feel herself welcomed upon equal ground where all are indeed equal, she was never led into any forgetfulness, thereby, of the difference of outward position, and of daily duty. Perhaps they whom God in His wise will, may have placed a little higher by gift and opportunity, lessen really nothing of their height to the eyes of others below, when they reach down willing hands to draw them, also, up.

One day, Aunt Faith had twisted her foot by a slip upon the stairs, and was kept at home. Glory, of course, was obliged to remain also, as Miss Henderson was confined, helpless, to her chair or sofa.

Faith Gartney and the minister walked down the pleasant lane, and along the quiet road to the village church, together.

Faith had fresh, white ribbons, to-day, upon her simple straw bonnet, and delicate flowers and deep green leaves about her face. She seemed like an outgrowth of the morning, so purely her sweet look and fair unsulliedness of attire reflected and interpreted, as it were, the significance of the day's own newness and beauty.

"Do you know," said Mr. Armstrong, presently, after the morning greeting had passed, and they had walked a few paces, silently, "do you know that you are one of Glory's saints, Miss Faith?"

Faith's wondering eyes looked out their questioning astonishment from a deep rosiness that overspread her face.

The minister was not apt to make remarks of at all a personal bearing. Neither was this allusion to sainthood quite to have been looked for, from his lips. Faith could scarcely comprehend.

"I found her this morning, as I came out to cross the field, sitting on the door-stone with her Bible and a rosary of beautiful, small, variously-tinted shells upon her lap. I stopped to speak with her, and asked leave to look at them. 'They were given to me when I was very little,' she said. 'A lady sent them from Rome. The Pope blessed them!' 'They are very beautiful,' I said, 'and a blessing, if that mean a true man's prayer, can never be worthless. But — I asked her, 'do you *use* these, Glory?' 'Not as she did once,' she said. She had almost forgotten about that. She knew the larger beads stood for saints, and the smaller ones between were prayers. 'But,' she went on, 'it isn't for my prayers I keep them now. I've named some of my saints' beads for the people that have done me the most good in my life, and been the kindest to me; and the little ones are thoughts, and things they've taught me. This large one, with the queer spots, is Miss Henderson; and this lovely rose-colored one is Miss Faith; and these are Katie Ryan and Bridget Foye; but you don't know about them.' And then she timidly told me that the white one next the cross was mine. The child humbled me, Miss Faith! It is nearly fearful, sometimes, to get a glimpse of what one is to some trustful human soul, who looks through one toward the Highest!"

Faith had tears in her eyes.

"Glory is such a strange girl," said she. "She seems to have an instinct for things that other people are educated up to."

"She has seized the spirit of the dead Roman calendar, and put it into this rosary. Our saints *are* the spirits through whom God wills to send us of His own. Whatever becomes to us a channel of His truth and love we must involuntarily canonize and consecrate. Woe, if by the same channel ever an offence cometh!"

"I never thought of it before," said Faith; "but I don't wonder the Romans like to believe as they do about the saints and the pope. If it only were true that we could know exactly into whose hands had come down directly what Christ gave to Peter!"

"We know what is better," said Mr. Armstrong. "We know that we can stand by Christ's side *with* Peter, and receive it to ourselves."

Faith's lips parted eagerly, and then closed again, like one afraid to speak.

"What is it, my child?" asked the minister, with a kind persuasiveness.

"Mr. Armstrong!" said Faith, "you draw me out to say things that I wonder, afterward, how I have dared! I suppose it is wrong—it must be—but I cannot help thinking, sometimes, why our Saviour did not come into the world to stay! It wants him so."

"Does He *not* stay?"

"In the way you mean—yes," replied Faith, gently and fearfully. "But that is so hard for people to believe and remember."

"I mean as literal a thing as the truth can be. I mean that when Christ said, 'I am with you to the end of the world,' he only said that which was—which, by the laws of things, could not help being—simply, and without metaphor, true."

Faith almost paused in her walk to listen.

"Events and deeds are not done with in the moment they are enacted. Does a sublime instant in history pass by into nothingness, except for the memory that it has been? God is the God of Abraham, Isaac, and Jacob. He is not the God of the dead, but of the living. It is only our finiteness that compels us to receive in succession, and pass over into what we call the past. The past is back again to whatever soul, by sympathy, lives keenly in any instant of it. It is all God's Present. We need not say, 'Oh, if we had lived in the days when Christ walked here upon the earth!' We do live wherever we truly find our life. Christ's Life—every moment of it—is an everlasting Presence in the earth. The hem of his garment sweeps to the farthest edge of being. He sits at the head of the feast; and sends the cup of blessing down; and it matters not whether John, upon his bosom, or Jude, or James, or Peter, or you and I, with what we call the nineteen centuries between, receive it. It is one Act—one Gift—forever!"

They were silent, then, again, until they had almost reached the church.

Mr. Armstrong turned to Faith once more, before they entered.

"Read all the Gospel scenes with that thought. Go back into them, and live them. And believe always, that if so your soul can go to Christ, across all time, His spirit can no less come to you!"

Are these too grave and solemn pages for a story? Grave and solemn is our life, also; and the deep thoughts do come, and no narration can be true in fact or purpose, which shall leave them out. I do not think the girl of eighteen who feels the soul within her, will pass them by unread, any more than if a high and earnest spirit, like that I seek here to delineate, have ever met her in her world, she can have done other than hail it reverently and gladly. Thank God, so His truth hath even already spread, that no wide circle can be drawn in fact or fancy which may not easily include some such! There is no life so frivolous that a holy day is not offered it once in seven. Shall we write books that tell of years, and have no Sabbaths in them? If I would do this, it would be impossible for me to tell the story of Faith's girlhood truly, and not give therein, however faintly and incidentally, something of the deeper influences that wrought upon her nature; nor could I speak of this life-friend of hers, and not show him as he was, in his daily word and living.

Perhaps Faith was nearly the only person in church, to-day, who did not notice that there were strangers in the pew behind the Gimps. When she came out, she was joined; and not by strangers. Margaret and Paul Rushleigh came eagerly to her side.

"We came out to Lakeside to stay a day or two with the Morrises; and ran away from them here, purposely to meet you. And we mean to be very good, and go to church all day, if you will take us home with you meanwhile."

Faith, between her surprise, her pleasure, her embarrassment, the rush of old remembrance, and a quick, apprehensive thought of Mis' Battis and her probable arrangements, made almost an awkward matter of her reply. But her father and mother came up, welcomed the Rushleighs cordially, and the five were presently on their way toward Cross Corners, and Faith had recovered sufficient self-possession to say something beyond mere words of course.

Paul Rushleigh looked very handsome! And very glad, too, to see shy Faith, who kept as invisible as might be at Margaret's other side, and looked there, in her simple spring dress contrasted with Margaret's rich and fashionable, though also simple and lady-like attire, like a field daisy beside a garden rose.

Margaret was charmed with everything. With being at Kinnicutt, with the day, with the sermon, with Cross Corners, and the house; most of all, with Faith's own bright chamber, where the blossoming elm-boughs were swaying in at the open windows, and with the room below, whither she was ushered when bonnet and mantle had been removed, and where the door was thrown back that gave out upon the grassy slope, fresh with its tender green, and let in the breaths of budding shrubs and sun-kissed soil.

Faith couldn't help being glad that the warm spring noontide allowed and suggested this arrangement.

"It's a little, old house;" said she to Miss Rushleigh, who was enthusiastically praising each new aspect; "but we can let in all out doors, you see, and that makes it large enough."

"Who wants brick and mortar in the country?" asked Margaret, with a disdain of all but what she saw before her.

Faith remembered, secretly, the winds and sleet of a few months back, and their closed doors and snuggery of half a house, and doubted whether her friend would quite have weathered and endured all this, for the after-joy of May or June. We stand, serene, at sunny points in life, and to them who smile at seeing us glad say nothing of the interval of storms!

Dinner was of no moment. There was only roast chicken, dressed the day before, and reheated and served with hot vegetables since their coming in, and a custard-pudding, and some pastry-cakes that Faith's fingers had shaped, and coffee; but they drank in balm and swallowed sunshine, and the essence of all that was to be concrete by-and-by in fruitful fields and gardens. And they talked of old times! Three years old, nearly! And Faith and Margaret laughed, and Mrs. Gartney listened, and dispensed dinner, or spoke gently now and then, and Paul did his cleverest with Mr Gartney, so that the latter gentleman declared afterward that "young Rushleigh was a capital fellow; well posted; his father's million did n't seem to have spoiled him yet."

Altogether, this unexpected visit infused great life at Cross Corners.

Why was it that Faith, when she thought it all over, tried to weigh so very nicely just the amount of gladness she had felt; and was dimly conscious of a vague misgiving, deep down, lest her father and mother might possibly be a little more glad than she was quite ready to have them? What made her especially rejoice that Saidie and the strawberries had not come yet?

There are certain shadows of feeling so faint, so indefinite, that when we look fully at them, they are no longer there. Faith could surely analyze neither her pleasure nor her doubt.

When Paul Rushleigh took her hand at parting, — Faith stood, ungloved, on the great door-stone under the elms, Paul and Margaret having accompanied her home from afternoon church, before setting out on their walk to Lakeside, whither they must return, they said, for the Morrises' late dinner, — he glanced down, as he did so, at the fair little fingers, and then up, inquiringly, at Faith's face. Her eyes fell, and the color rose, till it became an indignation at itself. She grew hot, for days afterward, many a time, as she remembered it. Who has not blushed at the self-suspicion of blushing?

Who has not blushed at the simple recollection of having blushed before? On Monday, this happened. Faith went over to the Old House, to inquire about Aunt Henderson's foot, and to sit with her, if she should wish it, for an hour. She chose the hour at which she thought Mr. Armstrong usually walked to the village. Somehow, greatly as she enjoyed all the minister's kindly words, and each moment of his accidental presence, she had, of late, almost invariably taken this time for coming over to see Aunt Faith. A secret womanly instinct, only, it was; waked into no consciousness, and but ignorantly aware of its own prompting.

To-day, however, Mr. Armstrong had not gone out. Some writing that he was tempted to do, contrary to his usual Monday habit, had detained him within. And so, just as Miss Henderson, having given the history of her slip, and the untoward wrenching of her foot, and its present condition, to Faith's inquiries, asked her suddenly, "if they hadn't had some city visitors yesterday, and what sent them flacketting over from Lakeside to church in the village?" the minister walked in. If he had n't heard, she might not have done it; but, with the abrupt question, came, as abruptly, the hot memory of yesterday; and with those other eyes, beside the double keenness of Aunt Faith's over her spectacles, upon her, it was so much worse if she should, that of course she could n't help doing it! She colored up, and up, till the very roots of her soft hair tingled, and a quick shame wrapped her as in a flaming garment.

The minister saw, and read. Not quite the obvious inference Faith might fear, — he had a somewhat profounder knowledge of nature than that, — but what persuaded him there was a thought, at least, between the two who met yesterday, more than of a mere chance greeting; it might not lie so much with Faith as with the other; yet it had the power, — even the consciousness of its unspoken being, to send the crimson to her face. What kept the crimson there and deepened it, he knew quite well. He knew the shame was at having blushed at all.

Nevertheless, Mr. Armstrong remembered that blush, and pondered it, almost as long as Faith herself. In the little time that he had felt himself her friend, he had grown to recognize so fully, and to prize so dearly, her truth, her purity, her high-mindedness, her reverence, that no new influence could show itself in her life, without touching his solicitous love. Was this young man worthy of a blush from Faith? Was there a height in his nature answering to the reach of hers? Was the quick, impulsive pain that came to him in the thought of how much that rose-hue of forehead and cheek might mean, an intuition of his stronger and more instructed soul of a danger to the child that she might not dream? Be it as it might, Roger Armstrong pondered. He would also watch.

CHAPTER XXI.

PRESSURE.

"To be warped, unconsciously, by the magnetic influence of all around
is the destiny, to a certain extent, of even the greatest souls."

OAKFIELD.

SOMETIMES there springs up in a quiet life a period when all its elements seem fermenting together; when, emphatically, in more than the common meaning of the common phrase, "something seems brewing;" when all sorts of unexpected conjunctures and combinations arise, and amid a multitude of strange and unforeseen forces, one is impelled forward to some new path.

It is for Life, — not so much, even, for Death, — that we are to be "ready." Ready for God's call, that comes to us in an hour when we think not, and demands all the strength we should have grown to, to enable us to decide and act. Ah! the many foolish ones, who, with lamps untrimmed, are in no plight to meet the exigence of circumstance, or the flash of opportunity, but are swayed hither or thither into ways that were never planned for them in God's projection of their lives, but wherein they stumble, or are left, darkly, while His golden moment goes by!

June came, and Saidie Gartney. Not for flowers, or strawberries, merely but for father's and mother's consent that, in a few weeks, when flowers and strawberries should have fully come, there should be a marriage feast made for her in the simple home, and she should go forth into the gay world again, the bride of a wealthy New York banker.

Aunt Etherege and Saidie filled the house. With finery, with bustle, with important presence.

Miss Gartney's engagement had been sudden; her marriage was to be speedy. Half-a-dozen seamstresses, and as many sewing-machines, were busy in New York, — hands, feet, and wheels, — in making up the delicate draperies for the *trousseau;* and Madame A—— was frantic with the heap of elaborate dresses that was thrust upon her hands, and must be ready for the thirtieth.

Mrs. Gartney and Faith had enough to do, to put the house and themselves in festival trim. Hendie was spoiled with having no lessons, and more toys and sugar-plums than he knew what to do with. Mr. Selmore's comings and goings made special ebullitions, weekly, where was only a continuous lesser effervescence before. Mis' Battis had not been able to subside into an arm-chair since the last day of May.

Faith found great favor in the eyes of her brother-in-law elect. He pronounced her a "*naïve, piquante* little person," and already there was talk of how pleasant it would be, to have her in Madison Square, and show her to the world. Faith said nothing to this, but in her heart she clung to Kinnicutt.

Glory thought Miss Gartney wonderful. Even Mr. Armstrong spoke to Aunt Faith of the striking beauty of her elder niece.

"I don't know how she *does* look," Aunt Faith replied with all her ancient gruffness. "I see a great show of flounces, and manners, and hair; but they don't look as if they all grew, natural. I can't make *her* out, amongst all that. Now *Faith's* just Faith. You see her prettiness the minute you look at her, as you do a flower's.

"There are not many like Miss Faith," replied Mr. Armstrong. "I never knew but one other who wore so the fresh, pure beauty of God's giving."

His voice was low and quiet, and his eye looked afar, as he spoke.

Glory went away, and sat down on the door-stone. There was a strange tumult at her heart. In the midst, a noble joy. About it, a disquietude, as of one who feels shut out, — alone.

"I don't know what ails me. I wonder if I aint glad! Of course, it's nothing to me. I aint in it. But it must be beautiful to be so! And to have such words said! *She* don't know what a sight the minister thinks of her! I know. I knew before. It's beautiful — but I aint in it. Only, I think I've got the feeling of it all. And I'm glad it's real, somewhere. Some way, I seem to have so much here, that never grows out into anything. Maybe I'd be beautiful if it did!"

So talked Glory, interjectionally, with herself.

In the midst of these excited days, there came two letters to Mr. Gartney.

One was from a gentleman in Michigan, in relation to some land Mr. Gartney owned there, taken years ago, at a very low valuation, for a debt. This was likely, from the rapid growth and improvement in the neighborhood, to become, within a few years, perhaps, a property of some importance.

"By-and-by," said he to his wife, to whom he had

handed the letter across the table for perusal, "I must try and get out there, and look up that Owasso farm of mine."

The other letter was from his son, James Gartney, in San Francisco. The young man urged his father to consider whether it might not be a good idea for him to come out and join him in California. "You are well out of business, there," he wrote, "and when you begin to feel like trying something again, why not come round? There is always plenty to be done here, and the climate would just suit you. That, and the voyage, would set you up, right off."

Mr. Gartney, by his year of comparative rest, and country air and living, had gained strength that he began to be impatient, now, to use. An invalid's first vigor is like a school-boy's coin, that "burns in his pocket." He is in a wonderful hurry to do something with it. Mrs. Gartney saw that Cross Corners would not limit him long, and began to feel her old anxiety creeping up, lest he should rush, impulsively, into risk and excitement and worry again.

James Gartney's proposal evidently roused his attention. It was a great deal to think of, certainly; but it was worth thinking of, too. James had married in San Francisco, had a pleasant home there, and was prospering. Many old business friends had gone from Mishaumok, in the years when the great flood of enterprise set westward across the continent, and were building up name and influence in the Golden Land. The idea found a place in his brain, and clung there. Only, there was Faith! But things might come round so that even this thought need be no hindrance to the scheme.

Changes, and plans, and interests, and influences were gathering; all to bear down upon one young life.

"More news!" said Mr. Gartney, one morning, coming in from his walk to the village post-office, to the pleasant sitting-room, or morning-room, as Mrs. Etherege and Saidie called it, where Faith was helping her sister write a list of the hundreds who were to receive Mr. and Mrs. Selmore's cards, — "At Home, in September, in Madison Square." "Whom do you think I met in the village, this morning?"

Everybody looked up, and everybody's imagination took a discursive leap among possibilities, and then everybody, of course, asked "Whom?"

"Old Jacob Rushleigh, himself. He has taken a house at Lakeside, for the summer. And he has bought the new mills just over the river. That is to give young Paul something to do, I imagine. Kinnicutt has begun to grow; and when places or people once take a start, there's no knowing what they may come to. Here's something for you, Faithie, that I dare say tells all about it."

And he tossed over her shoulder, upon the table, a letter, bearing her name, in Margaret Rushleigh's chirograph, upon the cover.

Faith's head was bent over the list she was writing; but the vexatious color, feeling itself shielded in her face, crept round till it made her ear-tips rosy. Saidie put out her forefinger, with a hardly perceptible motion, at the telltale sign, and nodded at Aunt Etherege behind her sister's back.

Aunt Etherege looked bland and sagacious.

Up stairs, a little after, these sentences were spoken in Saidie's room.

"Of course it will be," said the younger to the elder lady. "It's been going on ever since they were children. Faith hasn't a right to say no, now. And what else brought him up here after houses and mills?"

"I don't see that the houses and mills were necessary to the object. Rather cumbersome and costly machinery, I should think, to bring to bear upon such a simple purpose."

"Oh, the business plan is something that has come up accidentally, no doubt. Running after one thing, people very often stumble upon another. But it will all play in together, you'll see. Only, I'm afraid I shan't have the glory of introducing Faithie in New York!"

"It would be as good a thing as possible. And I can perceive that your father and mother count upon it, also. In their situation what a great relief it would be! Of course, Henderson never could do so mad a thing as take the child up by the roots, again, and transplant her to San Francisco! And I see plainly he has got that in his own head."

A door across the passage at this moment shut, softly, but securely.

Behind it, in her low chair by her sewing-table, sat the young sister whose fate had been so lightly decreed.

Was it all just so, as Saidie had said? Had she no longer a right to say no? Only themselves know how easily, how almost inevitably, young judgments and consciences are drawn on in the track beaten down for them by others. Many and many a life-decision has been made, through this *taken for granted* that bears with its mute, but magnetic power, upon the shyness and irresolution that can scarcely face and interpret its own wish or will.

It was very true, that, as Saidie Gartney had said, "this had been going on for years." For years, Faith had found great pleasantness in the companionship and evident preference of Paul Rushleigh. There had been nobody to compare with him in her young set in Mishaumok. She knew he liked her. She had been proud of it. The girlish fancy, that may be forgotten in after years, or may, fostered by circumstances, endure and blow into a calm and happy wifehood, had been given to him. And what troubled her now? Was it that always, when the decisive moment approaches, there is a little revulsion of timid feminine feeling, even amid the truest joy? Or was it that a new wine had been given into Faith's life, which would not be held in the old bottles? Was she uncertain — inconstant; or had she spiritually outgrown her old attachment? Or, was she bewildered, now, out of the discernment of what was still her heart's desire and need?

Paul was kind, and true, and manly. She recognized all this in him as surely as ever. If he had turned from, and forgotten her, she would have felt a pang. What was this, then, that she felt, as he came near, and nearer?

And then, her father! Had he really begun to count on this? Do men know how their young daughters feel when the first suggestion comes that they are not regarded as born for perpetual daughterhood in the father's house; Would she even encumber his plans, if she clung still to her maidenly life?

By all these subtleties does the destiny of woman close in upon her.

Margaret Rushleigh's letter was full of delight, and eagerness, and anticipation. She and Paul had been so charmed with Kinnicutt and Lakeside; and there had happoned to be a furnished house to let for the season close by the Morrises, and they had persuaded papa to take it. They were tired of the sea-shore, and Conway was getting crowded to death. They wanted a real summer in the country. And then this had turned up about the mills! Perhaps, now, her father would build, and they should come up every year. Perhaps Paul would stay altogether, and superintend. Perhaps — anything! It was all a delightful chaos of possibilities; with this thing certain, that she and Faith would be together for the next four months in the glorious summer shine and bloom.

Miss Gartney's wedding was simple. The stateliness and show were all reserved for Madison Square.

Mr. Armstrong pronounced the solemn words, in the shaded summer parlor, with the door open into the sweeter and stiller shade without.

Faith stood by her sister's side, in fair, white robes, and Mr. Robert Selmore was groomsman to his brother. A few especial friends from Mishaumok and Lakeside were present to witness the ceremony.

And then there was a kissing, — a hand-shaking, — a well-wishing, — a going out to the simple but elegantly arranged collation, — a disappearance of the bride to put on travelling array, — a carriage at the door, — smiles, tears, and good-byes, — Mr., Mrs., and Mr. Robert Selmore were off to meet the Western train, — and all was over.

Mrs. Etherege remained a few days longer at Cross Corners. As Mis' Battis judiciously remarked, "after a weddin' or a funeral, there ought to be somebody to stay awhile and cheer up the mourners."

This visit, that had been so full of happenings, was to

have a strange occurrence still to mark it, before all fell again into the usual order.

Aunt Etherege was to go on Thursday. On Wednesday, the three ladies sat together in the cool, open parlor, where Mr. Armstrong, walking over from the Old House, had joined them. He had the July number of the "Mishaumok" in his hand, and a finger between the fresh-cut leaves at a poem he would read them.

Just as he finished the last stanza, amid a hush of the room that paid tribute to the beauty of the lines and his perfect rendering of them, wheels came round from the high road into the lane.

"It is Mr. Gartney come back from Sedgely," said Aunt Etheredge, looking from her window, between the blinds. "Whom on earth has he picked up to bring with him?"

A thin, angular figure of a woman, destitute of crinoline, wearing big boots, and a bonnet that ignored the fashion, and carrying in her hand a black enamelled leather bag, was alighting as she spoke, at the gate.

"Mother!" said Faith, leaning forward, and glancing out, also, "it looks like — it is — Nurse Sampson!"

And she put her work hastily from her lap, and rose to go out at the side door, to meet and welcome her.

To do this, she had to pass by Mr. Armstrong. How came that rigid look, that deadly paleness, to his face? What spasms of pain made him clutch the pamphlet he held with fingers that grew white about the nails?

Faith stopped, startled.

"Mr. Armstrong! Are you not well?" said she. At the same instant of her pausing, Miss Sampson entered from the hall, behind her. Mr. Armstrong's eye, lifted toward Faith in an attempt to reply, caught a glimpse of the sharp, pronounced outlines of the nurse's face. Before Faith could comprehend, or turn, or cry out, the paleness blanched ghastlier over his features, and the strong man fell back, fainting.

With quick, professional instinct, Miss Sampson sprang forward, seizing, as she did so, an ice-water pitcher from the table.

"There, take this!" said she to Faith, "and sprinkle him with it, while I loosen his neck-cloth! — Gracious goodness!" she exclaimed, in an altered tone, as she came nearer to him for this purpose, "do it, some of the rest of you, and let me get out of his way! It was me!"

And she vanished out of the room.

CHAPTER XXII.

ROGER ARMSTRONG'S STORY.

"Even by means of our sorrows, we belong to the Eternal Plan."
HUMBOLDT

"Go in there," said Nurse Sampson to Mr. Gartney, calling him in from the porch, "and lay that man flat on the floor!"

Which Mr. Gartney did, wondering, vaguely, in the instant required for his transit to the apartment, whether bandit or lunatic might await his offices.

All happened in a moment; and in that moment, the minister's fugitive senses began to return.

"Lie quiet, a minute. Faith, get a glass of wine, or a little brandy."

Faith quickly brought both; and Mr. Armstrong, whom her father now assisted to the arm-chair again, took the wine from her hand, with a smile that thanked her, and deprecated himself.

"I am not ill," he said. "It is all over now. It was the sudden shock. I did not think I could have been so weak."

Mrs. Gartney had gone to find some hartshorn. Mrs. Etherege, seeing that the need for it was passing, went out to tell her sister so, and to ask the strange woman who had originated all the commotion, what it could possibly mean. Mr. Gartney, at the same instant, caught a glimpse of his horse, which he had left unfastened at the gate, giving indications of restlessness, and hastened out to tie him, and to call Luther, whom he had been awaiting when Miss Sampson hailed him at the door.

Faith and Mr. Armstrong were left alone.

"Did I frighten you, my child?" he asked, gently. "It was a strange thing to happen! I thought that woman was in her grave. I thought she died, when —. I will tell you all about it some day, soon, Miss Faith. It was the sad, terrible page of my life."

Faith's eyes were lustrous with sympathy. Under all other thought was a beating joy, — not looked at yet, — that he could speak to her so! That he could snatch this chance moment to tell her, only, of his sacred sorrow!

She moved a half-step nearer, and laid her hand, softly, on the chair-arm beside him. She did not touch so much as a fold of his sleeve; but it seemed, somehow, like a pitying caress.

"I am sorry!" said she. And then the others came in.

Mr. Gartney walked round with his friend to the old house.

Miss Sampson began to recount what she knew of the story. Faith escaped to her own room at the first sentence. She would rather have it as Mr. Armstrong's confidence.

Next morning, Faith was dusting, and arranging flowers in the east parlor, and had just set the "hill-side door," as they called it, open, when Mr. Armstrong passed the window and appeared thereat.

"I came to ask, Miss Faith, if you would walk up over

the Ridge. It is a lovely morning, and I am selfish enough to wish to have you to myself for a little of it. By-and-by, I would like to come back, and see Miss Sampson."

Faith understood. He meant to tell her this that had been heavy upon his heart through all these years. She would go. Directly, when she had brought her hat, and spoken with her mother.

Mrs. Etherege and Mrs. Gartney were sitting together in the guest-chamber, above. At noon, after an early dinner, Mrs. Etherege was to leave.

Mr. Armstrong stood upon the door-stone below, looking outward, waiting. If he had been inside the room, he would not have heard. The ladies, sitting by the window, just over his head, were quite unaware and thoughtless of his possible position.

He caught Faith's clear, sweet accent first, as she announced her purpose to her mother, adding, —

"I shall be back, auntie, long before dinner."

Then she crossed the hall into her own room, made her slight preparation for the walk, and went down by the kitchen staircase, to give Parthenia some last word about the early dinner.

"I think," said Mrs. Etherege, in the keenness of her worldly wisdom, "that this minister of yours might as well have a hint of how matters stand. It seems to me he is growing to monopolize Faith, rather."

"Oh," replied Mrs. Gartney, "there is nothing of that! You know what nurse told us, last evening. It isn't quite likely that a man would faint away at the memory of one woman, if his thoughts were turned, the least, in that way, upon another. No, indeed! She is his Sunday scholar,

and he treats her always as a very dear young friend. But that is all."

"Maybe. But is it quite safe for her? He is a young man yet, notwithstanding those few gray hairs."

"Oh, Faith has tacitly belonged to Paul Rushleigh these three years!"

Mr. Armstrong heard it all. He turned the next moment, and met his "dear young friend" with the same gentle smile and manner that he always wore toward her, and they walked up the Ridge-path, among the trees together.

No landscape gardener could have planned so beautiful an illusion as Nature had made here behind the house at Cross Corners.

This natural ridge,— that sloped up from the lane in a bank along one side, and on the other sunk down into a hollow, beyond which were the cornfields and potato-patches,— crowned and clad with wild shrubbery and trees, ended like a sloping promontory that melted down into the level, scarcely a rod beyond the "hill-side door."

Over the cool, grassy path,— up among the lilacs and evergreens, and barberries,— until they were shut in upon the crest, by the verdure and the blue,— they kept on, in a silence wherein their spirits felt each other, and could wait for words.

A boulder of rock, scooped into smooth hollows that made pleasant seats, was the goal, usually, of the Ridge-walk. Here Faith paused, and Mr. Armstrong made her sit down and rest.

Standing there before her, he began his story.

"One summer,— years ago,"— he said, "I went to the city of New Orleans. I went to bring thence, with me, a dear friend — her who was to have been my wife."

The deep voice trembled, and paused. Faith could not look up, her breath came quickly, and the tears were all but ready.

"She had been there, through the winter and spring, with her father, who, save myself, was the only near friend she had in all the world.

"The business which took him there detained him until later in the season than Northerners are accustomed to feel safe in staying. And still, important affairs hindered his departure.

"He wrote to me, that, for himself, he must risk a residence there for some weeks yet; but that his daughter must be placed in safety. There was every indication of a sickly summer. She knew nothing of his writing, and he feared would hardly consent to leave him. But, if I came, she would yield to me. Our marriage might take place there, and I could bring her home. Without her, he said, he could more quickly despatch what remained for him to do; and I must persuade her of this, and that it was for the safety of all that she should so fulfil the promise which was to have been at this time redeemed, had their earlier return been possible.

"In the New Orleans papers that came by the same mail, were paragraphs of deadly significance. The very cautiousness with which they were worded weighted them the more.

"Miss Faith! my friend!"—and, as Roger Armstrong spoke, the strong right hand clutched, with a nervous grasp of pain, the bole of a young tree by which he stood, — "in that city of pestilence, was my life! Night and day I journeyed, till I reached the place. I found the address which had been sent me,—there were only strangers there! Mr. Waldo had been, but the very day before, seized with the fatal endemic, and removed to a fever-hospital. Miriam had refused to leave him, and had gone with him, — into plague and death!

"Was I wrong, child? Could I have helped it? I followed. Ah! God lets strange woes, most fearful horrors, into this world of His! I cannot tell you, if I would, what I saw there! Pestilence — death — corruption!

"In the midst of all, among the gentle sisters of charity, I found a New England woman, — a nurse, — her whom I met yesterday. She came to me on my inquiry for Mr. Waldo. He was dead. Miriam had already sickened, — was past hope. I could not see her. It was against the rule. She would not know me.

"I only remember that I refused to be sent away. I think my brain reeled with the weariness of sleepless nights and the horror of the shock.

"I cannot dwell upon the story. It was ended quickly. When I struggled back, painfully, to life, from the disease that struck me, too, down, there were strange faces round me, and none could even tell me of her last hours. The nurse, — Miss Sampson, — had been smitten — was dying.

"They sent me to a hospital for convalescents. Weeks after, I came out, feeble and hopeless, into my lonely life!

"Since then, God, who had taken from me the object I had set for myself, has filled its room with His own work. And, doing it, He has not denied me to find many a chastened joy.

"Dear, young friend!" said he, with a tender, lingering emphasis, — it was all he could say then, — all they had left him to say, if he would, — "I have told you this, because you have come nearer into my sympathies than any in all those years that have **been my years of** strangerhood and sorrow! You have made me think, in your fresh, maidenly life, **and your soul-earnestness,** of Miriam!

"When your way broadens **out** into busy sunshine, **and** mine lies otherwhere, do not forget me!"

A solemn baptism of mingled grief and joy seemed to touch the soul of Faith. One hand covered her face, that was bowed down, weeping. The other lay in her companion's, who had taken it as he uttered these last words. So **it** rested a moment, and then its fellow came to it, and, between the two, held Roger Armstrong's reverently, while **the** fair, tearful face lifted itself **to his.**

"I do thank you so!" And that was all.

Faith **was** his " dear young friend!" How the words in which her mother limited his thoughts of her to commonplace, widened, when she spoke them to herself, into a great beatitude! She never thought of more, — scarcely whether more could be. This great, noble, purified, God-loving soul that stood between her and heaven, like the mountain-peak, bathing its head in clouds, and drawing **lightnings down,** leaned over her, and blessed her thus!

He had even likened her **to Miriam.** He had made her nearest, next to her. However their differing paths might lie, **he had** begged her to remember him. What could happen to her that should take away this joy? She **was** strong for all life, all duty, henceforth.

She never suspected her own heart, even when the re- **membrance** of Paul came **up** and took a tenderness **from the** thought how he, too, might love, and learn from, this her friend. She turned back with a new gentleness to all other love, as one does from a prayer!

CHAPTER XXIII.

QUESTION AND ANSWER.

"Unless you can swear, 'For life, for death'
Oh, fear to call it loving!"
Mrs. Browning.

FAITH sent Nurse Sampson in to talk with Mr. Armstrong. Then he learned all that he had longed to know, but had never known before; that which took him to his lost bride's death-bed, and awoke out of the silent years for him a moment refused to him in its passing.

Miss Sampson came from her hour's interview, with an unbending of the hard lines of her face, and a softness, even, in her eyes, that told of tears.

"If ever there was an angel that went walking about in black broadcloth, that man is the one," said she.

And that was all she would say.

"I'm staying," she exclaimed, in answer to their enquiries, "with a half-sister of mine at Sedgely. Mrs. Crabe, the blacksmith's wife. You see, I'd got run down, and had to take a rest. Resting is as much a part of work as doing, when it's necessary. I had a chance to go to Europe with an invaleed lady; but I allers hate such half-way contrivances. I either want to work with all my might, or be lazy with all my might. And so I've come here to do nothing, as hard as ever I can."

"I know well enough," she said again, afterward, "that something's being cut out for me, tougher'n anything I've had yet. I never had an hour's extra rest in my life, but I found out, precious soon, what it had been sent for. I'm going to stay on all summer, as the doctor told me to; but I'm getting strong, already; and I shall be just like a tiger before the year's out. And then it'll come, whatever it is. You'll see."

Miss Sampson staid until the next day after, and then Mr. Gartney drove her back to Sedgely.

In those days it came to pass that Glory found she had a "follower."

Luther Goodell, who "did round" at Cross Corners, got so into the way of straying up the field-path in his nooning hours, and after chores were done at night, that Miss Henderson at last, in her plain, outright fashion, took the subject up, and questioned Glory.

"If it means anything, and you mean it shall mean anything, well and good. I shall put up with it; though what anybody wants with men-folks cluttering round, is more than I can understand. But, if you don't want him, he shan't come. So tell me the truth, child. Yes, or no. Have you any notion of him for a husband?"

Glory blushed her brightest at these words; but there was no falling of the eye, or faltering of the voice, as she spoke with answering straightforwardness and simplicity.

"No ma'am. I don't think I shall ever have a husband."

"No ma'am's enough. The rest you don't know anything about. Most likely you will."

"I should n't want anybody, ma'am, that would be likely to want me."

And Glory walked out into the milk-room with the pans she had been scalding.

It was true. This woman-child would go all through life as she had begun; discerning always, and reaching spiritually after, that which was beyond; which in that "kingdom of heaven" was hers already; but which to earthly having and holding should never come.

God puts such souls oftener than we think, into such life. These are His vestals.

Miss Henderson's foot had not grown perfectly strong. She, herself, said, coolly, that she never expected it to. More than that, she supposed, now she had begun, she should keep on going to pieces.

"An old life," she said, "is just like old cloth when it begins to tear. It'll soon go into the rag-bag, and then to the mill that grinds all up, and brings us out new and white again!"

"Glory McWhirk," said she, on another day after, "if you could do just the thing you would like best to do, what would it be?"

"To-day, ma'am? or any time?" asked Glory, puzzled as to how much her mistress's question included.

"Ever. If you had a home to live in, say, and money to spend?"

Glory had to wait a moment before she could so grasp such an extraordinary hypothesis as to reply.

"Well?" said Miss Henderson, with slight impatience.

"If I had, — I should like best to find some little children without any fathers or mothers, as I was, and dress them up, as you did me, and curl their hair, and make a real good time for them, every day!"

"You would! Well, that's all. I was curious to know what you'd say. I guess those beans in the oven want more hot water."

The Rushleighs had come to Lakeside. **Every day, nearly,** saw Paul, or Margaret, or both, at Cross Corners.

Faith led them through her beautiful wood-walks; they strolled away for whole mornings, and made little picnics; not deigning to come back to damask table-cloths and regular dinners; **Paul read** them beautiful poems, and whole **chapters out of new** and charming books, and sang wild ballads, and climbed impossible places to get Faith all the farthest off and fairest wild flowers.

Faith was often, also, at Lakeside.

Old Mr. Rushleigh treated her with a benignant fatherliness and looked **upon her with** an evident fondness and pride that threw heavy weight in the scale of his son's chances. **And** Madam Rushleigh, as she began **to be** called, since Mrs. Philip had entered the family, **petted her** in the old, graceful, gracious fashion; **and Margaret** loved her, simply, and from her heart.

There was nothing she **could** break **away from, if she had** wished; there was **everything that** bound and multiplied **the** fine, invisible network about her fancy and her will.

With Paul himself it had not been as in the days of bouquets, and " Germans," and bridal association in Mishaumok. They were all living and enjoying together a beautiful idyl. Nothing seemed special, — nothing **was** embarrassing.

Faith thought, in these days, that she was **very happy.**

Mr. Armstrong relinquished her, **almost** imperceptibly, to her younger friends. **In** the pleasant twilights, though, when her day's pleasures **and occupations** were ended, he would often come over, **as of old,** and sit **with them in the** summer parlor or under the elms.

Or Faith would go up the beautiful Ridge-walk with him; and he would have a thought for her that was higher than any she could reach, by herself, or with the help of any other human soul.

And so, — her best nature fed, — no want left craving and unfilled, — she hardly knew what it was that made her so utterly content; but the brightness of her life, like that of day, seemed to come from all around, overflowing upon her from the whole illumined world.

And the minister? How did his world look to him? Perhaps, as if clouds that had parted, sending a sunbeam across from the west upon the dark sorrow of the morning, had shut again, inexorably, leaving him still to tread the nightward path under the old, leaden sky.

A day came, that set him thinking of all this — of the years that were past, of those that might be to come.

Mr. Armstrong was not quite so old as he had been represented. A man cannot go through plague and anguish, as he had done, and "keep," as Nurse Sampson had said, long ago, of women, "the baby face on." There were lines about brow and mouth, and gleams in the hair, that seldom come so early.

This day he completed one-and-thirty years.

The same day, last month, had been Faith's birthday. She was nineteen.

Roger Armstrong thought of the two together.

He thought of these twelve years that lay between them. Of the love, — the loss, — the stern and bitter struggle, — the divine amends and holy hope that they had brought to him; and then of the innocent girl-life she had been living in them; then, how the two paths had met so, in these last few, beautiful months.

Whither, and how far apart, trended they now?

He could not see. He waited,—leaving the end with God.

A few weeks went by, in this careless, holiday fashion with Faith and her friends; and then came the hour when she must face the truth for herself and for another, and speak the word of destiny for both.

She had made a promise for a drive around the Pond Road. Margaret and her brother were to come for her, and to return to Cross Corners for tea.

At the hour fixed, she sat, waiting, under the elms, hat and mantle on, and whiling the moments of delay with a new book Mr. Armstrong had lent her.

Presently, the Rushleighs' light, open, single-seated wagon drove up.

Paul had come alone.

Margaret had a headache, but thought that after sundown she might feel better, and begged that Faith would reverse the plan agreed upon, and let Paul bring her home to tea with them.

Paul took for granted that Faith would keep to her engagement with himself. It was difficult to refuse. She was ready, waiting. It would be absurd to draw back, sensitively, now, she thought. Besides, it would be very pleasant; and why should she be afraid? Yet she wished, very regretfully, that Margaret were there.

She shrank from *tête-à-têtes*,—from anything that might help to precipitate a moment she felt herself not quite ready for.

She supposed she did care for Paul Rushleigh as most girls cared for lovers; that she had given him reason to expect she should; she felt, instinctively, whither all this pleased acquiescence of father and mother, and this warm welcome and encouragement at Lakeside, tended; and she had a dim prescience of what must, some time, come of it: but that was all in the far-off by-and-by. She would not look at it yet. She was quite happy and content in this bright summer-life of the present. Why should people want to hurry her on to more?

There is much that is apparently inconsistent in the varying moods of young girls, to whom their own wishes are, as yet, a mystery.

If Faith felt, ordinarily, a blithe content, there were moments, nevertheless, when she was afraid.

She was afraid, now, as she let Paul help her into the wagon, and take his place at her side.

She had been frightened by a word of her mother's, when she had gone to her, before leaving, to tell how the plan had been altered, and ask if she had better do as was wished of her.

Mrs. Gartney had assented with a smile, and a "Certainly, if you like it, Faith; indeed, I don't see how you can very well help it; only —"

"Only what, mother?" asked Faith, a little fearfully.

"Nothing, dear," answered her mother, turning to her with a little caress. But she had a look in her eyes that mothers wear when they begin to see their last woman's sacrifice demand itself at their hands.

"Go, darling. Paul is waiting."

It was like giving her away.

So they drove down, through by-ways, among the lanes, toward the Wachaug road.

Summer was in her perfect flush and fulness of spendor The smell of new-mown hay was in the air.

As they came upon the river, they saw the workmen busy in and about the new mills. Mr. Rushleigh's buggy stood by the fence; and he was there, among his mechanics, with his straw hat and seer-sucker coat on, inspecting and giving orders.

"What a capital old fellow the governor is!" said Paul, in the fashion young men use, now-a-days, to utter their affections.

"Do you know he means to set me up in these mills he is making such a hobby of, and give me half the profits?"

Faith had not known. She thought him very good.

"Yes; he would do anything, I believe, for me,— or anybody I cared for."

Faith was silent; and the strange fear came up in heart and throat.

"I like Kinnicutt, thoroughly."

"Yes," said Faith. "It is very beautiful here."

"Not only that. I like the people. I like their simple fashions. One gets at human life and human nature here. I don't think I was ever, at heart, a city boy. I don't like living at arm's-length from everybody. People come close together, in the country. And — Faith! what a minister you've got here! What a sermon that was he preached last Sunday! I've never been what you might call one of the serious sort; but such a sermon as that must do anybody good."

Faith felt a warmth toward Paul as he said this, which was more a drawing of the heart than he had gained from her by all the rest.

"My father says he will keep him here, if money can do it. He never goes to church at Lakeside, now. It needs just such a man among mill-villages like these, he says

My father thinks a great deal of his work-people. He says nobody ought to bring families together, and build up a neighborhood, as a manufacturer does, and not look out for more than the money. I think he'll expect a great deal of me, if he leaves me here, at the head of it all. More than I can ever do, by myself."

"Mr. Armstrong will be the very best help to you," said Faith. "I think he means to stay. I'm sure Kinnicutt would seem nothing without him now."

They were in the Pond Road. At this moment, they were passing a bend, where a great elm leaned over from the wood-side, and on the bank, opposite, lay a mossy log. Here some child had sat down to rest, and left a handful of wild flowers, that were fading there.

Faith carried, through all her life, a daguerreotype of this little scene, to its minutest detail, flashed upon her soul by these next words that were spoken, as they passed slowly by.

"Faith! Will you help me to make a home here?"

She could not speak. A great shock had fallen upon her whole nature, as if a thunder-bolt she had had presentiment of, burst, warningless, from a clear blue sky.

They drove on for minutes, without another word.

"Faith! You don't answer me. Must I take silence as I please? It can't be that you don't care for me!"

"No, no!" cried Faith, desperately, like one struggling for voice through a nightmare. "I do care. But — Paul! I don't know! I can't tell. Let me wait, please. Let me think."

"As long as you like, darling," said he, gently and tenderly. "You know all I can tell you. You know I have cared for you all my life. And I'll wait now till you tell me I may speak again. Till you put on that little ring of mine, Faith!"

There was a little loving reproach in these last words.

"Please take me home, now, Paul!"

They were close upon the return path around the Lake. A look of disappointed pain passed over Paul Rushleigh's features. This was hardly the happy reception, however shy, he had hoped and looked for. Still he hoped, however. He could not think she did not care for him. She, who had been the spring of his own thoughts and purposes for years. But, obedient to her wish, he touched his horse with the lash, and urged him homeward.

How many minutes, how many miles, they might have counted, as they sat side by side, in that intense consciousness that was speechless, neither thought.

Paul helped her from the wagon at the little white gate at Cross Corners, and then they both remembered that she was to have gone to Lakeside to tea.

"What shall I tell Margaret?" he asked.

"Oh, don't tell her anything! I mean — tell her, I couldn't come to-night. And, Paul — forgive me! I do want so to do what is right!"

"Isn't it right to let me try and make you happy all your life?"

A light had broken upon her, — confusedly, it is true, — yet that began to show her to herself more plainly than any glimpse she had had before, as Paul's words, simple, yet burning with his strong sure love, came to her, with their claim to honest answer.

She saw what it was he brought her; she felt it was less she had to give him back. There was something in the world she might go missing all the way through life, if she took this lot that lay before her now. Would he not miss a something in her, also? Yet, must she needs insist on the greatest, the rarest, that God ever sends? Why should she, more than others? Would she wrong him more, to give him what she could, or to refuse him all?

"I ought — if I do —" she said, tremulously, "to care as you do!"

"You never can, Faith!" cried the young man, impetuously. "I care as a man cares! Let me love you! care a little for me, and let it grow to more!"

Men, till something is accorded, are willing to take so little! And then, straightway, the little must become so entire!

"Well, I declare!" exclaimed Mis' Battis, as Faith came in. "Who'd a thought o' seeing you home to tea! I spose you aint had none?"

The fire was down, — the kitchen stove immaculate in blackness from fresh polish, and the relict sat in her wooden rocking-chair opposite the door that stood open into the sitting-room, with her knitting in her hands, working at it, dreamily, in the twilight.

"Yes — no. That is, I don't want any. Where is my mother?"

"She and your pa's gone down to Dr. Wasgatt's. I knew 't would be contrary to the thirty-nine articles that they should get away from there without their suppers, and so I let the fire right down, and blacked the stove."

"Never mind," said Faith, abstractedly. "I don't feel hungry." And she went away, up stairs.

"'M!" said Mis' Battis, significantly, to herself, running a released knitting-needle through her hair, "Don't tell me! I've ben through the mill!"

Half-an-hour after, she came up to Faith's door.

"The minister's down stairs," said she, "Hope to goodness he's had *his* supper!"

"Oh, if I dared!" thought Faith; and her heart throbbed tumultuously. "Why can't there be somebody to tell me what I ought to do?"

If she had dared, how she could have leaned upon this friend! How she could have trusted her conscience and her fate to his decision!

And still the light that lighted her to herself was but a glimmer!

There was a moment when a word was almost on her lips, that might have changed, who knows? so much that was to come after!

"Does anything trouble you to-night, Miss Faith?" asked Mr. Armstrong, watching her sad, abstracted look in one of the silent pauses that broke their attempts at conversation. "Are you ill, or tired?"

"Oh, no!" answered Faith, quickly, from the surface, as one often does when thoughts lie deep. "I am quite well. Only — I am sometimes puzzled."

"About what is? Or about what ought to be?"

"About doing. So much depends. I get so tired — feeling how responsible everything makes me. I wish I were a little child again! Or that somebody would just take me and tell me where to go, and where to stay, and what to do, and what not. From minute to minute, as the things come up."

Roger Armstrong, with his great, chastened soul, yearned over the child as she spoke; so gladly he would have taken her, at that moment, to his heart, and bid her lean on him for all that man might give of help, — of love, of leading

If she had told him, in that moment, all her doubt, as for the instant of his pause she caught her breath with swelling impulse to do!

"'And they shall all be led of God;'" said the minister. "It is only to be willing to take His way rather than one's own. All this that seems to depend painfully upon one's self, depends, then, upon Him. The act is human — the consequences become Divine."

Faith was silenced then. There was no appeal to human help from that. Her impulse throbbed itself away into a lonely passiveness again.

There was a distance between these two that neither dared to pass.

A word was spoken between mother and daughter as they parted for the night.

"Mother! I have such a thing to think of, — to decide!"

It was whispered low, and with cheek hidden on her mother's neck, as the good-night kiss was taken.

"Decide for your own happiness, Faithie. We have seen and understood for a long time. If it is to be as we think, nothing could give us a greater joy for you."

Ah! how much had father and mother seen and understood?

The daughter went her way, to wage her own battle in secret; to balance and fix her decision between her own heart and God. So we find ourselves left, at the last, in all the great crises of our life.

Late that night, while Mr. and Mrs. Gartney were felicitating each other, cheerily, upon the great good that had fallen to the lot of their cherished child, that child sat by her open window, looking out into the summer night the tossing elm-boughs whispering weird syllables in her ears, and the stars looking down upon her soul-struggle, so silently, from so far!

"He had cared for her all his life." And who had been to her, in the happy years of the unthinking past, what he had been? Had she a right to do other than to go on in this, seemingly, her appointed path of life? Was not this the "high and holy work of love" that next awaited her? For father and mother she had done, in her girlish sacrifice and effort, what she could. Now, did not a greater work rise before her for others? and no less, at the same time, perhaps, for them?

To take anxiety from them, — to gratify what she perceived to have been a cherished wish and hope of theirs for her, — to leave them without care, save for the little brother for whom they would wish to do so much, and for whom they could do so much better when their cares for her were ended?"

And then, to help Paul, as he had asked her, to make a home here. To build up about them all things beautiful and true. Influence, — and all good that comes of influence and opportunity. To keep near them the lofty council they both would love, — to be guided by it, — to carry it out, — to live so in a pure and blessed friendship, that should exalt them both. What might not God will that she should be to Paul, — that each should be to the other?

Or, to cast down utterly all these hopes of father, mother, and lover, — to dash aside the opportunity set in her way. recklessly, — impiously, it might be! To carry, all her life, a burden upon her heart and soul, the anguish she had laid on one who loved her!

And all, because, caring for him as she surely did, she had a doubt as to whether she might quite care as he did, — as it was possible for her to care!

He had said she could not feel as he. That he felt as a man. Perhaps it was so. That a woman's love must needs be different.

Woman's necessity is to lose herself — to give herself away. If she be hindered from doing this, in the sweet and utter forgetfulness of a noble and unthwarted affection, her next impulse is to self-sacrifice.

There are nuns; there are nurses like Mehitable Sampson; there are sisters and patronesses of charity; there are hundreds — thousands — like Faith Gartney, who marry from a pure, blind reaching for a holy sphere of good. They have entreated God to lead them. They have given up self, and sought His work of Him. Does He not guide? Does He not give it?

The whole, long story, that He only sees, in its unfolding shall surely show.

"Mr. Rushleigh's here!" shouted Hendie, precipitating himself, next morning, into the breakfast-room, where, at a rather later hour than usual, Mrs. Gartney and Faith were washing and wiping the silver and china, and Mr. Gartney still lingered in his seat, finishing somebody's long speech, reported in the evening paper of yesterday.

"Mr. Rushleigh's here, on his long-tailed black horse! And he says he'll give me a ride, but not yet. He wants to see papa. Make haste, papa."

Faith dropped her towel, and as Mr. Gartney rose to go out and meet his visitor, just whispered, hurriedly, to her mother, —

"I'll come down again. I'll see him before he goes." And escaped up the kitchen staircase to her own room.

Paul Rushleigh came, he told Mr. Gartney, because, although Faith had not authorized him to appeal to her father to ratify any consent of hers, he thought it right to let him know what he had already said to his daughter. He did not wish to hurry Faith. He only wished to stand openly with Mr. Gartney in the matter, and would wait, then, till she should be quite ready to give him her own answer.

He explained the prospect his father offered him, and the likelihood of his making a permanent home at Kinnicutt.

"That is," he added, "if I am to be so happy as to have a home, anywhere, of my own."

Mr. Gartney was delighted with the young man's unaffected warmth of heart and noble candor.

"I could not wish better for my daughter, Mr. Rushleigh," he replied. "And she is a daughter whom I may fairly wish the best for, too."

Paul Rushleigh grasped the hand held out to him, in a strong gratitude for the favor shown himself, and mute, eloquent concurrence in the father's honest tribute to his child's worth.

Mr. Gartney rose. "I will send Faith," said he.

"I do not *ask* for her," answered Paul, a flush of feeling showing in his cheek. "I did not come, expecting it; — my errand was one I owed to yourself; — but Faith knows quite well how glad I shall be if she chooses to see me."

As Mr. Gartney crossed the hall from parlor to sitting-room, a light step came over the front staircase.

Faith passed her father, with a downcast look, as he motioned with his hand toward the room where Paul stood, waiting. The bright color spread to her temples as she glided in.

She held, but did not wear, the little turquoise ring.

Paul saw it, as he came forward eagerly.

A thrill of hope, or dread, — he scarce knew which, —

quivered suddenly at his heart. Was he to take it back, or place it on her finger as a pledge?

"I have been thinking, Paul," said she, tremulously, and with eyes that fell again away from his, after the first glance and greeting, "almost ever since. And I do not think I ought to keep you waiting to know the little I can tell you. I do not think I understand myself. I cannot tell, certainly, how I ought — how I do feel. I have liked you very much. And it was very pleasant to me before all this. I know you deserve to be made very happy. And if it depends on me, I do not dare to say I will not try to do it. If you think, yourself, that this is enough, — that I shall do the truest thing so, — I will try."

And the timid little fingers laid the ring into his hand, to do with as he would.

What else could Paul have done?

With the strong arm that should henceforth uphold and guard her, he drew her close; and with the other hand slipped the simply jewelled round upon her finger. For all word of answer, he lifted it, so encircled, to his lips.

Faith shrank and trembled.

Hendie's voice sounded, jubilant, along the upper floor, toward the staircase.

"I will go, now, if you wish. Perhaps I ought," said Paul. "And yet, I would so gladly stay. May I come again by-and-by?"

Faith uttered a half-audible assent, and as Hendie's step came nearer down the stairs, and passed the door, straight out upon the grass-plat, toward the gate, and the long-tailed black horse that stood there, she escaped again to her own chamber.

Hendie had his ride. Meanwhile, his sister, down upon

her knees at her bedside, struggled with the mystery and doubt of her own heart. Why could she not feel happier? Would it never be otherwise? Was this all life had for her, in its holiest gift, henceforth? But, come what might, she would have God, always!

So, without words, only with tears, she prayed, and at last, grew calm.

CHAPTER XXIV.

CONFLICT.

> O Life, O Beyond,
> *Art* thou fair? — *art* thou sweet?"
> MRS. BROWNING.

WE live two lives. A life of our deepest thought and feeling, that gets stirred but seldom; and a surface-life among things and words.

The great events that come to us wear two aspects. One when we look at them from the inmost, and measure them in all their mighty relation to what is everlasting; and again another as they effect only the little outward details of doing.

One hour, we are alone before God, and the soul's grasp stretches out toward the Infinite. All that befalls or may befall it, then seems great, momentous. We sleep, — we rise, — we are our daily petty selves again, — presences and voices come about that call us back into our superficial round, — and, underneath, for weal or woe, the silenced tide of our real being surges onward — whither?

So the river freezes over, and bears a merriment upon its bosom. So the great earth whereon we dwell wears its crust of hills and plains and cities above its everlasting fires.

There followed days that almost won Faith back into her outward life of pleasantness.

Margaret came over with Madam Rushleigh, and felicitated herself and friend, impetuously. Paul's mother thanked her for making her son happy. Old Mr. Rushleigh kissed her forehead with a blessing. And Mr. and Mrs. Gartney looked upon their daughter as with new eyes of love. Hendie rode the black horse every day, and declared that "everything was just as jolly as it could be!"

Paul drove her out, and walked with her, and talked of his plans, and all they would do and have together.

And she let herself be brightened by all this outward cheer and promise, and this looking forward to a happiness and use that were to come. But still she shrank and trembled at every lover-like caress, and still she said, fearfully, every now and then, —

"Paul, — I don't feel as you do. What if I don't love you as I ought?"

And Paul called her his little oversensitive, conscientious Faithie, and persuaded himself and her that he had no fear — that he was quite satisfied.

When Mr. Armstrong came to see her, gravely and tenderly wishing her joy, and looked searchingly into her face for the pure content that should be there, she bent her head into her hands and wept.

She was very weak, you say? She ought to have known her own mind better? Perhaps. I speak of her as she was. There are mistakes like these in life; there are hearts that suffer thus, unconscious of their ail.

The minister waited while the momentary burst of emotion subsided, and something of Faith's wonted manner returned.

"It is very foolish of me," she said, "and you must think me very strange. But, somehow, tears come easily when one has been feeling a great deal. And such kind words from you touched me."

"My words and thoughts will always be kind for you, my child. And I know very well that tears may mean sweeter and deeper things than smiles. I will not try you with much talking now. You have my affectionate wishes and my prayers. If there is ever any help that I can give, to you who have so much loving help about you, count on me as an earnest friend, always."

The hour was past when Faith, if she could ever, could have asked of him the help she did most sorely need.

And so, with a gentle hand-clasp, he went away.

Mr. Gartney began to be restless about Michigan. He wanted to go and see this wild estate of his. He would have liked to take his wife, now that haying would soon be over, and he could spare the time from his farm, and make it a pleasant summer journey for them both. But he could neither leave Faith, nor take her, well, it seemed. Hendie might go. Fathers always think their boys ready for the world when once they are fairly out of the nursery.

One day, Paul came to Cross Corners with news.

Mr. Rushleigh had affairs to be arranged and looked to, in New York, — matters connected with the mills, which had, within a few weeks, begun to run, — he had been there, once, about them; he could do all quite well, now, by letter, and an authorized messenger; he could not just now very well leave Kinnicutt. Besides, he wanted Paul to see and know his business friends, and to put himself in the way of valuable business information. Would Faith spare him for a week or two, — he bade his son to ask.

Madam Rushleigh would accompany Paul; and before his return he would go with his mother to Saratoga, where her daughter Gertrude and Mrs. Philip Rushleigh were, and where he was to leave her for the remainder of their stay.

Margaret liked Kinnicutt better than any watering-place; and she and her father had made a little plan of their own, which, if Faith would go back with him, they would explain to her.

So Faith went over to Lakeside to tea, and heard the plan.

"We are going to make our first claim upon you, Faith," said the elder Mr. Rushleigh, as he led his daughter-in-law elect out on the broad piazza under the Italian awnings, when the slight summer evening repast was ended. "We want to borrow you, while madam and the yonker are gone. Your father tells me he wishes to make a western journey Now, why not send him off at this very time? I think your mother intends accompanying him?"

"It had been talked of," Faith said; "and perhaps her father would be very glad to go when he could leave her in such good keeping. She would tell him what Mr. Rushleigh had been so kind as to propose."

It was a suggestion of real rest to Faith, — this free companionship with Margaret again, in the old girlish fashion, — and the very thoughtful look, that was almost sad, which had become habitual to her face, of late, brightened into the old, careless pleasure, as she spoke.

Mr. Rushleigh noted. A little doubt, like a quick shade, crossed him, for the first time.

It was almost like a look of relief. And Paul was to be away!

Paul and his mother came out on the piazza, and Madam Rushleigh drew Faith to a place between them, on the wide Indian settee.

Margaret went to the piano, and sang her twilight songs. And the sweet tones floated out from the open windows, and lingered about them as they sat there; and then diffused themselves away upon the still, warm air, into faint vibrations, lost to human hearing; yet spreading, — who can tell? perhaps, — in a rare, ethereal joy of melody, the mere soul of music, whereof the form, like all other form, may die, while the spirit, once evoked, lives on forever, and reaching with each thinned, successive wave, some listening, adapted sense in the great deep of being.

The elegant comfort, the refined pleasantness, the family joy that reigned in the Rushleighs' home, and that welcomed and took Faith in, and made her an essential part of it, — how could it help but win her to a glad content? All these accompanying relationships and circumstances made an exterior sphere for her that was so suited to her feeling and her taste, that in it she always lost, for the moment, her doubt, and accepted, involuntarily, the obvious good of this, her *secondary* life.

It was only when she forgot all else, and turned her thought, self-searchingly, to her tie with him who was to be the life-long, unchanging centre, henceforth, of whatever world, in all the years to come, might gather and shift about her, that the fear and the shrinking came back.

She was happier, somehow, when father, mother, and sister, with their winning endearments, were all about her with him, than when he claimed her to himself, and sought to speak or show his tenderness.

Old Mr. Rushleigh saw something in this that began to seem to him more than mere maidenly shyness.

By-and-by, Margaret called her brother to sing with her.

"Come, Faithie," said Paul as he rose, drawing her gently by the hand. "I can't sing unless you go, too."

Faith went; more, it seemed, of his will, than her own.

"How does that appear to you?" said Mr. Rushleigh to his wife. "Is it all right? Does the child care for Paul?"

"Care!" exclaimed the mother, almost surprised into too audible speech. "How can she help caring? And hasn't it grown up from childhood with them? What put such a question into your head? I should as soon think of doubting whether I care for you."

It was easier for the father to doubt, jealously, for his son, than for the mother to conceive the possibility of indifference in the woman her boy had chosen.

"Besides," added Mrs. Rushleigh, "why, else, should she have accepted him? I *know* Faith Gartney is not mercenary, or worldly ambitious."

"I am quite sure of that, as well," answered her husband. "It is no doubt of her motive or her worth, — I can't say it is really a doubt of anything; but, Gertrude, she must not marry the boy unless her whole heart is in it! A sharp stroke is better than a life-long pain."

"I'm sure I can't tell what has come over you! She can't ever have thought of anybody else! And she seems quite one of ourselves."

"Yes; that's just the uncertainty," replied Mr. Rushleigh. "Whether it isn't as much Margaret, and you and I, as Paul. Whether she fully knows what she is about. She can't marry the family, you know. We shall die, and go off, and Heaven knows what; Paul must be the whole world to her, or nothing. I hope he hasn't hurried her, — or let her hurry herself."

"Hurry! She has had years to make up her mind in!"

Mrs. Rushleigh, woman as she was, would not understand.

"We shall go, in three days," said Paul, when he stood in the moonlight with Faith at the little white gate under the elms, after driving her home; "and I must have you all the time to myself, until then!"

Faith wondered if it were right that she shouldn't quite care to be "had all the time to himself until then"? Whether such demonstrativeness and exclusiveness of affection was ever a little irksome to others as to her?

Faith thought and questioned, often, what other girls might feel in positions like her own, and tried to judge herself by them; it absolutely never occurred to her to think how it might have been if another than Paul had stood in this relation toward herself.

The young man did not quite have his own way, however. His father went down to Mishaumok on one of the three days, and left him in charge at the mills; and there were people to see, and arrangements to make; but some part of each day he did manage to devote to Faith, and they had walking and driving together, and every night Paul staid to tea at Cross Corners.

On the last evening, they sat together, by the hill-side door, in the summer parlor.

"Faithie," said Paul, a little suddenly, "there is something you must do for me — do you know?"

"What is it?" asked Faith, quite calmly.

"You must wear this, now, and keep the forget-me-not for a guard."

He held her hand, that wore the ring, in one of his, and there was a flash of diamonds as he brought the other toward it.

Then Faith gave a quick, strange cry.

"I can't! I can't! Oh, Paul! don't ask me!" And her hand was drawn from the clasp of his, and her face was hidden in both her own.

Paul drew back — hurt, silent.

"If I could only wait!" she murmured. "I don't dare, yet!"

She could wear the forget-me-not, as she wore the memory of all their long young friendship; it belonged to the past; but this definite pledge for the future, — these diamonds!

"Do you not quite belong to me, even yet?" asked Paul, with a resentment, yet a loving and patient one, in his voice.

"I told you," said Faith, "that I would try — to be to you as you wish; but, Paul! if I could n't be so, truly? — I don't know why I feel so uncertain. Perhaps it is because you care for me too much. Your thought for me is so great, that mine, when I look at it, never seems worthy."

Paul was a man. He could not sue, too cringingly, even for Faith Gartney's love.

"And I told you, Faith, that I was satisfied to be allowed to love you. That you should love me a little, and let it grow to more. But if it is not love at all, — if I frighten you, and repel you, — I have no wish to make you unhappy. I must let you go. And yet — oh, Faith!" he cried, — the sternness all gone, and only the wild love sweeping through his heart, and driving wild words before it, — "it can't be that it is no love, after all! It would be too cruel!"

At those words, "I must let you go," spoken apparently with calmness, as if it could be done, Faith felt a bound of freedom in her soul. If he would let her go, and care for her in the old way, only as a friend! But the strong pas sionate accents came after; and the old battle of doubt and pity and remorse surged up again, and the cloud of their strife dimmed all perception, save that she was very, very wretched.

She sobbed, silently.

"Don't let us say good-bye, so," said Paul. "Don't let us quarrel. We will let all wait, as you wish, till I come home again."

So he still clung to her, and held her, half-bound.

"And your father, Paul? And Margaret? How can I let them receive me as they do, — how can I go to them as I have promised, in all this indecision?"

"They want you, Faith, for your own sake. There is no need for you to disappoint them. It is better to say nothing more until we do know. I ask it of you, — do not refuse me this, — to let all rest just here; to make no difference until I come back. You will let me write, Faith?"

"Why, yes, Paul," she said, wonderingly.

It was so hard for her to comprehend that it could not be with him, any longer, as it had been; that his written or his spoken word could not be, for a time, at least, mere friendly any more.

And so she gave him, unwittingly, this hope to go with.

"I think you *do* care for me, Faith, if you only knew it!" said he, half sadly and very wistfully, as they parted.

"I do care, very much," Faith answered, simply and earnestly. "I never can help caring. It is only that I am afraid I care so differently from you!"

She was nearer loving him at that moment, than she had ever been.

Who shall attempt to bring into accord the seeming contradictions of a woman's heart?

CHAPTER XXV.

A GAME AT CHESS.

"Life's burdens fall, its discords cease,
 I lapse into the glad release
Of nature's own exceeding peace."
WHITTIER.

"I DON'T see," said Aunt Faith, "why the child can't come to me, Henderson, while you and Elizabeth are away. I don't believe in putting yourself under obligations to people till you 're sure they 're going to be something to you. Things don't always turn out according to the Almanac."

"She goes just as she always has gone to the Rushleighs," replied Mr. Gartney. "Paul is to be away. It is a visit to Margaret. Still, I shall be absent at least a fortnight, and it might be well that she should divide her time, and come to Cross Corners for a few days, if it is only to see the house opened and ready. Luther can have a bed here, if Mis' Battis should be afraid."

Mis' Battis was to improve the fortnight's interval for a visit to Factory Village.

"Well, fix it your own way," said Miss Henderson. "I 'm ready for her, any time. Only, if she is going to peak and pine as she has done ever since this grand match was settled for her, Glory and I 'll have our hands full, nursing her, by then you get back!"

"Faith is quite well," said Mrs. Gartney. "It is natural for a girl to be somewhat thoughtful when she decides for herself such an important relation."

"Symptoms differ, in different cases. *I* should say she was taking it pretty hard," said the old lady.

Mr. and Mrs. Gartney left home on Monday.

Faith and Mis' Battis remained in the house a few hours after, setting all things in that dreary "to rights" before leaving, which is almost, in its chillness and silence, like burial array. Glory came over to help; and when all was done, — blinds shut, windows and doors fastened, fire out, ashes removed, — stove blackened, — Luther drove Mis' Battis and her box over to Mrs. Pranker's, and Glory took Faith's little bag for her to the Old House.

This night she was to stay with her aunt. She wanted just this little pause and quiet before going to the Rushleighs'.

"Tell Aunt Faith I'm coming," said she, as she let herself and Glory out at the front door, and then, locking it, put the key in her pocket. "I'll just walk up over the Ridge first, for a little coolness and quiet, after this busy day."

It had been truly so busy, that Faith had had no time for facing her intruding thoughts; but put them all off, and thrust them back, as it were, into the antechamber of her mind, to be bidden in when she should be more at leisure; and even yet, she would not let them crowd upon her with their importunate errands. She wanted just this little time for respite. This Monday evening should be all peaceful. There was a natural reaction from the tense strain that had been upon thought and feeling, that made this at once an instinct and a possibility. She held herself in a passiveness that would, for awhile, neither feel nor consider.

She walked up the shady path to the boulder rock, and cradled herself in its stony hollow, — just where she had sat and listened, weeks before, to Roger Armstrong's story.

The summer sweetness, distilled all day by the glowing sun out of all growing things, came up to and around her. Beauty and stillness folded her as in a garment. She was in God's world still! Whatever world of fear and doubt and struggle her spirit might be groping into, dimly, things outside her were unchanged. She would come back into, and live in them for a few brief hours of utter and child-like calm.

There was the peace of a rested body and soul upon her face when she came down again a half hour after, and crossed the lane, and entered, through the stile, upon the field-path to the Old House. Heart and will had been laid asleep, — earthly plan and purpose had been put aside in all their incompleteness and uncertainty, — and only God and Nature had been permitted to come near.

Mr. Armstrong walked down and met her midway in the field.

"How beautiful mere simpleness and quiet are," said Faith. "The cool look of trees and grass, and the stillness of this evening time, are better even than flowers, and bright sunlight, and singing of birds!"

"'He maketh me to lie down in green pastures: He leadeth me beside the still waters: He restoreth my soul: He leadeth me in the paths of righteousness for His name's sake.'"

They did not disturb the stillness by more words. They came up together, in the hush and shadow, to the pleasant doorstone, that offered its broad invitation to their entering feet, and where Aunt Faith at this moment stood, watching and awaiting them.

"Go into the blue bedroom, and lay off your things, child," she said, giving Faith a kiss of welcome, "and then come back and we'll have our tea."

Faith disappeared through passages and rooms beyond.

Aunt Henderson turned quickly to the minister.

"You're her spiritual adviser, aint you?" she asked abruptly.

"I ought to be," answered Mr. Armstrong.

"Why don't you advise her then?"

"Spiritually, I do and will, in so far as so pure a spirit can need a help from me. But, — I think I know what you mean, Miss Henderson, — spirit and heart are two. I am a man; and she is — what you know."

Miss Henderson's keen eyes fixed themselves, for a minute, piercingly and unflinchingly, on the minister's face. Then she turned, without a word, and went into the house to see the tea brought in. She knew, now, all there was to tell.

Faith's face interpreted itself to Mr. Armstrong. He saw that she needed, and would have, rest. Rest, this night, from all that of late had given her weariness and trouble. So, he did not even talk to her in the way they mostly talked together; he would not rouse, ever so distantly, thought, that might, by so many subtle links, bear round upon her hidden pain. But he brought, — after tea, when the faint little shaded lamp, that hardly quarrelled with the twilight, or, if it did, made nothing more than a drawn battle of it, so that dor-bugs and mosquitoes could not make up their minds, positively, that they should do better inside than out, was lit in the southeast room, — a tiny chess-board, and set the delicate carved men upon it, and asked her if she knew the game.

"A little," she said. "What everybody always owns to knowing — the moves."

"Suppose we play."

It was a very pleasant novelty, — sitting down with this grave, earnest friend to a game of skill, — and seeing him bring to it all the resource of power and thought that he bent, at other times, on more important work.

Whatever Roger Armstrong did, he did with the might that was in him.

"Not that, Miss Faith! You don't mean that! You put your queen in danger."

"My queen is always a great trouble to me," said Faith, smiling, as she retracted the half-made move. "I think I do better when I give her up in exchange."

"Excuse me, Miss Faith; but that always seems to me a cowardly sort of game. It is like giving up a great power in life because one is too weak to claim and hold it."

"Only I make you lose yours too."

"Yes, there is a double loss and inefficiency. Does that make a better game, or one pleasanter to play?"

"There are two people, in there, talking riddles; and they don't even know it," said Miss Henderson to her handmaid, in the kitchen close by.

Perhaps Mr. Armstrong, as he spoke, did discern a possible deeper significance in his own words; did misgive himself that he might rouse thoughts so; at any rate, he made rapid, skilful movements on the board, that brought the game into new complications, and taxed all Faith's attention to avert their dangers to herself.

For half an hour, there was no more talking.

Then Faith's queen was put in helpless peril.

"I must give her up," said she. "She is all but gone.

A few moves more, and all Faith's hope depended on one little pawn, that might be pushed to queen and save her game.

"How one does want the queen-power at the last!" said she. "And how much easier it is to lose it, than to get it back."

"It is like the one great, leading possibility, that life, in some sort, offers each of us," said Mr. Armstrong. "Once lost, — once missed, — we may struggle on without it, — we may push little chances forward to partial amends; but the game is changed; its soul is gone."

As he spoke he made the move that led to obvious checkmate.

Glory came in to the cupboard, now, and began putting up the tea-things she had brought from washing.

Mr. Armstrong had done just what, at first, he had meant not to do. Had he bethought himself better, and did he seize the opening to give vague warning where he might not speak more plainly? Or, had his habit, as a man of thought, discerning quick meaning in all things, betrayed him into the instant's forgetfulness?

However it might be, Glory caught glimpse of two strange pained faces over the little board and its mystic pieces.

One, pale, — downcast, — with expression showing a sudden pang; the other, suffering also, yet tender, self-forgetful, loving, — looking on.

"I don't know whichever is worst," she said afterward, without apparent suggestion of word or circumstance, to her mistress; "to see the beautiful times that there are in the world, and not be in 'em, — or to see people that might be in 'em, and aint!"

They were all out on the front stoop, later. They sat in the cool, summer dusk, and looked out between the arched lattices, where the vines climb up, seeing the stars rise, far away, eastwardly, in the blue; and Mr. Armstrong, talking with Faith, managed to win her back into the calm he had, for an instant, broken; and to keep her from pursuing the thought that by-and-by would surely come back, and which she would surely want all possible gain of strength to grapple with.

Faith met his intention bravely, seconding it with her own. These hours, to the last, should still be restful. She would not think, to-night, of those words that had startled her so, — of all they suggested or might mean, — of life's great possibility lost to him, away back in the sorrowful past, as she also, perhaps was missing it, — relinquishing it, — now.

She knew not that his thought had been utterly self-forgetful. She believed that he had told her, indirectly, of himself, when he had spoken those dreary syllables, — "the game is changed. Its soul is gone!"

Singularly, that night again, as on the night so long ago, when Faith had come on her little visit of exploration to Kinnicutt, the lesson read them from the Bible was that miracle of the loaves and fishes.

A comfort came to Faith, as she listened; as the comfort we need at the moment always does come, by the instant gift of the Spirit, through whatever Gospel-words may be its vehicle.

The loaves might be few and small; life might be scant and insufficient seemingly; yet a touch Divine should multiply the food, and make it ample!

Nevertheless, — did she remember this? That, but the next day after, the disciples, with this recognized Divineness at their side, stood self-rebuked, because they had neglected to make for themselves such human provision as they might have done?

CHAPTER XXVI.

LAKESIDE.

> " Look! are the southern curtains drawn?
> Fetch me a fan, and so begone!
>
> . . . .
>
> Rain me sweet odors on the air,
> And wheel me up my Indian chair;
> And spread some book not overwise
> Flat out before my sleepy eyes."
>
> O. W. HOLMES.

THE Rushleighs' breakfast-room at Lakeside was very lovely in a summer's morning.

Looking off, northwestwardly, across the head of the Pond, the long windows, opening down to the piazza, let in all the light and joy of the early day, and that indescribable freshness born from the union of woods and water.

Faith had come down long before the others, this fair Wednesday morning.

Mr. Rushleigh found her, when he entered, sitting by a window, — a book upon her lap, to be sure, — but her eyes away off over the lake, and a look in them that told of thoughts horizoned yet more distantly.

Last night, he had brought home Paul's first letter.

When he gave it to her, at tea time, with a gay and kindly word, the color that deepened vividly upon her face, and the quiet way in which she laid it down beside her plate, were nothing strange, perhaps; but — was he wrong? the eyes that drooped so quickly as the blushes rose, and then lifted themselves again so timidly to him as he next addressed her, were surely brimmed with feeling that was not quite, or wholly glad.

And now, this wistful, silent, musing, far-off look!

"Good morning, Faithie!"

"Good morning." And the glance came back, — the reverie was broken, — Faith's spirit informed her visible presence again, and bade him true and gentle welcome. "You haven't your morning paper yet? I'll bring it. Thomas left it in the library, I think. He came back from the early train half an hour ago."

"Can't you women tell what's the matter with each other?" said Mr. Rushleigh to his daughter, who entered by the other door, as Faith went out into the hall. "What ails Faith, Margaret?"

"Nothing of consequence, I think. She is tired with all that has been going on, lately. And then she's the shyest little thing!"

"It's a sort of shyness that don't look so happy as it might, it seems to me. And what has become of Paul's diamonds, I wonder? I went with him to choose some, last week. I thought I should see them next upon her finger."

Margaret opened her eyes widely. Of course, this was the first she had heard of the diamonds. Where could they be, indeed? Was anything wrong? They had not surely quarrelled!

Faith came in with the paper. Thomas brought up breakfast. And presently, these three, with all their thoughts of and for each other, that reached into the long years to come, and had their roots in all that had gone by, were gathered at the table, seemingly with no further anxiety than to know whether one or another would have toast or muffins, — eggs or raspberries.

Do we not — and most strangely and incomprehensibly — live two lives?

"I must write to my mother, to-day," said Margaret, when her father had driven away to the mills, and they had brought in a few fresh flowers from the terrace for the vases, and had had a little morning music, which Margaret always craved, "as an overture," she said "to the day."

"I must write to my mother; and you, I suppose, will be busy with answering Paul?"

A little consciousness kept her from looking straight in Faith's face, as she spoke. Had she done so, she might have seen that a paleness came over it, and that the lips trembled.

"I don't know," was the answer. "Perhaps not, to-day."

"Not to-day? Won't he be watching every mail? I don't know much about it, to be sure; but I fancied lovers were such uneasy, exacting creatures!"

"Paul is very patient," said Faith, — not lightly as Margaret had spoken, but as one self-reproached, almost, for abusing patience, — " and they go to-morrow to Lake George. He won't look for a letter until he gets to Saratoga."

She had calculated her time as if it were the minutes of a reprieve.

"I had n't thought of that," said Margaret. "How came you to reckon so closely? But, for me, I must write, simply because I have just heard from mamma. My ideas are like champagne — good for nothing after the first effervescence. And the cork is drawn, always, the minute I get a letter myself! If I wait till next day, it may as well never be answered; and, very likely, never will!"

When Paul Rushleigh, with his mother, reached Saratoga, he found two letters there, for him. One kind, simple, but reticent, from Faith — a mere answer to that which she could answer, of his own. The other was from his father.

"There seems," he wrote to his son, toward the close, "to be a little cloud upon Faith, somehow. Perhaps it is one you would not wish away. It may brighten up and roll off, at your return. You, possibly, understand it better than I. Yet I feel, in my strong anxiety for your true good, impelled to warn you against letting her deceive herself and you, by giving you less than, for her own happiness and yours, she ought to be able to give. Do not marry the child, Paul, if there can be a doubt of her entire affection for you. You had better go through life alone, than with a wife's half-love. If you have reason to imagine that she feels bound by anything in the past to what the present cannot heartily ratify, — release her. I counsel you to this, not more in justice to her, than for the saving of your own peace. She writes you to-day. It may be that the antidote comes with the hurt. I may be quite mistaken. But I hurt you, my son, only to save a sorer pain. Faith is true. If she says she loves you, believe her, and take her, though all the world should doubt. But if she is fearful, — if she hesitates, — be fearful, and hesitate yourself, lest your marriage be no true marriage before heaven!"

Paul Rushleigh thanked his father, briefly, for his admonition, in reply. He wrote, also, to Faith — affectionately, but with something, at last, of her own reserve. He should not probably write again. In a week, or less, he would be home.

And behind, and beyond all this, that could be put on paper, was the hope of a life, — the sharp doubt of days, — waiting the final word!

In a week, he would be home! A week! It might bring much!

Wednesday had come round again.

Dinner was nearly ended at Lakeside. Cool jellies, and creams, and fruits, were on the table for dessert. Steaming dishes of meats and vegetables had been gladly sent away, but slightly partaken. The day was sultry. Even now, at five in the afternoon, the heat was hardly mitigated from that of midday.

They lingered over their dessert, and spoke, rather languidly, of what might be done after.

"For me," said Mr. Rushleigh, "I must go down to the mills again, before night. If either, or both of you, like a drive, I shall be glad to have you with me."

"Those hot mills!" exclaimed Margaret. "What an excursion to propose!"

"I could find you a very cool corner, even in those hot mills," replied her father. "My little sanctum, up stairs, that overlooks the river, and gets its breezes, is the freshest place I have been in, to-day. Will you go, Faith?"

"Oh, yes! she'll go! I see it in her eyes!" said Margaret. "She is getting to be as much absorbed in all those frantic looms and things, — that set me into a fever just to think of, whizzing and humming all day long in this horrible heat, — as you are! I believe she expects to help Paul oversee the factory, one of these days, she is so fierce to peer into and understand everything about it. Or else, she means mischief! You had a funny look in your face, Faithie, the other day, when you stood there by the great rope that hoists the water-gate, and Mr. Blasland was explaining it to us!"

"I was thinking, I remember," said Faith, "what a strange thing it was to have one's hand on the very motive power of it all. To see those great looms, and wheels, and cylinders, and spindles, we had been looking at, and hear nothing but their deafening roar all about us, and to think that even I, standing there with my hand upon the rope, might hush it all, and stop the mainspring of it in a minute!"

Ah, Faithie! Did you think, as you said this, how your little hand lay, otherwise, also, on the mainspring and motive of it all? One of the three, at least, thought of it, as you spoke.

"Well,—your heart's in the spindles, I see!" rejoined Margaret. "So, don't mind me. I haven't a bit of a plan for your entertainment, here. I shouldn't, probably, speak to you, if you staid. It's too hot for anything but a book, and a fan, and a sofa by an open window!"

Faith laughed; but, before she could reply, a chaise rolled up to the open front door, and the step and voice of Doctor Wasgatt were heard, as he inquired for Miss Gartney.

Faith left her seat, with a word of excuse, and met him in the hall.

"I had a patient up this way," said he, "and came round to bring you a message from Miss Henderson. Nothing to be frightened at, in the least; only that she isn't quite so well as ordinary, these last hot days, and thought perhaps you might as lief come over. She said she was expecting you for a visit there, before your folks get back. No, thank you;" as Faith motioned to conduct him to the drawing-room,—"can't come in. Sorry I couldn't offer to take you down; but I've got more visits to make, and they lie round the other way."

"Is Aunt Faith ill?"

"Well,—no. Not so but that she'll be spry again in a day or two; especially if the weather changes. That ancle of hers is troublesome, and she had something of an ill turn last night, and called me over this morning. She seems to have taken a sort of fancy that she'd like to have you there."

"I'll come."

And Faith went back, quickly, as Doctor Wasgatt departed, to make his errand known, and to ask if Mr. Rushleigh would mind driving her round to Cross Corners, after going to his mills.

"Wait till to-morrow, Faithie," said Margaret, in the tone of one whom it fatigues to think of an exertion, even for another. "You'll want your box with you, you know; and there isn't time for anything to-night."

"I think I ought to go now," answered Faith. "Aunt Henderson never complains for a slight ailment, and she might be ill again to-night. I can take all I shall need before to-morrow in my little morocco bag. I won't keep you waiting a minute," she added, turning to Mr. Rushleigh.

"I can wait twenty, if you wish," he answered, kindly.

But in less than ten, they were driving down toward the river.

Margaret Rushleigh had betaken herself to her own cool chamber, where the delicate straw matting, and pale green, leaf-patterned chintz of sofa, chairs, and hangings, gave a feeling of the last degree of summer lightness and daintiness, and the gentle air breathed in from the southwest, sifted, on the way, of its sunny heat, by the green draperies of vine and branch it wandered through.

Lying there, on the cool, springy cushions of her couch, — turning the fresh-cut leaves of the August "Mishaumok," — she forgot the wheels and the spindles — the hot mills, and the ceaseless whirr.

Just at that moment of her utter comfort and content, a young factory girl dropped, fainting, in the dizzy heat, before her loom.

CHAPTER XXVII.

AT THE MILLS.

> "For all day the wheels are droning, turning,—
> Their wind comes in our faces,—
> Till our hearts turn,—our head with pulses burning,—
> And the walls turn in their places."
>
> Mrs. Browning.

FAITH sat silent by Mr. Rushleigh's side, drinking in, also, with a cool content, the river air that blew upon their faces as they drove along.

"Faithie!" said Paul's father, a little suddenly, at last,—"do you know how true a thing you said a little while ago?"

"How, sir?" asked Faith, not perceiving what he meant.

"When you spoke of having your hand on the mainspring of all this?"

And he raised his right arm, motioning with the slender whip he held, along the line of factory buildings that lay before them.

A deep, blazing blush burned, at his word, over Faith's cheek and brow. She sat and suffered it under his eye,—uttering not a syllable.

"I knew you did *not* know. You did not think of it so. Yet it is true, none the less.—Faith! Are you happy? Are you satisfied?"

Still a silence, and tears gathering in the eyes.

"I do not wish to distress you, my dear. It is only a little word I should like to hear you speak. I must, so far as I can, see that my children are happy, Faith."

"I suppose," said Faith, tremulously, struggling to speech, — "one cannot expect to be utterly happy in this world."

"One does expect it, forgetting all else, at the moment when is given what seems to one life's first, great good, — the earthly good that comes but once. I remember my own youth, Faithie. Pure, present content is seldom over-wise."

"Only," said Faith, still tremblingly, "that the responsibility comes with the good. That feeling of having one's hand upon the mainspring is a fearful one."

"I am not given," said Mr. Rushleigh, "to quoting Bible at all times; but you make a line of it come up to me. 'There is no fear in love. Perfect love casteth out fear.'"

"Be sure of yourself, dear child. Be sure you are content and happy; and tell me so, if you can; or, tell me otherwise, if you must, without a reserve or misgiving," he said again, as they drove down the mill-entrance; and their conversation, for the time, came, necessarily, to an end.

Coming into the mill-yard, they were aware of a little commotion about one of the side doors.

The mill-girl who had fainted sat here, surrounded by two or three of her companions, slowly recovering.

"It is Mary Grover, sir, from up at the Peak," said one of them, in reply to Mr. Rushleigh's question. "She hasn't been well for some days, but she's kept on at her work and the heat, to-day, was too much for her. She'd ought to be got home, if there was any way. She can't ever walk."

"I'll take her, myself," said the mill-owner, promptly. "Keep her quiet here a minute or two, while I go in and speak to Blasland."

But first he turned to Faith again. "What shall I do with you, my child?"

"Dear Mr. Rushleigh," said she, with all her gratitude for his just spoken kindness to herself and her appreciation of his ready sympathy for the poor work-girl, in her voice, — "don't think of me! It's lovely out there over the foot-bridge, and in the fields; and that way, the distance is nearly nothing to Aunt Faith's. I should like the walk, — really."

"Thank you," said Mr. Rushleigh. "I believe you would. Then I'll take Mary Grover up to the Peak."

And he shook her hand, and left her standing there, and went up into the mill.

Two of the girls who had come out with Mary Grover, followed him and returned to their work. One, sitting with her in the door-way, on one of the upper steps, and supporting her yet dizzy head upon her shoulder, remained.

Faith asked if she could do anything, and was answered, no, with thanks.

She turned away, then, and walked over the planking above the race-way, toward the river, where a pretty little foot-bridge crossed it here, from the end of the mill-building.

Against this end, projected, on this side, a square, tower-like appendage to the main structure, around which one must pass to reach the foot-bridge. A door at the base opened upon a staircase, leading up. This was the entrance to Mr. Rushleigh's "sanctum," above, which communicated, also, with the second story of the mill.

Here Faith paused. She caught, from around the corner, a sound of the angry voices of men.

"I tell you, I'll stay here till I see the boss!"

"I tell you, the boss won't see you. He's done with you."

"Let him *be* done with me, then; and not go spoiling my chance with other people! I'll see it out with him, somehow, yet."

"Better not threaten. He won't go out of his way to meddle with you; only it's no use your sending anybody here after a character. He's one of the sort that speaks the truth and shames the devil."

"I'll let him know he aint boss of the whole country round! D—d if I don't!"

Faith turned away from hearing more of this, and from facing the speakers; and took refuge up the open staircase.

Above, — in the quiet little counting-room, shut off by double doors at the right from the great loom-chamber of the mill, and opening at the front by a wide window upon the river that ran tumbling and flashing below, spanned by the graceful little bridge that reached the green slope of the field beyond, — it was so cool and pleasant, — so still with continuous and softened sound, — that Faith sat down upon the comfortable sofa there, to rest, to think, to be alone, a little.

She had Paul's letter in her pocket; she had his father's words fresh upon ear and heart. A strange peace came over her, as she placed herself here; as if, somehow, a way was soon to be opened and made clear to her. As if she should come to know herself, and to be brave to act as God should show her how

She heard, presently, Mr. Rushleigh's voice in the mill-yard, and then the staircase door closed and locked below. Thinking that he should be here no more, to-night, he had shut and fastened it.

It was no matter. She would go through the mill, by-and-by, and look at the looms; and so out, and over the river, then, to Aunt Faith,

CHAPTER XXVIII.

LOCKED IN.

"How idle it is to call certain things godsends! as if there were any thing else in the world." HARE.

IT is accounted a part of the machinery of invention when, in a story, several coincident circumstances, that apart, would have had no noticeable result, bear down together, with a nice and sure calculation upon some catastrophe or *denouement* that develops itself therefrom.

Does not God work out our human fate by the bee-lines of His Providence? From points afar and seemingly separate, the threads of agency begin. And, straight to one fore-ordered purpose, move on, undeviatingly, as we trace them, to the converging point, where the divine meaning and plan shall be consummated.

God, — let it be said reverently, — is the Great Novelist, and Architect of circumstance. When we see the lives of men, that he writes out daily, in actual fact, about us, can we think, for an instant, that our poor imagining and contriving can go beyond His infinite possibilities, — His hourly accomplishments? Can transcend, by any ingenuity, His groupings and combinings, when a thing is willed to be?

Last night, a man, — an employé in Mr. Rushleigh's factory, — had been kept awake by one of his children, taken suddenly ill. A slight matter, — but it has to do with our story.

Last night, also, Faith, — Paul's second letter just received, — had lain sleepless for hours, fighting the old battle over, darkly, of doubt, pity, half-love, and indecision. She had felt, or had thought she felt, — thus, or so, — in the days that were past. Why could she not be sure of her feeling now?

The new wine in the old bottles, — the new cloth in the old garment, — these, in Faith's life, were at variance. What satisfied once, satisfied no longer. Was she to blame? What ought she to do? There was a seething — a rending. Poor heart, that was likely to be burst and torn, — wonderingly, helplessly, — in the half-comprehended struggle!

So it happened, that, tired with all this, sore with its daily pressure and recurrence, this moment of strange peace came over her, and soothed her into rest.

She laid herself back, there, on the broad, soft, old-fashioned sofa, and with the river breeze upon her brow, and the song of its waters in her ears, and the deadened hum of the factory rumbling on, — she fell asleep.

A heavy sleep it was; as if some waiting angel bore her soul away, away, — far off from all earthly sound and association, — and left her body there to utter rest.

And so, — strangely, perhaps, but it was so, — the factory-bell, at the far end of the long building, sent its clang out on the air that seized and bore it from the river, and the busy operatives hurried out from their place of toil, and streamed in long lines homeward, and the rumbling hushed, and left only the noise of falling and rushing waters in her ears, — and still Faith slumbered on.

How long it had been, she could not tell; she knew **not**

whether it were evening, or midnight, or near the morning; but she felt **cold and** cramped; everything **save** the busy river was still, and the daylight was **all** gone, and **stars out** bright in the deep, moonless sky, when she awoke.

Awoke, bewilderedly, and came **slowly to the** comprehension that she was here alone. That **it** was night, — that nobody could know it, — that she **was** locked up here, in **the great** dreary **mill.**

She raised herself upon the sofa, and sat **in a terrified** amaze. She took **out her** watch, and tried **to** see, by the starlight, the time. The slender black hands upon its golden face were invisible. It ticked, — **it was going.** She **knew,** by that, it could not be far beyond midnight, **at the** most. She was chilly, in her white dress, **from** the night air. She went to the open window, and looked **out** from it, before she drew it down. Away, **over** the **fields, and up** and down **the river, all** was **dark, solitary.**

Nobody knew it, — she **was here alone.**

She shut the window, **softly, afraid of the sounds herself** might **make.** She opened the double doors from the counting-room, and stood on **the outer threshold, and looked into the mill.** The heavy looms **were still.** They stood like great, dead creatures, smitten **in the midst of busy motion.** There was an awfulness in being **here, the only** breathing, moving thing, — in darkness, — **where so lately** had been the deafening hum of rolling wheels, **and** clanking shafts, and flying shuttles, and busy, moving **human** figures. It **was as if the** world itself were stopped, **and she forgotten** on its mighty, silent corse.

Should she find her way to the great bell, ring it, and make **an alarm?** She thought of this; and then she reasoned with herself that **she was hardly so badly off, as to** justify her, quite, in doing that. It would rouse the village, it would bring Mr. Rushleigh down, perhaps,— it would cause a terrible alarm. And all that she might be spared a few hours longer of loneliness and discomfort. She was safe. It would soon be morning. The mill would be opened early. She would go back to the sofa, and try to sleep again. Nobody could be anxious about her. The Rushleighs supposed her to be at Cross Corners. Her aunt would think her detained at Lakeside. It was really no great matter. She would be brave, and quiet.

So she shut the double doors again, and found a coat of Paul's, or Mr. Rushleigh's, in the closet of the counting-room, and lay down upon the sofa, covering herself with that.

For an hour or more, her heart throbbed, her nerves were excited, she could not sleep. But at last she grew calmer, her thought wandered from her actual situation,— became indistinct,— and slumber held her again, dreamily.

There was another sleeper, also, in the mill whom Faith knew nothing of.

Michael Garvin, the night-watchman,— the same whose child had been ill the night before,— when Faith came out into the loom-chamber, had left it but a few minutes, going his silent round within the building, and recording his faithfulness by the half-hour pin upon the watch-clock. Six times he had done this, already. It was half-past ten.

He had gone up, now, by the stairs from the weaving-room, into the third story. These stairs ascended at the front, from within the chamber.

Michael Garvin went on nearly to the end of the room above,— stopped, and looked out at a window. All still, all safe apparently.

He was very tired. What harm in lying down somewhere in a corner, for five minutes? He need not shut his eyes. He rolled his coat up for a pillow, and threw it against the wall beneath the window. The next instant he had stretched his stalwart limbs along the floor, and before ten minutes of his seventh half hour were spent, — long before Faith, who thought herself all alone in the great building, had lost consciousness of her strange position, — he was fast asleep.

Fast asleep, here, in the third story!

So, since the days of the disciples, men have grown heavy and forgotten their trust. So they have slumbered upon decks, at sea. So sentinels have lain down at picket-posts, though they knew the purchase of that hour of rest might be the leaden death!

Faith Gartney dreamed, uneasily.

She thought herself wandering, at night, through the deserted streets of a great city. She seemed to have come from somewhere afar off, and to have no place to go to.

Up and down, through avenues sometimes half familiar, sometimes wholly unknown, she went wearily, without aim, or end, or hope. "Tired! tired! tired!" she seemed to say to herself. "Nowhere to rest, — nobody to take care of me!"

Then, — city, streets, and houses disappeared; the scenery of her dream rolled away, and opened out, and she was standing on a high, bare cliff, away up in wintry air; threatening rocky avalanches overhanging her, — chill winds piercing her, — and no pathway visible downward. Still crying out in loneliness and fear. Still with none to comfort or to help.

Standing on the sheer edge of the precipice, — behind

her, suddenly, a crater opened. A hissing breath came up, and the chill air quivered and scorched about her. Her feet were upon a volcano! A lake of boiling, molten stone heaved, — huge, brazen, bubbling, — spreading wider and wider, like a great earth-ulcer, eating in its own brink continually. Up in the air over her, reared a vast, sulphurous canopy of smoke. The narrowing ridge beneath her feet burned, — — trembled. She hovered between two destructions.

Instantly, — in that throbbing, agonizing moment of her dream, just after which one wakes, — she felt a presence, — she heard a call, — she thought two arms were stretched out toward her, — there seemed a safety and a rest near by; she was borne by an unseen impulse, along the dizzy ridge that her feet scarce touched, toward it; she was taken, — folded, held; smoke, fire, the threatening danger of the cliff, were nothing, suddenly, any more. Whether they menaced still, she thought not; a voice she knew and trusted was in her ear; a grasp of loving strength sustained her; she was utterly secure.

So vividly she felt the presence, — so warm and sure seemed that love and strength about her, — that waking out of such pause of peace, before her senses recognized anything that was real without, she stretched her hands, as if to find it at her side, and her lips breathed a name, — the name of Roger Armstrong.

Then she started to her feet. The kind, protecting presence faded back into her dream.

The horrible smoke, the scorching smell, were true.

A glare smote sky and trees and water, as she saw them from the window.

There was fire near her!

Could it be among the buildings of the mill?

The long, main structure ran several feet beyond the square projection within which she stood. Upon the other side, close to the front, quite away, of course, from all observation hence, joined, at right angles, another building, communicating and forming one with the first. Here were the carding rooms. Then beyond, detached, were houses for storage and other purposes connected with the business.

Was it from one of these the glare and smoke and suffocating burning smell were pouring?

Or, lay the danger nearer, — within these close, contiguous walls?

Vainly she threw up the one window, and leaned forth.

She could not tell.

At this moment, Roger Armstrong, also, woke from out a dream.

In this strange, second life of ours, that replaces the life of day, do we not meet interiorly? Do not thoughts and knowledges cross, from spirit to spirit, over the abyss, that lip, and eye, and ear, in waking moments, neither send nor receive? That even mind itself is scarcely conscious of? Is not the great deep of being, wherein we rest, electric with a sympathetic life, — and do not warnings and promises and cheer pulse in upon us, mysteriously, in these passive hours of the flesh, when soul only is awake and keen?

Do not two thoughts, two consciousnesses, call and answer to each other, mutely, in twin dreams of night?

Roger Armstrong came in, late, that evening, from a visit to a distant sick parishioner. Then he sat, writing, for an hour or two longer.

By-and-by he threw down his pen, — pushed back his

arm-chair before his window, — stretched his feet, wearily, into the deep, old-fashioned window-seat, — leaned his head back, and let the cool breeze stir his hair.

So it soothed him into sleep.

He dreamed of Faith. He dreamed he saw her stand, afar off, in some solitary place, and beckon, as it were, visibly, from a wide, invisible distance. He dreamed he struggled to obey her summons. He battled with the strange inertia of sleep. He strove, — he gasped, — he broke the spell and hastened on. He plunged, — he climbed, — he stood in a great din that bewildered and threatened; there was a lurid light that glowed intense about him as he went; in the midst of all, — beyond, — she beckoned still!

"Faith! Faith! What danger is about you, child?"

These words broke forth from him aloud, as he started to his feet, and stretched his hands, impulsively, out before him, toward the open window.

His eyes flashed wide upon that crimson glare that flooded sky and field and river.

There was fire at the mills!

Not a sound, yet, from the sleeping village.

The heavy, close-fitting double doors between the counting-room and the great mill-chamber were shut. Only by opening these and venturing forth, could Faith gain certain knowledge of her situation.

Once more she pulled them open and passed through.

A blinding smoke rushed thick about her, and made her gasp for breath. Up through the belt-holes in the floor, toward the farther end of the long room, sprang little tongues of flame that leaped higher and higher, even while she strove for sight, that single, horrified, suffocating instant, and gleamed, mockingly, upon the burnished shafts of silent looms.

In at the windows on the left, came the vengeful shine of those other windows, at right angles, in the adjacent building. The carding-rooms, and the whole front of the mill, below, were all in flames!

In frantic affright, in choking agony, Faith dashed herself back through the heavy doors, that swung on springs, and closed tightly once more after her.

Here, at the open window, she took breath. Must she wait here, helpless, for the fiery death?

Down below her, the narrow brink. — the rushing river. No foothold, — no chance for a descent. Behind her, only those two doors, barring out flame and smoke!

And the little foot-bridge, lying in the light across the water, and the green fields, stretching away, cool and safe beyond. A little farther — her home!

"Fire!"

She cried the fearful word out upon the night, uselessly. There was no one near. The village slumbered on, away there to the left. The strong, deep shout of a man might reach it, but no tone of hers. There were no completed or occupied dwelling-houses, as yet, about the new mills. Mr. Rushleigh was putting up some blocks; but, for the present, there was nothing nearer than the village proper of Kinnicutt on the one hand, and as far, or farther, on the other the houses at Lakeside.

The flames themselves, alone, could signal her danger, and summon help. How long would it be first?

Thoughts of father, mother, and little brother, — thoughts of the kind friends at Lakeside, parted from but a few hours before, — thoughts of the young lover to whom the answer he waited for should be given, perhaps, so awfully; — through all, lighting, as it were, suddenly and searchingly, the deep places of her own soul, the thought, — the feeling, rather, of that presence in her dream; of him who had led her, taught her, lifted her so, to high things; — brought her nearer, by his ministry, to God! Of all human influence or love, his was nearest and strongest, spiritually, to her, now!

All at once, across these surging, crowding, agonizing feelings, rushed an inspiration for the present moment.

The water-gate! The force-pump!

The apparatus for working these lay at this end of the building. She had been shown the method of its operation; they had explained to her its purpose. It was perfectly simple. Only the drawing of a rope over a pulley, — the turning of a faucet. She could do it, if she could only reach the spot.

Instantly and strangely, the cloud of terror seemed to roll away. Her faculties cleared. Her mind was all alert and quickened. She thought of things she had heard of years before, and long forgotten. That a wet cloth about the face would defend from smoke. That down low, close to the floor, was always a current of fresher air.

She turned a faucet that supplied a basin in the counting-room, held her handkerchief to it, and saturated it with water. Then she tied it across her forehead, letting it hang before her face like a veil. She caught a fold of it between her teeth.

And so, opening the doors between whose cracks the pent-up smoke was curling, she passed through, crouching down, and crawled along the end of the chamber, toward the great rope in the opposite corner.

The fire was creeping thitherward, also, to meet her. Along from the front, down the chamber on the opposite side, the quick flames sprang and flashed, momentarily higher, catching already, here and there, from point to point, where an oiled belt or an unfinished web of cloth attracted their hungry tongues.

As yet, they were like separate skirmishers, sent out in advance; their mighty force not yet gathered and rolled together in such terrible sheet and volume as raged beneath.

She reached the corner where hung the rope.

Close by, was the faucet in the main pipe fed by the force-pump. Underneath it, lay a coil of hose, attached and ready.

She turned the faucet, and laid hold of the long rope. A few pulls, and she heard the dashing of the water far below. The great wheel was turning.

The pipes filled. She lifted the end of the coiled hose, and directed it toward the forward part of the chamber, where flames were wreathing, climbing, flashing. An impetuous column of water rushed, eager, hissing, upon blazing wood and heated iron.

Still keeping the hose in her grasp, she crawled back again, half stifled, yet a new hope of life aroused within her, to the double doors. Before these, with the little counting-room behind her, as her last refuge, she took her stand.

How long could she fight off death? Till help came?

All this had been done and thought quickly. There had been less time than she would have believed, since she first woke to the knowledge of this, her horrible peril.

The flames were already repulsed. The mill was being flooded. Down the belt-holes the water poured upon the fiercer blaze below, that swept across the **forward and central** part of the great spinning-room, from side to side.

At this moment, **a cry, close at hand.**

"Fire!"

A man was swaying by a rope, down from a third-story window.

"Fire!" came again, instantly, **from without, upon** another side.

It was a voice hoarse, excited, strained. A tone Faith had never heard before; yet she knew, by a mysterious intuition, from whom it came. She dropped the hose, still pouring out its torrent, to the floor, and sprang back, through the doors, to the counting-room window. The voice came from the river-side.

A man was dashing down the green slope, upon the foot-bridge.

Faith stretched her arms out, as a child might, wakened in pain and terror. A cry, in which were uttered the fear, the horror, that were now first fully felt, as a possible safety appeared, and the joy, that itself came like a sudden pang, escaped her, piercingly, thrillingly.

Roger Armstrong looked upward as he sprang upon the bridge.

He caught the cry. He saw Faith stand there, in her white dress, that had been wet and blackened in her battling with the fire.

A great soul-glance of courage and resolve flashed from his eyes. He reached his uplifted arms toward her, answering hers. He uttered not a word.

"Round! round!" cried Faith. "The door upon the other side!"

Roger Armstrong, leaping to the spot, and Michael Garvin, escaped by the long rope that hung vibrating from his grasp, down the brick wall of the building, met at the staircase door.

"Help me drive that in!" cried the minister.

And the two men threw their stalwart shoulders against the barrier, forcing lock and hinges.

Up the stairs rushed Roger Armstrong.

Answering the crash of the falling door, came another and more fearful crash within.

Gnawed by the fire, the timbers and supports beneath the forward portion of the second floor had given way, and the heavy looms that stood there had gone plunging down. A horrible volume of smoke and steam poured upward, with the flames, from out the chasm, and rushed, resistlessly, everywhere.

Roger Armstrong dashed into the little counting-room. Faith lay there, on the floor. At that fearful crash, that rush of suffocating smoke, she had fallen, senseless. He seized her, frantically, in his arms to bear her down.

"Faith! Faith!" he cried, when she neither spoke nor moved. "My darling! Are you hurt? Are you killed? Oh, my God! must there be another?"

Faith did not hear these words, uttered with all the passionate agony of a man who would hold the woman he loves to his heart, and defy for her even death.

She came to herself in the open air. She felt herself in his arms. She only heard him say, tenderly and anxiously, in something of his old tone, as her consciousness returned, and he saw it, —

"My dear child!"

But she knew then all that had been a mystery to her in herself before.

She knew that she loved Roger Armstrong. That it was not a love of gratitude and reverence, only; but that her very soul was rendered up to him, involuntarily, as a woman renders herself but once. That she would rather have died there, in that flame and smoke, held in his arms, — gathered to his heart, — than have lived whatever life of ease and pleasantness, — aye, even of use, — with any other! She knew that her thought, in those terrible moments before he came, had been, — not father's or mother's, only; not her young lover, Paul's; but, deepest and mostly, his!

CHAPTER XXIX.

HOME.

> The joy that knows there *is* a joy —
> That scents its breath, and cries, 't is there;
> And, patient in its pure repose,
> Receiveth so the holier share.

Faith's thought and courage saved the mill from **utter** destruction.

For one fearful moment, when that **forward** portion of the loom-floor fell through, **and flame,** and vapor, and smoke rioted **together in a wild alliance of fury, all** seemed lost. But the great water-wheel was plying **on;** the river fought the fire; **the** rushing, exhaustless streams were pouring out **and down,** everywhere; and the crowd that in a few moments after **the first** alarm, and Faith's rescue, gathered at the spot, found its work half done.

A little later, there were only sullen smoke, defeated, smouldering fires, blackened timbers, the burned carding-rooms, and the ruin at the front, to tell the awful story of the **night.**

Mr. Armstrong had carried Faith into **one of** the unfinished factory houses. Here he was obliged to leave her for a few moments, after making such a rude couch for her as was possible, with a pile **of** clean shavings, and his own coat, which he insisted, against all **her** remonstrances, upon spreading above them.

"The first horse and **vehicle** which comes, Miss Faith, I shall impress for your **service,**" he said; "and to do that I must leave **you.** I have made that frightened watchman promise to say nothing, at present, of your being here; **so** I trust the **crowd may** not annoy you. I shall not **be** gone long, nor far away."

The first horse and vehicle which **came was the one** that had brought her there in the afternoon but just past, yet that seemed, strangely, to have been so long ago.

Mr. Rushleigh found her lying here, quiet, **amid the** growing tumult,— exhausted, patient, waiting.

"**My** little Faithie!" he cried, coming up **to** her with hands outstretched, and **a** quiver of strong feeling in **his** voice. "**To** think **that you** should **have** been **in this** horrible danger, and we **all lying in our** beds, **asleep! I** do not quite understand **it all.** You must tell **me,** by-and-by. Armstrong has told me what you have *done.* You **have** saved me half my property here, — do you know it, child? Can I ever thank you for your courage?"

"Oh, Mr. **Rushleigh!**" cried Faith, rising as he came to **her,** and holding her hands to his, "don't thank me! and don't wait here! They'll **want you,**—and, oh! **my** kind friend! there **will** be nothing **to thank me for, when I** have told you what I must. I have been very near to death, and I have seen life *so* clearly! I know now what **I did** not know yesterday, — what I could not answer you then!"

"**Let it be as it** may, I am sure it will be right and true, **and I** shall honor you, Faith! And we must bear what is, for it has come of the will of God, and not by any fault of **yours.** Now, **let** me take you home."

"May I do that in your stead, Mr. Rushleigh?" asked Roger Armstrong, who entered at this moment, with garments he had brought from somewhere to wrap Faith.

"I must go home," said Faith. "To Aunt Henderson's."

"You shall do as you like," answered Mr. Rushleigh. "But it belongs to us to care for you, I think."

"You do, — you have cared for me already," said Faith earnestly.

And Mr. Rushleigh helped to wrap her up, and kissed her forehead tenderly, and Roger Armstrong lifted her into the chaise, and seated himself by her, and drove her away from out the smoke and noise and curious crowd that had begun to find out she was there, and that she had been shut up in the mill, and had saved herself and stopped the fire; and would have made her as uncomfortable as crowds always do heroes or heroines, — had it not been for the friend beside her, whose foresight and precaution had warded it all off.

And the mill-owner went back among the villagers and firemen, to direct their efforts for his property.

Glory McWhirk had been up and watching the great fire, since Roger Armstrong first went out.

She had seen it from the window of Miss Henderson's room, where she was to sleep to-night; and had first carefully lowered the blinds lest the light should waken her mistress, who, after suffering much pain, had at length, by the help of an anodyne, fallen asleep; and then she had come round softly to the southwest room, to call the minister.

The door stood open, and she saw him sitting in his chair, asleep. Just as she crossed the threshold to come toward him, he started, and spoke those words out of his restless dream.

"Faith! Faith! What danger is about you, child?"

They were instinct with his love. They were eager with his visionary fear. It only needed a human heart to interpret them.

Glory drew back as he sprang to his feet, and noiselessly disappeared. She would not have him know that she had heard this cry with which he waked.

"He dreamed about her! and he called her Faith. How beautiful it is to be cared for so!"

Glory, — while we have so long been following Faith, — had no less been living on her own, peculiar, inward life, that reached to, that apprehended, that seized ideally, — that was denied, so much!

God leads some through life toward Himself, as a mother wins a child, making its first feeble steps; with good held always in sight, and always out beyond the grasp. There are those, who perceiving, longing, falling short, continually put off, still struggle on and keep the best in view. There are those again, who sit down, tamely, by the way, and turn to some inferior, easy joy.

As Glory had seen, in the old years, children happier than herself, wearing beautiful garments, and "hair that was let to grow," she saw those about her now whom life enfolded with a grace and loveliness she might not look for; about whom fair affections, "let to grow," clustered radiant, and enshrined them in their light.

She saw always something that was beyond; something she might not attain; yet, expectant of nothing, but blindly true to the highest within her, she lost no glimpse of the greater, through lowering herself to the less.

Her soul of womanhood asserted itself; longing, ignorantly, for a soul love. "To be cared for, so!"

But she would rather recognize it afar, — rather have her joy in knowing the joy that might be, — than shut herself from knowledge in the content of a common, sordid lot.

She did not think this deliberately, however; it was not reason, **but** instinct. She renounced unconsciously. **She** bore denial, and never knew she was denied.

Of course, the thought of daring to covet what she saw, had never crossed her, in her humbleness. It was quite away from her. It was something with which she had nothing to do. "But it must be beautiful to be like Miss Faith." And she thanked God, mutely, that she had this beautiful life near her, and could look on it every day.

She could not marry Luther Goodell.

> "A vague unrest
> And a nameless longing filled her breast;"

But, unlike the maiden of the ballad, she could not smother it down, to break forth, by-and-by, defying the "burden of life," in sweet bright vision, grown **to a** keen torture then.

Faith had read to **her** this story of Maud, one day.

"**I** should n't have done so," she had said, when it was **ended.** I 'd rather have kept that one minute under the apple-trees to live on all the rest of my days!"

She could not marry Luther Goodell.

Would it have been better that she should? That she should have gone down from her dreams into a plain man's life, and made a plain man happy? Some women, of far higher mental **culture** and social place. **have** done this, and, seemingly, **done** well. **Only** God and their own hearts know **if the seeming** be true.

Glory waited. "Everybody need n't marry," she said. This night, with those words **of Mr.** Armstrong's in her ears, revealing to her so much, she stood **before that window of** his and watched the fire.

Doors were open behind her, leading through to Miss Henderson's chamber. She would hear her mistress if **she** stirred.

If she had known what she did not know, — that **Faith** Gartney stood at this moment in that burning mill, looking forth despairingly on those bright waters and green fields **that lay between it and this home of hers,** — that were so near her, she might discern each shining pebble and the separate grass-blades in the scarlet light, yet so infinitely far, so gone from her forever, — had she known all this, without knowing **the** help and hope that were coming, — she would yet have said "How beautiful it would be to be like Miss Faith!"

She watched **the fire** till it began **to deaden, and the** glow paled out into the starlight.

By-and-by, up from the direction of the river-road, she **saw a chaise** approaching. It was stopped at the corner, **by the** bar-place. Two figures descended from it, and **entered upon** the field-path through the stile.

One, — yes, — it was surely the minister! The other, — a woman. Who?

Miss **Faith!**

Glory met them upon **the door-stone.**

Faith held her finger up.

"I was afraid of disturbing my aunt," said she.

"Take care of her, Glory," said her companion. "She has been in frightful danger."

"At the fire! And you —"

"I was there in time, thank God!" spoke Roger Armstrong, from his soul.

The two girls passed through to the blue bedroom, softly.

Mr. Armstrong went back to the mills again, with horse and chaise.

Glory shut the bedroom door.

"Why, you are all wet, and draggled, and smoked!" said she, taking off Faith's outer, borrowed garments. "What *has* happened to you, — and how came you there, Miss Faith?"

"I fell asleep in the counting-room, last evening, and got locked in. I was coming home. I can't tell you now, Glory. I don't dare to think it all over, yet. And we must n't let Aunt Faith know that I am here."

These sentences they spoke in whispers.

Glory asked no more; but brought warm water, and bathed and rubbed Faith's feet, and helped her to undress, and put her night-clothes on, and covered her in bed with blankets, and then went away softly to the kitchen, whence she brought back, presently, a cup of hot tea, and a biscuit.

"Take these, please," she said.

"I don't think I can, Glory. I don't want anything."

"But he told me to take care of you, Miss Faith!"

That, also, had a power with Faith. Because he had said that, she drank the tea, and then lay back, — so tired!

"I waited up till you came, sir, because I thought you would like to know," said Glory, meeting Mr. Armstrong once more upon the door-stone, as he returned a second time from the fire. "She's gone to sleep, and is resting beautiful!"

"You are a good girl, Glory, and I thank you," said the minister; and he put his hand forth, and grasped hers as he spoke. "Now go to bed, and rest, yourself."

It was reward enough.

From the plenitude that waits on one life, falls a crumb that stays the craving of another.

CHAPTER XXX.

AUNT HENDERSON'S MYSTERY.

Oh, the little birds sang east, and the little birds sang west,
And I said in underbreath, — All our life is mixed with death,
    And who knoweth which is best?

' Oh, the little birds sang east, and the little birds sang west,
And I smiled to think God's greatness flowed around our incompleteness, —
    Round our restlessness, His rest."
MRS. BROWNING.

" So the dreams depart,
So the fading phantoms flee,
And the sharp reality
Now must act its part."
WESTWOOD.

IT was a little after noon of the next day, when Mr. Rushleigh came to Cross Corners.

Faith was lying back, quite pale, and silent, — feeling very weak after the terror, excitement, and fatigue she had gone through, — in the large easy-chair which had been brought for her into the southeast room. Miss Henderson had been removed from her bed to the sofa here, and the two were keeping each other quiet company. Neither could bear the strain of nerve to dwell long or particularly on the events of the night. The story had been told, as simply as it might be; and the rest and the thankfulness were all they could think of now. So there were deep thoughts and few words between them. **On Faith's part, a** patient waiting for a trial yet before her.

"It's Mr. Rushleigh, come over to see Miss Faith. Shall I bring him in?" asked Glory, at the door.

"Will you mind it, aunt?" asked Faith.

"I? No," said Miss Henderson. "Will you mind my being here? **That's the** question. **I**'d take myself off, without asking, if I could, you know."

"Dear Aunt Faith! There is something I have to say to Mr. Rushleigh which will be very hard to say, but no **more so** because you will be by to hear it. It is better so. I shall only have to say it **once.** I am glad you should be with me."

"Brave little Faithie!" **said Mr.** Rushleigh, coming **in** with hands outstretched. "**Not ill, I hope?**"

"Only tired," Faith answered. "**And a** little **weak, and** foolish," as the tears would come, in answer to his cordial **words.**

"I am sorry, Miss Henderson, that I could not have persuaded this little girl to go home with me last night,— this morning, rather. But she would come to you."

"She did just right," **Aunt** Faith replied. "It's the proper place for her to come **to. Not but that we** thank you all the same. You're **very kind.**"

"Kinder than I have deserved," whispered Faith, **as he** took his seat beside her.

Mr. Rushleigh would not let her lead him that way yet. He ignored **the** little whisper, and by a gentle question or two drew from **her** that which he had come, especially, to learn and speak of to-day,— the story of the fire, and her own knowledge of, and share in it, as she alone could tell it.

Now, for the first time, as she recalled it to explain her motive for entering the **mill at all, the** rough conversation **she** had overheard **between the two men** upon the river bank, suggested to Faith, as the mention of it was upon her lips, **a** possible clue to the origin of **the mischief. She** paused, suddenly, **and** a look of dismayed hesitation came over **her** face.

"I ought to tell you all, I suppose," she continued. "But pray, sir, do not conclude anything hastily. The two things may have had nothing to do with each other."

And then, reluctantly, she repeated the angry threat that had come **to her** ears.

Pausing, timidly, **to** look up in **her listener's face, to** judge of its expression, a smile there surprised **her.**

"See how truth is always best," said Mr. Rushleigh. "**If** you had kept back your knowledge of this, you would have sealed up a painful doubt for your own tormenting. That man, James Regan, **came to me this** morning. **There is good in** the **fellow,** after all. **He told me, just** as you have, **and as Hardy** did, the words he spoke in passion. **He was afraid, he said, they** might be brought up against him. And so he came to 'own up,' and account for his time; and to **beg me** to believe that he never had any definite thought of harm. I told him I did believe it; and then the poor fellow, rough as he is, turned pale, and burst into tears. Last night gave him a lesson, I think, that will go far to take the hardness out of him. Blasland says, 'he worked **like five** men and a horse,' at the fire."

Faith's face glowed as she listened, at the nobleness of **these two;** of **the** generous, Christian gentleman, — of the coarse workman, who wore **his nature,** like his garb, — the worse part of an every-day.

Fire and loss are not all calamity, when such as this comes of them.

Her own recital was soon finished.

Mr. Rushleigh listened, giving his whole sympathy to the danger she had faced, his fresh and fervent acknowledgment and admiring praise to the prompt daring she had shown, as if these things, and nought else, had been in either mind.

At these thanks, — at this praise, — Faith shrank.

"Oh, Mr. Rushleigh!" she interrupted, with a low, pained, humbled entreaty, — "don't speak so! Only forgive me, — if you can!"

Her hands lifted themselves with a slight, imploring gesture toward him. He laid his own upon them, gently, soothingly.

"I will not have you trouble or reproach yourself, Faith," he answered, meeting her meaning, frankly, now. "There are things beyond our control. All we can do is to be simply true. There is something, I know, which you think lies between us to be spoken of. Do not speak at all, if it be hard for you. — I will tell the boy that it was a mistake — that it cannot be."

But the father's lip was a little unsteady, to his own feeling, as he said the words.

"Oh, Mr. Rushleigh!" cried Faith. "If everything could only be put back as it was, in the old days before all this!"

"But that is what we can't do. Nothing goes back precisely to what it was before."

"No," said Aunt Faith, from her sofa. "And never did, since the days of Humpty Dumpty. You might be glad to, but you can't do it. Things must just be made the best of, as they are. And they're never just alike, two minutes together. They're altering, and working, and going on, all the time. And that's a comfort, too, when you come to think of it."

"There is always comfort, somehow, when there has been no wilful wrong. And there has been none here, I am sure."

Faith, with the half-smile yet upon her face, called there by her aunt's quaint speaking, bent her head, and burst into tears.

"I came to re-assure and to thank you, Faith — not to let you distress yourself so," said Mr. Rushleigh. "Margaret sent all kind messages; but I would not bring her. I thought it would be too much for you, so soon. Another day, she will come. We shall always claim old friendship, my child, and remember our new debt; though the old days themselves cannot quite be brought back again as they were. There may be better days, though, even, by-and-by."

"Let Margaret know, before she comes, please," whispered Faith. "I don't think I could tell her."

"You shall not have a moment of trial that I can spare you. But — Paul will be content with nothing, as a final word, that does not come from you."

"I will see him when he comes. I wish it. Oh, sir! I am so sorry!"

"And so am I, Faith. We must all be sorry. But we are *only* sorry. And that is all that need be said."

The conversation, after this, could not be prolonged. Mr. Rushleigh took his leave, kindly, as he had made his greeting.

"Oh, Aunt Faith! What a terrible thing I have done!"

"What a terrible thing you came near doing, you mean.

child! Be thankful to the Lord, — He's delivered you from it! And look well to the rest of your life, after all this. Out of fire and misery you must have been saved for something!"

Then Aunt Faith called Glory, and told her to bring an egg, beat up in milk, — "to a good froth, mind; and sugared and nutmegged, and a teaspoonful of brandy in it."

This she made Faith swallow, and then bade her put her feet up on the sofa, and lean back, and shut her eyes, and not speak another word till she'd had a nap.

All which, strangely enough, Faith, — wearied, troubled, yet relieved, — obeyed.

For the next two days, what with waiting on the invalids, — for Faith was far from well, — and with answering the incessant calls at the door of curious people flocking to inquire, Glory McWhirk was kept busy and tired. But not with a thankless duty, as in the days gone by, that she remembered; it was heart-work now, and brought heart-love as its reward. It was one of her "real good times."

Mr. Armstrong talked and read with them, and gave hand-help and ministry also, just when it could be given most effectually.

It was a beautiful lull of peace between the conflict that was past, and the final pang that was to come. Faith accepted it with a thankfulness. Such joy as this was all life had for her, henceforth. There was no restlessness, no selfishness in the love that had so suddenly asserted itself, and borne down all her doubts. She thought not of it, as love, any more. She never dreamed of being other to Mr. Armstrong than she was. Only, that other life had become impossible to her. Here, if she might not elsewhere, she had gone back to the things that were. She could be quite content and happy, so. It was enough to rest in such a friendship. If only she had once seen Paul, and if he could but bear it!

And Roger Armstrong, of intent, was just what he had always been, — the kind and earnest friend, — the ready helper; — no more. He knew Faith Gartney had a trouble to bear; he had read her perplexity, — her indecision; he had feared, unselfishly, for the mistake she was making. Miss Henderson had told him, now, in few, plain words, how things were ending; he strove, in all pleasant and thoughtful ways, to soothe and beguile her from her harassment. He dreamed not how the light had come to her that had revealed to her the insufficiency of that other love. He laid his own love back, from his own sight.

So, calmly, and with what peace they might, these hours went on.

"I want to see that Sampson woman," said Aunt Faith, suddenly, to her niece, on the third afternoon of their being together. "Do you think she would come over here if I should send for her?"

Faith flashed a surprised look of inquiry to Miss Henderson's face.

"Why, aunt?" she asked.

"Never mind why, child. I can't tell you now. Of course it's something, or I shouldn't want her. Something I should like to know, and that I suppose she could tell me. Do you think she'd come?"

"Why, yes, auntie. I don't doubt it. I might write her a note."

"I wish you would. Mr. Armstrong says he'll drive

over. And I'd like to have you do it right off. Now, don't ask me another word about it, till she's been here."

Faith wrote the note, and Mr. Armstrong went away.

Miss Henderson seemed to grow tired, to-day, after her dinner, and at four o'clock she said to Glory, abruptly, —

"I'll go to bed. Help me into the other room."

Faith offered to go too, and assist her. But her aunt said. no, she should do quite well with Glory. "And if the Sampson woman comes, send her in to me."

Faith was astonished, and a little frightened.

What could it be that Miss Henderson wanted with the nurse? Was it professionally that she wished to see her? She knew the peculiar whim, or principle, Miss Sampson always acted on, of never taking cases of common illness. She could not have sent for her in the hope of keeping her merely to wait upon her wants as an invalid, and relieve Glory? Was her aunt aware of symptoms in herself, foretokening other or more serious illness?

Faith could only wonder, and wait.

Glory came back, presently, into the southeast room, to say to Faith that her aunt was comfortable, and thought she should get a nap. But that whenever the nurse came, she was to be shown in to her.

The next half-hour, that happened which drove even this thought utterly from Faith's mind.

Paul Rushleigh came.

Faith lay, a little wearily, upon the couch her aunt had quitted; and was thinking, at the very moment, — with that sudden, breathless anticipation that sweeps over one, now and then, of a thing awaited apprehensively, — of whether this Saturday night would not probably bring him home, — when she caught the sound of a horse's feet that stopped before the house, and then a man's step upon the stoop.

It was his. The moment had come.

She sprang to her feet. For an instant she would have **fled,**—anywhither. Then she grew strangely calm and strong. She must meet him quietly. She must tell **him** plainly. Tell him, if need be, all she knew herself. **He had** a right to all.

Paul came in, looking grave; and greeted her with a **gentle reserve.**

A moment, they stood there **as** they had met, she with face pale, sad, that dared not lift itself; he, not trusting himself to the utterance of **a** word.

But he had come there, not to reproach, or **to** bewail; not even to plead. To hear,—-to bear with firmness,—what she had to tell him. And there was, in truth, a new strength and nobleness in look and tone, when, presently, he spoke.

If he had **had** his way,—if all had gone prosperously **with him,**—he would have been, still,—recipient of his father's bounty, and accepted of his childish love,—scarcely **more than a** mere, happy **boy.** This pain, this struggle, this first rebuff of life, crowned him, a man.

Faith might have **loved him,** now, if she had so seen him, **first.**

Yet the hour would come when he should know that it had been better as it was. That so he should grow to **that** which, otherwise, he had never been.

"Faith! My father has told **me.** That it must be all over. That it was a mistake. I have come to hear it from you."

Then he laid in her hand his father's letter.

"This came **with yours,"** he said. "After this, I expected all **the** rest."

Faith took the open sheet, mechanically. With half-blinded eyes, she glanced over the few earnest, fatherly, generous lines. When she came to the last, she **spoke, low.**

"Yes That is it. He saw it. It would have been no true marriage, Paul, before heaven!"

"Then **why did I** love you, Faith?" cried the young man, impetuously.

"**I don't know,**" she said, meditatively, as if she really **were to** answer that. "Perhaps you will come **to** love again, differently, yet, **Paul;** and then you may know why this has been."

"I know," said Paul, sadly, "that you have been outgrowing me, Faith. I have felt that. I know I've been nothing but a careless, merry fellow, living an outside sort of life; and I suppose it was only **in** this outside companionship you liked me. But there might be something **more** in me, yet; and you might have brought **it out,** maybe. You *were* bringing it out. You, and the responsibilities **my** father put upon me. But it's too late, now. **It can't** be helped."

"Not too late, Paul, for that noble part of you to grow. It was that **I came so** near really loving at the last. But, — Paul! a woman don't want to lead her husband. She wants to be led. I have thought," she added, timidly, "so much of that verse in the Epistle, — '**the** head of the woman is the man, and the head **of the man is Christ, and the head** of Christ is God.'"

"You came *near* loving me!" cried Paul, catching at this sentence, only, out of all that should, by-and-by, nevertheless, come out in letters of light upon his thought and **memory.** "Oh, Faith! you may, yet! **It is n't all quite over?**"

Then Faith Gartney knew she must say it all. All,— though the hot crimson flushed up painfully, and the breath came quick, and she trembled from head to foot, there, where she stood. But the truth, mighty, and holy in its might, came up from heart to lip, and the crimson paled, and the breath grew calm, and she stood firm with her pure resolve, even in her maidenly shame, before him.

There are instants, when all thought of the moment itself, and the look and the word of it, are overborne and lost.

"No, Paul. I will tell you truly. With my little, childish heart, I loved you. With the love of a dear friend, I hold you still, and shall hold you, always. But, Paul!— no one else knows it, and I never knew it till I stood face to face with death,— with my *soul* I have come to love another!"

Deep and low these last words were — given up from the very innermost, and spoken with bowed head and streaming eyes.

Paul Rushleigh took her hand. A manly reverence in him recognized the pure courage that unveiled her woman's heart, and showed him all.

"Faith!" he said, "you have never deceived me. You are always noble. Forgive me that I have made you struggle to love me!"

With these words, he went.

Faith flung herself upon the sofa, and hid her face in its cushion, hearing, through her sobs, the tread of his horse as he passed down the road.

This chapter of her life-story was closed.

CHAPTER XXXI.

NURSE SAMPSON'S WAY OF LOOKING AT IT.

> "I can believe, it shall you grieve,
>   And somewhat you distrain;
> But afterward, your paines hard,
>   Within a day or twain,
> Shall soon aslake; and ye shall take
>   Comfort to you again."
>
> OLD ENGLISH BALLAD.

GLORY looked in, once, at the southeast room, and saw Faith lying, still with hidden face; and went away softly, shutting the door behind her as she went.

When Mr. Armstrong and Miss Sampson came, she met them at the front entrance, and led the nurse directly to her mistress, as she had been told.

Mr. Armstrong betook himself to his own room. Perhaps the hollow Paul Rushleigh's horse had pawed at the gate-post, and the closed door of the keeping-room, revealed something to his discernment that kept him from seeking Faith just then.

There was a half-hour of quiet in the old house. A quiet that overbrooded very much.

Then Nurse Sampson came out, with a look on her face that made Faith gaze upon her with an awed feeling of expectation. She feared, suddenly, to ask a question.

It was not a long-drawn look of sympathy. It was not surprised, nor shocked, nor excited. It was a look of business. As if she knew of work before her to do. As if Nurse Sampson were in her own proper element, once more.

Faith knew that something, — she could not guess what, — something terrible, she feared, — had happened, or was going to happen, to her aunt.

It was in the softening twilight that Miss Henderson sent for her to come in.

Aunt Faith leaned against her pillows, looking bright and comfortable, even cheerful; but there was a strange gentleness in look and word and touch, as she greeted the young girl who came to her bedside with a face that wore at once its own subduedness of fresh-past grief, and a wondering, loving apprehension of something to be disclosed concerning the kind friend who lay there, invested so with such new grace of tenderness.

Was there a twilight, other than that of day, softening, also, around her?

"Little Faith!" said Aunt Henderson. Her very voice had taken an unwonted tone.

"Auntie! It is surely something very grave! Will you not tell me?"

"Yes, child. I mean to tell you. It may be grave. Most things are, if we had the wisdom to see it. But it isn't very dreadful. It's what I've had warning enough of, and had mostly made up my mind to. But I wasn't quite sure. Now, I am. I suppose I've got to bear some pain, and go through a risk that will be greater, at my years, than it would have been if I'd been younger. And I may die. That's all."

The words, of old habit, were abrupt. The eye and voice were tender with unspoken love.

Faith turned to Miss Sampson, who sat by.

"And then, again, she may n't," said the nurse. "I shall stay and see her through. There 'll have to be an operation. At least, I think so. We 'll have the doctor over, to-morrow. And now, if there 's one thing more important than another, it 's to keep her cheerful. So, if you 've got anything bright and lively to say, speak out! If not, *keep* out! She 'll do well enough, I dare say."

Poor Faith! And, without this new trouble, there was so much that she, herself, was needing comfort for!

"You 're a wise woman, Nurse Sampson. But you don't know everything," said Aunt Faith. "The best thing to take people out of their own worries, is to go to work and find out how other folks' worries are getting on. — He 's been here, has n't he, child?"

It was not so hard for Aunt Faith, who had borne secretly, so long, the suspicion of what was coming, and had lived on, calmly, nevertheless, in her daily round, to turn thus from the announcement of her own state and possible danger, to thought and inquiry for the affairs of another, as it was for that other, newly apprised, and but half apprised, even, of what threatened, to leave the subject there, and answer. But she saw that Miss Henderson spoke only truth in declaring it was the best way to take her out of her worries; she read Nurse Sampson's look, and saw that she, at any rate, was quite resolved her patient should not be let to dwell longer on any painful or apprehensive thought, and she put off all her own anxious questionings, till she should see the nurse alone, and said, in a low tone, — yes; Paul Rushleigh had been there.

25*

"And you've told him the truth, like a woman, and he's heard it like a man?"

"I've told him it must be given up. **Oh, it was hard, auntie!**"

"You need n't worry. You've done just the **rightest** thing you could do."

"But it seems so selfish. As if my happiness were of so much more consequence than his. I've made him **so** miserable, I'm afraid!"

"Miss Sampson!" cried Aunt Faith, with all her old oddity and suddenness, "just tell this girl, if you know, what kind of a commandment a woman breaks, if she can't make up her mind to marry the first man that asks her! 'T aint in *my* Decalogue!"

"I can't tell what commandment she won't be likely to break, if she is n't pretty sure of her own mind before she *does* marry!" said Miss Sampson, energetically. "Talk of making a man miserable! Supposing you do for **a** little while? 'T won't last long. Right 's right, and settles itself. Wrong **never does**. And there is n't a greater wrong than **to marry the wrong** man. To him as well as to you. And **it won't** end there, — that 's the worst of it. There 's more concerned than just yourself and him; though you may n't **know how, or who.** It 's an awful thing to tangle up and disarrange **the** plans of Providence. And more of it 's done, I verily believe, in this matter of marrying, than any other way. It 's like mismatching anything else, — gloves or stockings, — and wearing the wrong ones together. They don't fit; and more 'n **that**, it spoils another pair. I believe, as true as **I live, if** the angels ever do cry over this miserable world, it 's when they see the souls they have paired off, all right, out of heaven, getting mixed up and mismated as they do down here! Why, it's fairly enough to account for all the sin and misery there is in the world! If it was n't for Adam and Eve and Cain, I should think it did!"

"But it's very hard," said Faith, smiling, despite all her saddening thoughts, at the characteristic harangue, "always to know wrong from right. People may make mistakes, if they mean ever so well."

"Yes, awful mistakes! There's that poor, unfortunate woman in the Bible. I never thought the Lord meant any reflection by what he said, — on her. She'd had six husbands. And he knew she had n't got what she bargained for, after all. Most likely she never had, in the whole six. And if things had got into such a snarl as that eighteen hundred years ago, how many people, do you think, by this time, are right enough in themselves to be right for anybody? I've thought it all over, many a time. I've had reasons of my own, and I've seen plenty of reasons as I've gone about the world. And my conclusion is, that matrimony's come to be more of a discipline, now-a-days, than anything else!"

It was strange cheer; and it came at a strange moment; with the very birth of a new anxiety. But so our moments and their influences are mingled. Faith was roused, strengthened, confirmed in her own thought of right, beguiled out of herself, by the words of these two odd, plain-dealing women, as she would not have been if a score of half-comprehending friends had soothed her indirectly with inanities, and delicate half-handling of that which Aunt Faith and Nurse Sampson went straight to the heart of, and brought out, uncompromisingly, into the light. So much we can endure from a true earnestness and simplicity, rough and homely though it be, which would be impertinent and intolerable if it came but with surface-sympathy.

She had a word that night from Roger Armstrong, when he came, late in the evening, from a conversation with Aunt Faith, and found her at the open door upon the stoop. It was only a hand-grasp, and a fervent "God bless you, child! You have been brave and true!" and he passed on. But a balm and a quiet fell deep into her heart, and a tone, that was a joy, lingered in her ear, and comforted her as no other earthly comfort could. But this was not all earthly; it lifted her toward heaven. It bore her toward the eternal solace there.

Aunt Faith would have no scenes. She told the others, in turn, very much as she had told Faith, that a suffering and an uncertainty lay before her; and then, by her next word and gesture, demanded that the life about her should go right on, taking as slightly as might be its coloring from this that brooded over her. Nobody had a chance to make a wail. There was something for each to do.

Miss Henderson, by Nurse Sampson's advice, remained mostly in her bed. In fact, she had kept back the announcement of this ailment of hers, just so long as she could resist its obvious encroachment. The twisted ancle had been, for long, a convenient explanation of more than its own actual disability.

But it was not a sick-room, — one felt that, — this little limited bound in which her life was now visibly encircled. All the cheer of the house was brought into it. If people were sorry and fearful, it was elsewhere. Neither Aunt Faith nor the nurse would let anybody into "their hospital," as Miss Sampson said, "unless they came with a bright look for a pass." Every evening, the great Bible was opened there, and Mr. Armstrong read with them, and uttered for them words that lifted each heart, with its secret need and thankfulness, to heaven. **All** together, trustfully, and tranquilly, they waited.

Dr. Wasgatt had been called in. Quite surprised he was, at this new development. He "had thought there was something **a** little peculiar in her symptoms." But **he was** one of those Æsculapian worthies who, having lived a scientifically **uneventful** life, **plodding** quietly along in his profession among people **who had** mostly been ill after very ordinary fashions, and who required only the administering **of** stereotyped remedies, according to the old stereotyped order and rule, had quite forgotten to think of the possibility of any unusual complications. **If** anybody were taken ill of a colic, and sent for him and told him so, for a colic he prescribed, according to outward indications. The subtle signs that to a keener or more practised discernment, might have **betokened more, he never** thought **of** looking for. What then? All cannot be geniuses; **most** men just learn a trade. It is only a Columbus who, by the drift along the shore of the fact or continent he stands on, predicates another, far over, out of sight.

Surgeons were to come out from Mishaumok to consult. Mr. and Mrs. Gartney would be home, now, in a day or two, and Aunt Faith preferred to wait till then. Mis' Battis opened the Cross Corners house, and Faith went over, daily, to direct the ordering of things there.

"Faith!" said Miss **Henderson, on the Wednesday** evening when they were to look confidently for the return **of** their travellers next day, "come here child! I have something to say to you."

Faith was sitting alone there, with **her aunt, in the** twilight.

"There's one thing on my mind, that I ought to speak of,

as things have turned out. When I thought, a few weeks ago, that you were provided for, as far as outside havings go, I made a will, one day. Look in **that** right hand upper bureau drawer, and you'll find a key, with **a** brown ribbon to it. That'll unlock a black box on the middle shelf of the closet. Open it, and take out the paper that lies on the top, and bring it to me."

Faith did all this, silently.

"Yes, this is it," said Miss Henderson, putting on her glasses, which were lying on the counterpane, and unfolding the single sheet, written out in her **own** round, upright, old-fashioned hand. "**It**'s an old woman's whim; but if you don't like **it**, it shan't stand. Nobody knows of it, and nobody'll be disappointed. I had a longing to leave **some** kind of a happy life behind me, if I could, in the Old House. It's only an earthly clinging and hankering, maybe; but I'd somehow like to feel sure, being the last of the line, that there'd be time for my **bones to** crumble away comfortably into dust, before the old timbers should come **down.** I meant, once, you should have had it all; but it seemed as if you wasn't going to *need* it, and as if there was going to be other kind of work cut out for you to do. And I'm persuaded there is yet, somewhere. So I've done this; and I want you to know it beforehand, in case anything goes wrong, — no, not that, but unexpectedly, — with me."

She reached out the paper, and Faith took it from her **hand.** It was not long in reading.

A light shone out of Faith's eyes, through the tears that sprang to them, as she finished it, and gave it back.

"Aunt Faith!" **she** said, earnestly. "It is beautiful! I am so glad! But, auntie! You'll get well, I know, and begin it yourself!"

"No," said Miss Henderson, quietly. "I may get over this, and I don't say I shouldn't be glad to. But I'm an old tree, and the axe is lying, ground, somewhere, that's to cut me down before very long. Old folks can't change their ways, and begin new plans and doings. I'm only thankful that the Lord has sent me a thought that lightens all the dread I've had for years about leaving the old place; and that I can go, thinking maybe there'll be His work doing in it as long as it stands."

"I don't know," she resumed, after a pause, "how your father's affairs are now. The likelihood is, if he has any health, that he'll go into some kind of a venture again before very long. But I shall have a talk with him, and if he isn't satisfied I'll alter it so as to do something more for you."

"Something more!" said Faith. "But you have done a great deal, as it is! I didn't say so, because I was thinking so much of the other."

"It won't make an heiress of you," said Aunt Faith. "But it'll be better than nothing, if other means fall short. And I don't feel, somehow, as if you need be a burden on my mind. There's a kind of a certainty borne in on me, otherwise. I can't help thinking that what I've done has been a leading. And if it has, it's right. — Now put this back, and tell Miss Sampson she may bring my gruel.'

CHAPTER XXXII.

GLORY MCWHIRK'S INSPIRATION.

> "No bird am I to sing in June,
> And dare not ask an equal boon.
> Good nests and berries red are Nature's
> To give away to better creatures,—
> And yet my days go on, go on."
>
> MRS. BROWNING.

MR. and Mrs. Gartney arrived on Thursday.

Two weeks and three days they had been absent; and in that time how the busy sprites of change and circumstance had been at work! As if the scattered straws of events, that, stretched out in slender winrows, might have reached across a field of years, had been raked together, and rolled over,—crowded close, and heaped, portentous, into these eighteen days!

Letters had told them something; of the burned mill, and Faith's fearful danger and escape; of Aunt Henderson's continued illness, and its present serious aspect; and with this last intelligence, which met them in New York but two days since, Mrs. Gartney found her daughter's agitated note of pained avowal, that she "had come, through all this, to know herself better, and to feel sure that this marriage ought not to be;" that, in short, all was at length over between her and Paul Rushleigh.

It was a meeting full of thought, — where much waited for speech that letters could neither have conveyed nor satisfied, — when Faith and her father and mother exchanged the kiss of love and welcome, once more, in the little home at Cross Corners.

It was well that Mis' Battis had made waffles, and spread a tempting summer tea with these and her nice, white bread, and fruits and cream; and wished, with such faint impatience as her huge calm was capable of, that "they would jest set right down, while things was good and hot;" and that Hendie was full of his wonderful adventures by boat and train, and through the wilds; so that these first hours were gotten over, and all a little used to the old feeling of being together again, before there was opportunity for touching upon deeper subjects.

It came at length, — the long evening talk, after Hendie was in bed, and Mr. Gartney had been over to the old house, and seen his aunt, and had come back, to find wife and daughter sitting in the dim light beside the open door, drawn close in love and confidence, and so glad and thankful to have each other back once more!

First, — Aunt Faith; and what was to be done, — what might be hoped — what must be feared — for her. Then, the terrible story of the fire; and all about it, that could only be got at by the hundred bits of question and answer, and the turning over and over, and repetition, whereby we do the best, — the feeble best, — we can, to satisfy great askings and deep sympathies that never can be anyhow made palpable in words.

And, last of all, — just with the good-night kiss, — Faith and her mother had had it all before, in the first minutes they were left alone together, — Mr. Gartney said to his daughter, —

"You are quite certain, now, Faith?"

"Quite certain, father;" Faith answered, low, with downcast eyes, as she stood before him.

Her father laid his hand upon her head.

"You are a good girl; and I don't blame you; yet I thought you would have been safe and happy, so."

"I am safe and happy here at home," said Faith.

"Home is in no hurry to spare you, my child."

And Faith felt taken back to daughterhood once more.

Margaret Rushleigh had been to see her, before this. It was a painful visit, with the mingling of old love and new restraint; and the effort, on either side, to show that things, except in the one particular, were still unchanged.

Faith felt how true it was that "nothing could go back, precisely, to what it was before."

There was another visit, a day or two after the re-assembling of the family at Cross Corners. This was to say farewell. New plans had been made. It would take some time to restore the mills to working order, and Mr. Rushleigh had not quite resolved whether to sell them out as they were, or to retain the property. Mrs. Rushleigh wished Margaret to join her at Newport, whither the Saratoga party was to go within the coming week. Then there was talk of another trip to Europe. Margaret had never been abroad. It was very likely they would all go out in October.

Paul's name was never mentioned.

Faith realized, painfully, how her little hand had been upon the motive power of much that was all ended, now.

Two eminent medical men had been summoned from Mishaumok, and had held consultation with Dr. Wasgatt upon Miss Henderson's case. It had been decided to postpone the surgical operation for two or three weeks. Meanwhile, she was simply to be kept comfortable and cheerful, strengthened with fresh air, and nourishing food, and some slight tonics.

Faith was at the old house, constantly. Her aunt craved her presence, and drew her more and more to herself. The strong love, kept down by a stiff, unbending manner, so, for years, — resisting almost its own growth, — would no longer be denied or concealed. Faith Gartney had nestled herself into the very core of this true, upright heart, unpersuadable by anything but clear judgment and inflexible conscience.

"I had a beautiful dream last night, Miss Faith," said Glory, one morning, when Faith came over and found the busy handmaiden with her churn upon the door-stone. "about Miss Henderson. I thought she was all well, and strong, and she looked so young, and bright, and pleasant! And she told me to make a May-day. And we had it out here in the field. And everybody had a crown; and everybody was queen. And the little children danced round the old apple-tree, and climbed up, and rode horseback in the branches. And Miss Henderson was out there, dressed in white, and looking on. It don't seem so, — just to say it; but I couldn't tell you how beautiful it was!"

"Dreams are strange things," said Faith, thoughtfully. "It seems as if they were sent to us, sometimes, — as if we really had a sort of life in them."

"Don't they?" cried Glory, eagerly. "Why, Miss Faith, I've dreamed on, and on, sometimes, a whole story out! And, after all, we're asleep almost as much as we're awake. Why isn't it just as real?"

"I had a dream that night of the fire, Glory. I never shall forget it. I went to sleep there, on the sofa. And it seemed as if I were on the top of a high, steep cliff, with no way to get down. And all at once, there was fire behind me, — a burning mountain! And it came nearer, and nearer, till it scorched my very feet; and there was no way down. And then, — it was so strange! — I knew Mr. Armstrong was coming. And two hands took me, — just as his did, afterward, — and I felt so safe! And then I woke, and it all happened. When he came, I felt as if I had called him."

The dasher of the churn was still, and Glory stood, breathless, in a white excitement, gazing into Faith's eyes.

"And so you did, Miss Faith! Somehow, — through the dream-land, — you certainly did!"

Faith went in to her aunt, and Glory churned and pondered.

Were these two to go on, dreaming, and calling to each other "through the dream-land," and never, in the daylight, and their waking hours, speak out?

This thought, in vague shape, turned itself, restlessly, in Glory's brain.

Other brains revolved a like thought, also.

"Somebody talked about a 'ripe pear,' once. I wonder if that one is n't ever going to fall!"

Nurse Sampson wondered thus, as she settled Miss Henderson in her arm-chair before the window, and they saw Roger Armstrong and Faith Gartney walk up the field together in the sunset light.

"I suppose it would n't take much of a jog to do it. But, maybe, it's as well to leave it to the Lord's sunshine. He'll ripen it, if He sees fit."

"It's a pretty picture, anyhow. There's the new moon exactly over their right shoulders, if they'd only turn their heads to look at it. I don't think much of signs; but, somehow, I always *do* like to have that one come right!"

"Well, it's there, whether they've found it out, or not," replied Aunt Faith.

Glory sat on the flat door-stone. She had the invariable afternoon knitting-work in her hand; but hand and work had fallen to her lap, and her eyes were away upon the glittering, faint crescent of the moon, that pierced the golden mist of sunset. Close by, the evening star had filled his chalice of silver splendor.

"The star and the moon only see each other. I can see both. It is better."

She had come to the feeling of Roger Armstrong's sermon. To receive consciously, as she had through her whole life intuitively and unwittingly, all beauty of all being about her into the secret beauty of her own. She could be glad with the gladness of the whole world.

The two came up, and Glory rose, and stood aside.

"You have had thoughts, to-night, Glory," said the minister. "Where have they been?"

"Away, there," answered Glory, pointing to the western sky.

They turned, and followed her gesture; and from up there, at their right, beyond, came down the traditional promise of the beautiful young moon.

Glory had shown it them.

"And I've been thinking, besides," said Glory, "about that dream of yours, Miss Faith. I've thought of it all day. Please tell it to Mr. Armstrong?"

And Glory disappeared down the long passage to the kitchen, and left them standing there, together. She went straight to the tin-baker before the fire, and lifted the cover, to see if her biscuits were ready for tea. **Then she** seated herself **upon** a little bench that stood against **the** chimney-side, and leaned her head against the bricks, and looked **down** into the glowing coals.

"It was put into my head to do it!" she said, breathlessly, to herself. "I hope it was n't ridiculous!"

So she sat, and gazed on, into the coals. *They* were out there in the sunset, with the new moon and the bright star above them in the saffron depths.

They stood **alone,** except for each other, in this still, radiant beauty of all things.

Miss Henderson's window was around a projection **of** the rambling, irregular structure, which made the angle wherein the pleasant old door-stone lay.

"May I have your dream, Miss Faith?"

She need not be afraid to tell a simple dream. **Any** more, at this moment, than when she told it to Glory, **that** morning, on that very spot. Why did she feel, that if she should speak a syllable of **it now,** the truth that lay behind **it,** would **look out,** resistless, through its veil? That **she** could **not so keep** down **its** spirit-meaning, that it should not flash, electric, from her soul to his?

"It was only — that night," she said, tremulously. **"It** seemed very strange. Before the fire, I had the dream. **It** was a dream of fire and danger, — danger that I could not escape from. And I held out my hands, — and I found you there, — and you saved me. Oh, Mr. Armstrong! As **you** *did* save me, afterward!"

Roger Armstrong turned, and faced her. His deep, earnest **eyes, lit with a new,** strange radiance, smote upon hers, and held them spell-bound with their glance.

"I, too, dreamed that night," — said he, — "of an unknown peril **to you. You** beckoned **me.** I sprang from **out that** dream, and rushed into the night, — **until** I found you!"

Their two souls met, in that brief recital, and knew that they had **met** before. That, through the dream-land, **there** had been that call and answer.

Faith **neither spoke, nor** stirred, **nor trembled.** This **supreme moment of her life held her unmoved in its own mightiness.**

Roger Armstrong held out both his hands.

"**Faith!** In the sight of God, I believe you belong **to me!**"

At that solemn word, of force beyond all claim of a mere mortal love, Faith **stretched** her hands in answer, and laid them into his, and bowed her head above them.

"In the sight of God, I belong to you!"

So she gave herself. So she was taken. **As God's gift,** to the heart that had been earthly desolate so long.

There was no dread, no shrinking, in that moment. **A** perfect love cast out all fear.

And the new moon and the evening star shone down together in an absolute peace.

CHAPTER XXXIII.

LAST HOURS.

> In this dim world of clouding cares
>   We rarely know, till 'wildered eyes
>   See white wings lessening up the skies,
> The angels with us unawares.
>
> . . . . .
>
> Strange glory streams through life's wild rents,
>   And through the open door of death
>   We see the heaven that beckoneth
> To the beloved going hence."
>
> GERALD MASSEY.

"READ me the twenty-third Psalm," said Miss Henderson.

It was the evening before the day fixed upon by her physicians for the surgical operation she had decided to submit to.

Faith was in her place by the bedside, her hand resting in that of her aunt. Mr. Armstrong sat near, — an open Bible before him. Miss Sampson had gone down the field for a "snatch of air."

Clear upon the stillness fell the sacred words of cheer. There was a strong, sure gladness in the tone that uttered them, that told they were born anew, in the breathing, from a heart that had proved the goodness and mercy of the Lord.

In a solemn gladness, also, two other hearts received them, and said, silently, Amen!

"Now the fourteenth of St. John."

"'In my father's house are many mansions.' 'I will dwell in the house of the Lord, forever.' Yes. It holds us all. Under one roof. One family, — whatever happens! Now, put away the book, and come here; you two!"

It was done; and Roger Armstrong and Faith Gartney stood up, side by side, before her.

"I haven't said so before, because I wouldn't set people troubling beforehand. But in my own mind, I'm pretty sure of what's coming. And if I had n't felt so all along, I should now. When the Lord gives us our last earthly wish, and the kind of peace comes over that seems as if it couldn't be disturbed by anything, any more, we may know, by the hush of it, that the day is done. I'm going to bid you good-night, Faith, and send you home. Say your prayers, and thank God, for yourself and for me. Whatever you hear of me, to-morrow, take it for good news; for it *will* be good. — Roger Armstrong! Take care of the child! — Child! love your husband; and trust in him; for you may!"

Close, close, — bent Faith above her aunt, and gave and took that solemn good-night kiss.

"'The grace of our Lord Jesus Christ, and the love of God, and the communion of the Holy Ghost, be with us all. Amen!'"

With the word of benediction, Roger Armstrong turned from the bedside, and led Faith away.

And the deeper shadows of night fell, and enfolded the Old House, and the hours wore on, and all was still. Stillest, calmest of all, in the soul of her who had dwelt there for nearly threescore years and ten, and who knew, none the less, that it would be surely home to her wheresoever her place might be given her next, in that wide and beautiful "House of the Lord!"

It was a strange day that succeeded; when they sat, waiting so, through those morning hours, keeping such Sabbath as heart and life do keep, and are keeping, somewhere, always, in whatever busy work-day of the world, when great issues come to solemnize the time.

Almost as still at the Old House as at **Cross** Corners. **No hurry**. No bustle. Glory quietly doing her needful duties, and obeying all direction of the nurse. Mr. Armstrong in his own room, in readiness always, for any act or errand that might be required of him. Henderson Gartney alone in that ancient parlor at the front. The three physicians, and Miss Sampson shut with Aunt Faith into her room. A faint, breathless odor of ether creeping everywhere, even out into the summer air.

It was eleven o'clock, when a word was spoken to Roger Armstrong, and he took his hat and walked across the field. Faith, with pale, asking face, met him at the door.

"Well, — **thus far**;" was the message; and a kiss fell **upon** the uplifted forehead, and a look of boundless love and **sympathy into the** fair, anxious eyes. "All has been done; **and** she is comfortable. There may still be danger; but the worst is past."

Then a brazen veil fell from before the face of day. The sunshine looked golden again, and the song of birds rang out, unmuffled. The strange, Sabbath stillness might be broken. They could speak common words, once more.

Faith and her mother sat there, in the hill-side parlor, talking thankfully, and happily, with Roger Armstrong. **So** a half-hour passed **by**. Mr. Gartney would come, with further tidings, when he **had** been able **to** speak with the physicians.

The shadows of shrub and tree crept and shortened to

the lines of noon, and still, 'no word. They began to wonder, why.

Mr. Armstrong would go **back**. **He** might be wanted, somehow. They should hear again, immediately, unless he were detained.

He was **not detained.** They watched him up the field, **and** into **the angle of the door-way.** He was hidden there a moment, **but not more.** Then they saw him **turn,** as one lingering and reluctant, and retrace his steps toward them.

"Faith! Stay here, **darling!** Let me **meet him** first," said Mrs. Gartney.

Faith shrank back, fearful of she knew not what, into the room they had just quitted.

A sudden, panic dread **and terror seized** her. She felt her hearing sharpened, strained, involuntarily. **She** should catch that first **word,** however **it might** be spoken. She dared not hear it, yet. **Out at the** hill-side door, into the shade of the deep evergreens, she passed, with a quick impulse.

Thither Roger Armstrong followed, presently, and found **her.** With the keen instinct of a loving sympathy, he knew she fled from speech. So he put his arm about her, silently, **tenderly; and** led her on, and **up,** under **the** close, cool **shade, the way** their steps had come **to know so well.**

"**Take it** for good news, darling. **For it is good,**" he said, at last, when he had placed **her in the rocky seat, where** she had listened to so many treasured words, — to that old, holy confidence, — of his.

And there he comforted her.

A sudden sinking, — a prostration beyond what they had **looked** for, had surprised her attendants; and, almost with their notice of the change, the last, pale, gray shadow had swept up over the **calm, patient face,** and good Aunt Faith had passed away.

Away, — for a little. Not out of God's house. Not lost out of His household.

This was her will.

"I, Faith Henderson, spinster, in sound mind, and of my own will, direct these things.

"That to my dear grandniece, Faith Henderson Gartney, be **given** from me, as my bequest, that portion of my worldly property now invested in **two** stores in D—— Street, in the city of Mishaumok. That this property and interest be hers, for her own use and disposal, with my love.

"Also, that my plate, and my box of best house linen, which stands beside the press in the northwest chamber, be given **to** her, Faith Henderson Gartney; and that my nephew, Henderson Gartney, shall, according to his own pleasure **and** judgment, appropriate and dispose of any **books, or articles of old family** value and interest. But that **beds, bedding, and all heavy** household furniture, **with a** proper **number of** chairs and other movables, **be retained in the** house, for its necessary and suitable furnishing.

"And then, that all this residue of personal effects, and **my real estate in the Old** Homestead at Kinnicutt Cross Corners, and **my** shares in the Kinnicutt Bank, **be** placed in the **hands of** my nephew, Henderson Gartney, to be held in trust during the natural life **of** my worthy and beloved handmaiden, Gloriana McWhirk; for her to occupy said house, and use said furniture, and the income of said property, so long as she can find at least four orphan children to maintain therewith, and " **make a good time for, every day."**

Provided, that in case the said Gloriana McWhirk shall marry **or** shall **no longer so employ this** property**, or in case** that she shall die, **said** property is to revert **to** my above-named grand niece, Faith Henderson Gartney, for her and her heirs, to their use and behoof forever.

"And if there be any failure of a legal binding in this paper that I write, I charge it upon my nephew, Henderson Gartney, on his conscience, as I believe him to be a true and honest man, to see that these my effects are so disposed of, according to my plain will and intention.

                (Signed)   **FAITH HENDERSON.**

(Witnessed)
    ROGER ARMSTRONG,
    HIRAM WASGATT.
    LUTHER GOODELL.'

CHAPTER XXXIV

MRS. PARLEY GIMP

"The best laid schemes o' mice an' men
Gang aft agley."
BURNS.

KINNICUTT had got an enormous deal to talk about. The excitement of the great fire, and the curiosity and astonishment concerning Miss Gartney's share in the events of that memorable night had hardly passed into the quietude of things discussed to death and laid away, unwillingly, in their graves, when all this that had happened at Cross Corners poured itself, in a flood of wonder, upon the little community.

Not all, quite, at once, however. Faith's engagement was not, at first, spoken of publicly. There was no need, in this moment of their common sorrow, to give their names to the little world about them, for such handling as it might please. Yet the little world found plenty to say, and a great many plans to make for them none the less.

Miss Henderson's so long unsuspected, and apparently brief illness, her sudden death, and the very singular will whose provisions had somehow leaked out, as matters of the sort always do, made a stir and ferment in the place, and everybody felt bound to arrive at some satisfactory conclusion which should account for all, and to get a clear idea of what everybody immediately concerned would do, or ought, in the circumstances, to do next, before they, — the first everybodies, — could eat and sleep, and go comfortably about their own business again, in the ordinary way.

They should think Mr. Gartney would dispute the will. It couldn't be a very hard matter, most likely, to set it aside. All that farm, and the Old Homestead, and her money in the bank, going to that Glory McWhirk! Why, it was just ridiculous. The old lady must have been losing her faculties. One thing was certain, any way. The minister was out of a boarding-place again. So that question came up, in all its intricate bearings, once more.

This time Mrs. Gimp struck, while, as she thought, the iron was hot.

Mr. Parley Gimp met Mr. Armstrong, one morning, in the village street, and waylaid him to say that "his good lady thought she could make room for him in their family, if it was so that he should be looking out for a place to stay at."

Mr. Armstrong thanked him; but, for the present, he was to remain at Cross Corners.

"At the Old House?"

"No, sir. At Mr. Gartney's."

The iron was cold, after all.

Mrs. Parley Gimp called, one day, a week or two later, when the minister was out. A visit of sympathetic scrutiny.

"Yes, it was a great loss, certainly. But then, at her age, you know, ma'am! We must all expect these things. It was awfully sudden, to be sure. Must have been a terrible shock. Was her mind quite clear at the last ma'am?"

"Perfectly. Clear, and calm, and happy, through it all."

"That's very pleasant to think of now, I'm sure. But I hear she's made a very extraordinary arrangement about the property. You can't tell, though, to be sure, about all you hear, now-a-days."

"No, Mrs. Gimp. That is very true," said Mrs. Gartney.

"Everybody always expected that it would all come to you. At least, to your daughter. She seemed to make so much of her."

"My daughter is quite satisfied, and we for her."

"Well, I must say! — and so, Mr. Armstrong is to board here, now? A little out of the way of most of the parish, is n't it? I never could see, exactly, what put it into his head to come so far. Not but what he makes out to do his duty as a pastor, pretty prompt, too. I don't hear any complaints. He's rather off and on about settling, though. I guess he's a man that keeps his intentions pretty close to himself, — and all his affairs, for that matter. Of course he's a perfect right to. But I will say I like to know all about folks from the beginning. It aggravates me to have to begin in the middle. I tell Serena, it's just like reading a book when the first volume's lost. I don't suppose I'm much more curious than other people; but I *should* like to know just how old he is, for one thing; and who his father and mother were; and where he came from in the first place, and what he lives on; for 't aint our salary, I know that; he's given away more 'n half of it a' ready, — right here in the village. I've said to my husband, forty times, if I've said it once, 'I declare, I've a great mind to ask him myself, straight out, just to see what he'll say.'"

"And why not?" asked a voice, pleasantly, behind her.

Mr. Armstrong had come in, unheard by the lady in her own rush of words, and had approached too near, as this suddenly ceased, to be able to escape again unnoticed.

Mis' Battis told Luther Goodell afterward, that she "jest looked in from the next room, at that, and if ever a woman felt cheap, — all over, — and as if she hadn't a right to her own toes and fingers, and as if every thread and stitch on her turned mean, all at once, — it was Mrs. Gimp, that minit!"

"Has Faith returned?" Mr. Armstrong asked, of Mrs. Gartney, after a little pause in which Mrs. Gimp showed no disposition to develop into deed her forty times declared "great mind."

"I think not. She said she would remain an hour or two with Glory, and help her to arrange those matters she came in, this morning, to ask us about."

"I will walk over."

And the minister took his hat again, and with a bow to the two ladies, passed out, and across the lane.

"Faith!" ejaculated the village matron, her courage and her mind to meddle returning. "Well, that's intimate!"

It might as well be done now, as at any time. Mr. Armstrong, himself, had heedlessly precipitated the occasion. It had only been, among them, a question of how and when. There was nothing to conceal.

"Yes," replied Mrs. Gartney, quietly. "They will be married by-and-by."

"Did she go out the door, ma'am? Or has she melted down into the carpet? 'Cause, I have heerd of people sinkin' right through the floor," said Mis' Battis, who "jest looked in" a second time, as the bewildered visitor receded.

The pleasant autumn months, mellowing and brightening all things, seemed also to soften and gild their memories of the life that had ended, ripely and beautifully, among them.

Glory, after the first overwhelm of astonishment at what had befallen her, — made fully to understand that which she had a right, and was in duty bound to do, — entered upon the preparations for her work with the same unaffected readiness with which she would have done the bidding of her living mistress. It was so evident that her true humbleness was untouched by all. "It's beautiful!" and the tears and smiles would come together as she said it. "But then, Miss Faith — Mr. Armstrong! I never can do any of it unless you help me!"

Faith and Mr. Armstrong did help with heart and hand, and every word of counsel that she needed.

"I must buy some cotton and calico, and make some little clothes and tyers. Had n't I better? When they come, I'll have them to take care of."

And with the loving anticipation of a mother, she made up, and laid away, Faith helping her in all, her store of small apparel for little ones that were to come.

She had gone down, one day, to Mishaumok, and found out Bridget Foye, at the old number in High Street. And to her she had entrusted the care of looking up the children, — to be not less than five, and not more than eight or nine years of age, — who should be taken to live with her at "Miss Henderson's home," and "have a good time every day."

"I must get them here before Christmas," said Glory to her friends. "We must hang their stockings all up by the great kitchen chimney, and put sugar-plums and picture books in!"

She was going back eagerly into her child-life, — rather into the life her childhood wist of, but missed, — and would live it all over, now, with these little ones, taken already, before even they were seen or found, out of their strangerhood into her great, kindly heart!

A plain, capable, motherly woman had been obtained, by Mr. Armstrong's efforts and inquiry, who would live with Glory as companion and assistant. There was the dairywork to be carried on, still. This, and the hay-crops, made the principal income of the Old Farm. A few fields were rented for cultivation.

"Just think," cried Glory when the future management of these matters was talked of, "what it will be to see the little things let out a rolling in the new hay!"

Her thought passed so entirely over herself, as holder and arbiter of means, to the good, — the daily little joy, — that was to come, thereby, to others!

When all was counted and calculated, they told her that she might safely venture to receive, in the end, six children. But that, for the present, four would perhaps be as many as it would be wise for her to undertake.

"You know best," she said, "and I shall do whatever you say. But I don't feel afraid, — any more, that is, for taking six than four. I shall just do for them all the time, whether or no."

"And what if they are bad and troublesome, Glory?"

"Oh, they won't be," she replied. "I shall love them so!"

CHAPTER XXXV.

INDIAN SUMMER.

'Tis as if the benignant Heaven
Had a new revelation given,
  And written it out with gems;
  For the golden tops of the elms
And the burnished bronze of the ash
And the scarlet lights that flash
From the sumach's points of flame,
  Like blazonings on a scroll
Spell forth an illumined Name
  For the reading of the soul!

IT is of no use to dispute about the Indian Summer. I never found two people who could agree as to the time when it ought to be here, or upon a month and day when it should be decidedly too late to look for it. It keeps coming. After the Equinoctial, which begins to be talked about with the first rains of September, and is n't done with till the Sun has measured half-a-dozen degrees of south declination, all the pleasant weather is Indian Summer,—away on to Christmas-tide. For my part, I think we get it now and then, little by little, as "the kingdom" comes. That every soft warm, mellow, hazy, golden day, like each fair, fragrant life, is a part and outcrop of it; though weeks of gale and frost, or ages of cruel worldliness and miserable sin may lie between.

It was an Indian Summer day, then; and it was in October.

Faith and Mr. Armstrong walked over the brook, and round by Pasture Rocks, to the "little chapel," as Faith had called it, since the time, last winter, when she and Glory had met the minister there, in the still, wonderful, pure beauty that enshrined it on that "diamond morning."

The elms that stood then, in their icy sheen, about the meadows, like great cataracts of light, were soft with amber drapery, now; translucent in each leaf with the detained sunshine of the summer; and along the borders of the wood-walk, scarlet flames of sumach sprang out, vivid, from among the lingering green; and birches trembled with their golden plumes; and bronzed ash boughs, and deep crimsons and maroons and chocolate-browns and carbuncle red that crowned the oaks with richer and intenser hues, made up a wealth and massiveness of beauty wherein eye and thought revelled and were sated.

Over and about all, the glorious October light, and the dreamy warmth that was like a palpable love.

They stood on the crisp moss carpet of the "half-way rock," — the altar-crag behind them, with its cherubim that waved illumined wings of tenderer radiance now, — and gazed over the broad outspread of marvellous color; and thought of the summer that had come and gone since they had stood there, last, together, and of the beauty that had breathed alike on earth and into life, for them.

"Faith, darling! Tell me your thought," said Roger Armstrong.

"This was my thought," Faith answered, slowly. "That first sermon you preached to us, — that gave me such a hope, then, — that comes up to me so, almost as a warning, now! The poor, — that were to have the kingdom! And then, those other words, — 'how hardly shall they who have riches enter in!' And **I am** *so* rich! It frightens me."

"Entire happiness does make one **tremble**. Only, **if we** feel God in it, and stand but the more ready for His work, we may be safe."

"His work — yes," Faith answered. "But now he only gives me rest. It seems as if, somehow, I were not worthy **of a hard** life. As if all things had been made too easy for **me.** And I had thought, so, of some great and difficult thing to do."

Then Faith told him of the oracle that, years ago, had **first** wakened her to the thought of what life might be; of **the** "high and holy work" that she had dreamed of; and **of** her struggles to fulfil it, feebly, in the only ways that **as** yet had opened for her.

"And now — just to receive all, — love, and help, and care, — and to rest, and to be so wholly happy!"

"Believe, darling, that **we are** led, through **all**. That the oil of joy is but as an anointing for a nobler work. **It** is only so **I** dare to think of **it.** We shall have plenty to **do,** Faithie! And, perhaps, **to** bear. It will all be set before us, in good time."

"But nothing can be *hard* to do, any more. That is what makes me almost feel unworthy. Look at Nurse Sampson. Look at Glory. They have only their work, and the love of God to help them in it. And I — ! Oh, I am not poor any longer. The words don't seem to be for me."

"Let us take them with their double-edge of truth, then. Holding ourselves always poor, in sight of the infinite spiritual riches of the kingdom. Blessed are the poor, who **can** feel, even in the keenest earthly joy, how there is a fulness of life laid up in Him who gives it, of whose depth the best gladness here is but a glimpse and foretaste! We will not be selfishly or unworthily content, God helping us my little one!"

"It is so hard *not* to be content!" whispered Faith, as the strong, manly arm held her, in its shelter, close beside the noble, earnest heart.

"I think," said Roger Armstrong, afterward, as they walked down over the fragrant pathway of fallen pine leaves "that I have never known an instance of one more evidently called, commissioned, and prepared for a good work in the world, than Glory. Her whole life has been her education for it. It is not without a purpose, when a soul like hers is left to struggle up through such externals of circumstance. We can love and help her in it, Faith; and do something, in our way, for her, as she will do, in hers, for others."

"Oh, yes!" assented Faith, impulsively. "I have wished ——" but there she stopped.

"Am I to hear no more?" asked Mr. Armstrong, presently. "Have I not a right to insist upon the wish?"

"I forgot what I was coming to," said Faith, blushing deeply. "I spoke of it, one day, to mother. And she said it was a thing I couldn't decide for myself, now. That some one else would be concerned, as well as I."

"And some one else will be sure to wish as you do. Only there may be a wisdom in waiting. Faithie, — I have never told you yet, — will you be frightened if I tell you now, — that I am not a poor man, as the world counts poverty? My friend, of whom you know, in those terrible days of the commencing pestilence, having only his daughter and myself to care for, made his will; in provision against whatever might befall them there. By that will, — through the fearful sorrow that made it effective, — I came into possession of a large property. Your little inheritance, Faithie, goes into your own little purse for private expenditures or charities. But for the present, as it seems to me, Glory has ample means for all that it is well for her to undertake. By-and-by, as she gains in years and in experience, you will have it in your power to enlarge her field of good. 'Miss Henderson's Home' may grow into a wider benefit than even she, herself, foresaw."

Faith was not frightened. These were not the riches that could make her tremble with a dread lest earth should too fully satisfy. This was only a promise of new power to work with; a guaranty that God was not leaving her merely to care for and to rest in a good that must needs be all her own.

"We shall find plenty to do, Faithie!" Mr. Armstrong repeated; and he held her hand in his with a strong pressure that told how the thought of that work to come, and her sweet and entire association in it, leaped along his pulses with a living joy.

Faith caught it; and all fear was gone. She could not shrink from the great blessedness that was laid upon her, any more than Nature could refuse to wear her coronation robes, that trailed their radiance in this path they trod.

Life held them in a divine harmony.

The October sun, that mantled them with warmth and glory; the Indian Summer, that transfigured earth about them; all tints, — all redolence, — all broad beatitude of globe and sky, — were none too much to breathe out and make palpable the glad and holy auspice of the hour.

Mr. Gartney had gradually relinquished his half-formed thought of San Francisco. Already the unsettled and threatening condition of affairs in the country had begun to make men feel that the time was not one for new schemes or adventurous changes. Somehow, the great wheels, mercantile and political, had slipped out of their old grooves, and went laboring, as it were, roughly and at random, with fierce clattering and jolting, quite off the ordinary track; so that none could say whether they should finally regain it, and roll smoothly forward, as in the prosperous and peaceful days of the past, or should bear suddenly and irretrievably down to some horrible, unknown crash and ruin.

Henderson Gartney, however, was too restless a man to wait, with entire passiveness, the possible turn and issue of things.

Quite strong, again, in health, — so great a part of his burden and anxiety lifted from him in the marriages, actual and prospective, of his two daughters, — and his means augmented by the sale of a portion of his western property which he had effected during his summer visit thereto, — it was little to be looked for that he should consent to vegetate, idly and quietly, through a second winter at Cross Corners.

The first feeling of some men, apparently, when they have succeeded in shuffling off a load of difficulty, is a sensation of the delightful ease with which they can immediately shoulder another. As when one has just cleared a desk or drawer of rubbish, there is such a tempting opportunity made for beginning to stow away and accumulate again. Well! the principle is an eternal one. Nature does abhor a vacuum.

The greater portion of the ensuing months, therefore, Mr. Gartney spent in New York; whither his wife and children accompanied him, also, for a stay of a few weeks; during which, Faith and her mother accomplished the inevita ble shopping that a coming wedding necessitates; and set in train of preparation certain matters beyond the range of Kinnicutt capacity and resource.

Mr. Armstrong, too, was obliged to be absent from his parish for a little time. Affairs of his own required some personal attention. He chose these weeks while the others, also, were away.

It was decided that the marriage should take place in the coming spring; and that then the house at Cross Corners should become the home of Mr. Armstrong and Faith; and that Mr. Gartney should remove, permanently, to New York, where he had already engaged in some incidental and preliminary business transactions. His purpose was to fix himself there, as a shipping and commission merchant, concerning himself, for a large proportion, with California trade.

The house in Mishaumok had been rented for a term of five years. One change prepares the way for another. Things never go back precisely to what they were before.

Mr. Armstrong, after serious thought, had come to this conclusion of accepting the invitation of the Old Parish at Kinnicutt to remain with it as its pastor, because the place itself had become endeared to him for its associations; because, also, it was Faith's home, which she had learned to love and cling to; because she, too, had a work here, in assisting Glory to fulfil the terms of her aunt's bequest; and because, country parish though it was, and a limited sphere, as it might seem, for his means and talents, he saw the way here, not only to accomplish much direct good in the way of his profession, but as well for a wider exercise of power through the channel of authorship; for which a more onerous pastoral charge would not have left him the needful quiet or leisure.

So, with these comings and goings, these happy plans, and helpings and on-lookings, the late autumn weeks merged in winter, and days slipped almost imperceptibly by, and Christmas came.

Three little orphan girls had been welcomed into "Miss Henderson's Home." And only one of them had hair that would curl. But Glory gave the other two an extra kiss each, every morning

CHAPTER XXXV.

CHRISTMAS-TIDE.

"Through suffering and through sorrow thou hast past
To show us what a woman true may be;
They have not taken sympathy from thee,
Nor made thee any other than thou wast;

. . . . .

Nor hath thy knowledge of adversity
Robbed thee of any faith in happiness,
But rather cleared thine inner eye to see
How many simple ways there are to bless."
LOWELL.

"And if any painter drew her,
He would paint her unaware,
With a halo round the hair."
MRS. BROWNING.

THERE were dark portents abroad. Rumors, and threats, and prognostications of fear and strife teemed in the columns of each day's sheet of news, and pulsed wildly along the electric nerves of the land; and men looked out, as into a coming tempest, that blackened all the southerly sky with wrath; and only that the horror was too great to be believed in, they could not have eaten and drunken, and bought and sold, and planted and builded, as they did, after the age-old manner of man, in these days before the flood that was to come.

Civil war, like a vulture of hell, was swooping down from the foul fastness of iniquity that had hatched her in its high places, and that reared itself, audaciously, in the very face of Heaven.

And a voice, as of a mighty angel, sounded "Wo! wo! wo! to the inhabiters of earth!"

And still men but half heard and comprehended; and still they slept and rose, and wrought on, each in his own work, and planned for the morrow, and for the days that were to be.

And in the midst of all, came the blessed Christmas tide. Yes! even into this world that has rolled its seething burden of sin and pain and shame and conflict along the listening depths through waiting cycles of God's eternity, was Christ once born!

And little children, of whom is the kingdom, in their simple faith and holy unconsciousness, were looking for the Christmas good, and wondering only what the coming joy should be.

The shops and streets of Mishaumok were filled with busy throngs. People forgot, for a day, the fissure that had just opened, away there in the far South-land, and the fierce flames that shot up, threatening, from the abyss. What mattered the mass meetings, and the shouts, and the guns, along those shores of the Mexican Gulf? To-night would be Christmas Eve; and there were thousands of little stockings waiting to be hung by happy firesides, and they must all be filled for the morrow.

So the shops and streets were crowded, and people with arms full of holiday parcels jostled each other at every corner. It wasn't like the common days, when they passed by, self-absorbed, unknowing and unheeding what might be each other's object or errand. There was a common business to be done to-day. Everybody knew what everybody else was after; and the lady whose carriage waited at the door, half filled with costly purchases, stood elbow to elbow at the gay counter with one whose face was pale and wearied with the many thoughts and steps it cost her to make the three dollars in her pocket, which she dared not break till she had quite settled what every cent should go for, buy something for each one of five.

As the day wore on, the hurry and the crowd increased. Grave, dignified men might now and then be seen with queer packages in their arms, held awkwardly; for the errand-boys in the shops were overbusied and uncertain; and some things must be transported with especial care, and nothing, to-night, must fail of its destination. Dolls' arms and legs betrayed themselves through their long swathings, and here and there the nose or tail of a painted horse had pricked its way out of its paper wrapping; coat pockets hung heavy with sweet burdens; the neat, square parcels, fastened with colored twine, told of booksellers' treasures; all along the shifting sea of faces you read one gleam of pleased anticipation; coins had melted into smiles; the soul of Christmas was abroad; the "better to give than to receive" was the keynote of the kindly carnival.

There are odd encounters in this world-tumble that we live in. In the early afternoon, at one of the bright showcases, filled within and heaped without with toys, two women met, — as strangers are always meeting. with involuntary touch and glance, — borne together in a crowd, — atoms impinging for an instant, never to approach again, perhaps, in all the coming combinations of time.

These two women, though, had met before.

One, sharp, eager, — with a stylish-shabby air of dress about her, and the look of pretence that shopmen know, as admitted and asked prices, where she had no actual thought of buying, — holding by the hand a child of six, who dragged and teased, and got an occasional word that crushed him into momentary silence, but who, tired with the sights and the Christmas shopping, had nothing for it but to begin to drag and tease again; another, with bright, happy, earnest eyes and flushing cheeks, and hair rolled back in a golden wealth beneath her plain straw bonnet; bonnet, and dress, and all, of simple black; these two came face to face.

The shabby woman with the sharp look recognized nothing. Glory McWhirk knew Mrs. Grubbling, and the child of six that had been the Grubbling baby.

All at once, she had him in her arms; and as if not a moment had gone by since she held him so in the little, dark, upper entry in Budd Street, where he had toddled to her in his night-gown, for her grieved farewell, was hugging and kissing him, with the old, forgetting and forgiving love.

Mrs. Grubbling looked on in petrified amaze. Glory had transferred a fragrant white paper parcel from her pocket to the child's hands, and had thrust upon that a gay tin horse from the counter, before it occurred to her that the mother might, possibly, neither remember nor approve.

"I beg your pardon, ma'am, for the liberty; and it's very likely you don't know me. I'm Glory McWhirk, that used to live with you, and mind the baby."

And then she seized once more the big boy in whom the baby of olden time was merged, and well-nigh lost, and who had already plunged his fingers into the candies, and was satisfying himself as to the perfect propriety of all that had occurred, by the sure recognition of peppermint-stick. —

and had the hugs and kisses all over again, without ever waiting for a word of license.

Mrs. Grubbling was not in the least offended. There was an air of high respectability in the public avowal of this very nice-looking young woman that she had once "lived with her and tended baby." Also, in the fervor of attachment that evinced itself in these embraces. It spoke well, surely, for the employer. There are those who can take a credit to themselves, even from their failure to thwart and spoil a nobleness that has overlived their meanness. As they might, in their Pharisaism, from the very sunlight of God, whose spontaneous outflow no evil of man can quench or turn aside. The earth rolls on, and is not yet consumed. The blue sky is set safely above its smirch. No track of its sin lies foul across the firmament. Therefore, impotent sinners, rejoice in the day-shine, and think well of yourselves that heaven still smiles!

"I'm sure I'm glad to see you, Glory," said Mrs. Grubbling, patronizingly; "and I hope you've been doing well since you went away from me." As if she had been doing so especially well before, that there might easily be a doubt as to whether going farther had not been faring worse. I have no question that Mrs. Grubbling really fancied, at the moment, that the foundation of all the simple content and quiet prosperity that evidenced themselves at present in the person of her former handmaid, had been laid in Budd Street.

"And where are you living now?" proceeded she, as Glory resigned the boy to his mint-stick, and was saying good-bye.

"Out in Kinnicutt, ma'am; at Miss Henderson's; where I have been ever since."

She never thought of triumphing. She never dreamed

of what it would be to **electrify her** former mistress with the announcement that she whom she had since served had died, and left her, Glory McWhirk, the life-use of more than half her estate. That she dwelt now, as proprietress, where she **had been** a servant. Her humbleness and her faithfulness **were so entire that she** never thought of herself as occupying, in the eyes of others, such position. She was Miss **Henderson's** handmaiden, still; doing her behest, simply, **as if** she had but left her there **in** keeping, while she went a journey.

So she bade good-bye, and courtesied to Mrs. Grubbling, and gathered **up her** little parcels, and **went out.** Fortunately. **Mrs.** Grubbling was half-stunned, as it was. It is impossible **to** tell what might have resulted, had she then and there been made cognizant of more. Not to the shorn lamb, alone, always, are sharp winds beneficently tempered. There is a mercy, also, to the miserable wolf.

Glory had one trouble, to-day, that **hindered her pure, free** and utter enjoyment of what she had **to** do.

All day she had seen, here and there along the street, little forlorn and ragged ones, straying about aimlessly, as if by any chance, **a** scrap of Christmas cheer might even fall to them, **if only** they **kept out in** the midst of it. There was a distant wonder in **their faces,** as they met the buyers among the shops, and glanced **at** the fair, fresh burdens they carried; and around **the** confectioners' windows they would cluster, sometimes, two **or** three together, and *look;* as if one sense could take in what was denied so to **another.** She knew so well what the feeling of it was! To see the good times going on, and not be in 'em! She longed so to gather them all to herself, and take them home, and make a Christmas for them!

She could **only drop** the pennies **that came to her in**

change loose **into her** pocket, and give them, **one** by one, along the wayside. And she more than once offered a bright quarter, (**it was in** the days when quarters yet were, reader!) when she might have counted out the sum in lesser bits, that **so the** pocket should **be** kept supplied the longer.

Down by the ——— Railway Station, the streets were dim, and dirty, and cheerless. Inside, the passengers gathered about the stove, where the **red** coals gleamed cheerful in the already gathering dusk of the winter afternoon. A New York train was going out; and all **sorts** of people, — from the **well-to-do**, portly gentleman of business, with his good **coat buttoned** comfortably to his chin, his tickets bought, his wallet lined with bank-notes for his journey, and **secretly** stowed beyond the reach (if there be such a thing) of **pickpockets**, and the Mishaumok Journal, Evening Edition, damp from the press, unfolded **in his fingers,** to the care-for-naught, dare-devil little **news-boy who had** sold it to him, **and** who now **saunters** off, varying his monotonous **cry with —**

"Jour-nal, gentlemen! Eve-nin' 'dition! Georgy **out!**"

("What's that?" exclaims an inconsiderate.)

"Georgy out! **(Little brother o'** mine. Seen him any**where?)** Eve-nin' 'dition! Jour-nal, gentlemen!" and the shivering little candy-girl, threading her way with a silent imploringness among the throng, — were bustling up and down, in waiting-rooms, and on the platforms, till one would think, assuredly, that the centre **of all** the world's activity, at this moment, lay here; and **that** everybody *not* going **in** this particular express train to **New** York, must be utterly devoid of any aim **or** object in **life,** whatever.

So we do, always, **carry our** centre about **with us.** A little while ago all the world was buying dolls and tin horses. Horizons shift and ring themselves about us, and we, ourselves, stand always in the middle.

By-and-by, however, the last call was heard.

"Passengers for New York! Train ready! All aboard!"

And with the ringing of the bell, and the mighty gasping of the impatient engine, and a scuffle and scurry of a minute, in which carpet-bags and babies were gathered up and shouldered indiscriminately, the rooms and the platforms were suddenly cleared of all but a few stragglers, and half a dozen women with Christmas bundles, who sat waiting for trains to way stations.

Two little pinched faces, purple with the bitter cold, looked in at the door.

"It's good and warm in there. Less' go!"

And the older drew the younger into the room, toward the glowing stove.

They looked as if they had been wandering about in the dreary streets till the chill had touched their very bones. The larger of the two, a boy, — torn hopelessly as to his trowsers, dilapidated to the last degree as to his fragment of a hat, — knees and elbows making their way out into the world with the faintest shadow of opposition, — had, perhaps from this, a certain look of pushing knowingness that set itself, by the obscure and inevitable law of compensation, over against the gigantic antagonism of things he found himself born into; and you knew, as you looked at him, that he would, somehow, sooner or later, make his small dint against the great dead wall of society that loomed itself in his way; whether society or he should get the worst of it, might happen as it would.

The younger was a little girl. A flower thrown down in the dirt. A jewel encrusted with mean earth. Little feet in enormous coarse shoes, cracked and trodden down; **bare arms** trying **to** hide themselves under a bit of old woolen shawl; hair tangled beneath a squalid hood; out amidst all, a face of beauty that peeped, like an unconscious draft of God's own signing, upon humanity. Was there none to acknowledge it?

An official came through the waiting-room.

The boy showed a slink in his eyes, like one used to shoving and rebuff, and to getting off, round corners. **The girl** stood, innocent and unheeding.

"There! out with you! No vagrums here!"

Of course, they couldn't have all Queer Street in their waiting-rooms, these railway people; and the man's words were rougher than his voice. But these were two children, who wanted cherishing!

The slink in the boy's eye worked down, and became a sneak and a shuffle, toward the door. The girl was following.

"Stop!" called a woman's voice, sharp and authoritative. "Don't you stir a single step either of you, till you get warm! If there isn't any other way to fix **it,** I'll buy you both **a** ticket somewhere and then you'll be passengers."

It was a tall, thin, hoopless woman, with a carpet-bag, a plaid shawl, and an umbrella; and a bonnet that, since other bonnets had begun to poke, looked like a chaise top flattened back at the first spring. **In a** word, Mehitable Sampson.

Something twitched at the corners **of** the man's mouth as he glanced round **at** this sudden and singular champion. Something may have twitched under his comfortable waistcoat, **also.** At any rate, he passed on; and the children, — the brief battledore over in which they had been the shuttle cocks, — crept back, compliant with the second order, much amazed, toward the stove.

Miss Sampson began to interrogate.

"Why don't you take your little sister home?"

"This one ain't my sister." Children always set people right before they answer queries.

"Well, — whoever she is, then. Why don't you both go home?"

"Cause its cold there, too. And we was sent to find sticks."

"If she isn't your sister, who does she belong to?"

"She don't belong to nobody. She lived upstairs, and her mother died, and she came down to us. But she's goin' to be took away. Mother's got five of us, now. She's goin' to the poor-house. She's a regular little brick, though; aint yer, Jo?"

The pretty, childish lips that had begun to grow red and life-like again, parted, and showed little rows of milk-teeth, like white shells. The blue eyes and the baby smile went up, confidingly, to the young ragamuffin's face. There had been kindness here. The boy had taken to Jo, it seemed; and was benevolently evincing it, in the best way he could, by teaching her goodnatured slang.

"Yes; I'm a little brick," she lisped.

Miss Sampson's keen eyes went from one to the other, resting last and long on Jo.

"I shouldn't wonder," she said, deliberately, "if you was Number Four!"

"Whereabouts do you live?" suddenly, to the boy.

"Three doors round the corner. 'Taint number four, though. It's ninety-three."

"What's your name?"

"Tim Rafferty."

"Tim Rafferty! Did anybody ever trust you with a carpet-bag?"

"I've carried 'em up. But then they mostly goes along, and looks sharp."

"Well, now I'm going to leave you here, with this one. If anybody speaks to you, say you was left in charge. Don't stir till I come back. And — look here! if you see a young woman come in, with bright, wavy hair, and a black gown and bonnet; and if she comes and speaks to you, as most likely she will, tell her I said I shouldn't wonder if this was Number Four!"

And Nurse Sampson went out into the street.

When she came back, the children sat there, still; and Glory McWhirk was with them.

"I don't know as I'd any business to meddle; and I haven't made any promises; but I've found out that you can do as you choose about it, and welcome. And I couldn't help thinking you might like to have this one for Number Four."

Glory had already nestled the poor, tattered child close to her, and given her a cake to eat from the refreshment counter.

Tim Rafferty delivered up the carpet-bag, in proud integrity. To be sure, there were half a dozen people in the room who had witnessed its intrustment to his hands; but I think he would have waited there, all the same, had the coast been clear.

Miss Sampson gave him ten cents, and recounted to Glory what she had learned at number ninety-three.

"She's a strange child, left on their hands; and they're as poor as death. They were going to give her in charge to the authorities. The woman said she could n't feed her another day. That's about the whole of it. If Tim don't bring her back, they'll know where she is, and be thankful."

"Do you want to go home with me, and hang up your stocking, and have a Christmas?"

"My golly!" ejaculated Tim, staring.

The little one smiled shyly, and was mute. She did n't know what Christmas was. She had been cold, and now she was warm, and her mouth and hands were filled with sweet cake. And there were pleasant words in her ears. That was all she knew. As much as we shall comprehend at first, perhaps; when the angels take us up out of the earth-cold, and give us the first morsel of heavenly good to stay our cravings.

This was how it ended. Tim had a paper bag of apples and cakes, with some sugar pigs and pussy-cats put in at the top, and a pair of warm stockings out of Glory's bag, to carry home, for himself; and he was to say that the lady who came to see his mother had taken Jo away into the country. To Miss Henderson's, at Kinnicutt. Glory wrote these names upon a paper. Tim was to be a good boy, and some day they would come and see him again.

Then Nurse Sampson's plaid shawl was wrapped about little Jo, and pinned close over her rags to keep out the cold of Christmas Eve; and the bell rang presently; and she was taken out into the bright, warm car, and tucked up in a corner, where she slept all the hour that they were steaming over the road.

And so these three went out to Kinnicutt to keep Christmas at the Old House.

So Glory carried home the Christ-gift that had come to her.

Tim went back, alone, to number ninety-three. He had his bag of good things, and his warm stockings, and his wonderful story to tell. And there was more supper and breakfast for five than there would have been for six. Nevertheless, somehow, he missed the " little brick."

Out at Cross Corners, Miss Henderson's Home **was** all aglow. The long kitchen, which, by the outgrowth **of** the **house** for generations, had come to be a central room, was **flooded** with the clear blaze of a great pine knot, that crackled in the chimney; and open doors showed neat adjoining rooms, in and out which the gleams and shadows played, making **a** suggestive pantomime of hide and seek. **It was** a grand old place for Christmas games! **And** three little bright-faced girls sat round the knee of a tidy, cheery old woman, who told them, in a quaint Irish brogue, the story of the " little rid hin," that was caught by the fox, and got away, again, safe, to her own little house in the woods, where she " lived happy **iver** afther, an' got a fine little brood of chickens to live wid her; an' pit 'em all intill warrum stockings and shoes, **an'** round-o **caliker** gowns."

And they carped at no discrepancies or improbabilities; **jut** seized all eagerly, and fused it in their quick imagina**tions to** one beautiful meaning; which, whether it were of chicken-comfort, overbrooded with warm love, or of a clothed, contented childhood, in safe shelter, mattered not a **bit.**

Into this warm, blithe scene came Glory, just as the fable was ended for the fourth time, bringing the last little chick, flushed and rosy from a bath ; born into beauty, like Venus from the sea; her fair hair, **combed** and glossy, hanging about her neck in curls; and wrapped, not in a " round-o-caliker," but in **a** scarlet flannel night-gown, comfortable

friends who had helped and sympathized in all, and said, with a quick overflow of feeling, that could find only the old words wherein to utter herself, —

"Such a time as this! Such a beautiful time! And to think that I should be in it!"

Miss Henderson's will was fulfilled.

A happy, young life had gathered again about the ancient hearthstone that had seen two hundred years of human change.

The Old House, wherefrom the last of a long line had passed on into the Everlasting Mansions, had become God's heritage.

Nurse Sampson spent her Christmas with the Gartneys.

They must have her again, they told her, at parting, for the wedding; which would be in May.

"I may be a thousand miles off, by that time. But I shall think of you, all the same, wherever I am. My work is coming. I feel it. There's a smell of blood and death in the air; and all the strong hearts and hands'll be wanted. You'll see it."

And with that, she was gone.

CHAPTER XXXVII.

THE WEDDING JOURNEY.

> "The tree
> Sucks kindlier nurture from a soil enriched
> By its own fallen leaves; and man is made,
> In heart and spirit, from deciduous hopes
> And things that seem to perish."

> "A stream always among woods or in the sunshine is pleasant to see and happy in itself. Another, forced through rocks, and choked with sand, under ground, cold, dark, comes up able to heal the world."
>
> FROM "SEED GRAIN."

"SHALL we plan a wedding journey, Faith?"

It was one evening in April that Mr Armstrong said this. The day for the marriage had been fixed for the first week in May.

Faith had something of the bird-nature about her. Always, at this moment of the year, a restlessness, akin to that which prompts the flitting of winged things that track the sunshine and the creeping greenness that goes up the latitudes, had used to seize her, inwardly. Something that came with the swelling of tender buds, and the springing of bright blades, and the first music born from winter silence, had prompted her with the whisper, — "Abroad! abroad! Out into the beautiful earth!"

It had been one of her unsatisfied longings. She had

thought, what **a joy it would be if she could** have said, frankly, "Father, **mother! let us have a** pleasant journey in the lovely weather!"

And now, that one stood at her side, who would have **taken her in** his tender guardianship whithersoever she might **choose,** — now that there was no need for hesitancy in her wish, — **this** child, who **had never been beyond the Hudson, who had** thought longingly of Catskill, and Trenton, and Niagara, and had seen them only in her **dreams,** — felt, inexplicably, **a contrary impulse,** that said within her, " Not yet!" Somehow, she did **not** care, **at** this great and beautiful **hour of her life, to** wander away into strange **places. Its holy** happiness belonged to home.

" **Not** now. Unless **you** wish **it.** Not on purpose. **Take** me **with** you, sometime, when, perhaps, you would have gone alone. Let it *happen*."

" **We** will just begin **our** quiet life, **then,** darling, shall **we?** The life that is to be our real blessedness, and that has **no** need to give itself a holiday, as yet. And let the work-days and the holidays be portioned as God pleases?"

" **It will be better,** — happier," Faith answered, timidly. " Besides, with all this fearful tramping to war through the whole land, how can one feel like pleasure-journeying? And then ——" there was another little reason that peeped out last. — "they would have been so sure to make a fuss about us in New York!"

The adjuncts of life had been much to her in those restless days when a dark doubt lay over its deep reality. She **had** found a passing cheer and relief in them, then. Now, she was so sure, **so quietly content!** It was a joy too sacred to be intermeddled with.

So a family group, only, gathered in the hill-side parlor, on the fair May morning wherein good, venerable Mr. Holland said the words that made Faith Gartney and Roger Armstrong one.

It was all still, and bright, and simple. Glory, standing modestly by the door, said within herself, "it was like a little piece of heaven."

And afterward, — not the bride and groom, — but father, mother, and little brother, said good-bye, and went away upon their journey, and left them there. In the quaint, pleasant home, that was theirs now, under the budding elms, with the smile of the May promise pouring in.

And Glory made a May-day at the Old House, by-and-by. And the little children climbed in the apple-branches, and perched there, singing, like the birds.

And was there not a white-robed presence with them, somehow, watching all?

Nearly three months had gone. The hay was down. The distillation of sweet clover was in all the air. The little ones at the Old House were out, in the lengthening shadows of the July afternoon, rolling and revelling in the perfumed, elastic heaps.

Faith Armstrong stood with Glory, in the porch-angle, looking on.

Calm and beautiful. Only the joy of birds and children making sound and stir across the summer stillness.

Away over the broad face of the earth, out from such peace as this, might there, if one could look, — unroll some vision of horrible contrast? Were blood, and wrath, and groans, and thunderous roar of guns down there under that far, fair horizon, stooping in golden beauty to the cool, green hills?

Faith walked down the field-path, presently, to meet her husband, coming up. He held in his hand an open **paper,** that he had brought, just now, from the village.

There was news.

Rout, horror, confusion, death, dismay.

The field of Manassas had **been** fought. The Union armies were falling back, **in** disorder, upon Washington.

Breathlessly, with pale faces, and with hands that grasped each other in a deep excitement that could not come to speech, they read those columns, together.

Down there, on those Virginian plains, was this.

And they were here, in quiet safety, among the clover blooms, and the new-cut hay. Elsewhere, men were mown.

"Roger!" said Faith, when, by-and-by, they had grown calmer over the fearful tidings, and had had Bible words of peace and cheer for the fevered and bloody rumors **of** men, — "mightn't we take our wedding journey, now?"

All the bright, early summer, **in those** first months of their life together, they had been finding work to do. Work they had hardly dreamed of, when Faith had feared she might be left to a mere, unworthy, selfish rest and happiness.

The old New England spirit had roused itself, mightily, in the little country **town.** People had forgotten their own needs, **and** the provision they were wont to make, **at** this time, **each** household for itself. Money and material, and quick, willing hands were found, and a good work went on; and kindling zeal, and noble sympathies, and hearty prayers wove themselves in, with toil of thread and needle, to homely fabrics, and embalmed, with every finger-touch, all whereon they labored.

They had remembered the old struggle wherein their

country had been born. They were glad and proud to bear their burden in this grander one wherein she was to be born anew, to higher life.

Roger Armstrong and his wife had been the spring and soul and centre of all.

And now, Faith said, — "Roger! may n't we take our wedding journey?"

Not for a bridal holiday, — not for gay change and pleasure, — but for a holy purpose, went they out from home.

Down among the wounded, and war-smitten. Bearing comfort of gifts, and helpful words, and prayers. Doing whatsoever they found to do, now; seeking and learning what they might best do, hereafter. Truly, God left them not without a work. A noble ministry lay ready for them, at this very threshold of their wedded life.

In the hospital at Georgetown, they found Nurse Sampson.

"I told you so," she said. "I knew it was coming. And the first gun brought me down here to be ready. I've been out to Western Virginia; and I came back here when we got the news of this. I shall follow round, wherever the clouds roll."

In Washington, still another meeting awaited them.

Paul Rushleigh, in a Captain's uniform, came, one day, to the table of their hotel.

The first gun had brought him, also, where he could be ready. He had sailed for home, with his father, upon the reception, abroad, of the tidings of the fall of Sumter.

"Your country will want you, now, my son," had been the words of the brave and loyal gentleman. And, like another Abraham, he had set his face toward the mount of sacrifice.

There was a new light in the young man's eye. A soul awakened there. A purpose, better than any plan or hope of a mere happy living in the earth.

He met his old friends frankly, generously; and, seemingly, without a pang. They were all one now, in the sublime labor that, in their several spheres, lay out before them.

"You were right, Faith," he said, as he stood with them, and spoke briefly of the past, before they parted. "I shall be more of a man, than if I'd had my first wish. This war is going to make a nation of men. I'm free, now, to give my heart and hand to my country, as long as she needs me. And by-and-by, perhaps, if I live, some woman may love me with the sort of love you have for your husband. I feel now, how surely I should have come to be dissatisfied with less. God bless you both!"

"God bless you, Paul!"

www.ingramcontent.com/pod-product-compliance
Lightning Source LLC
Chambersburg PA
CBHW031426230426
43668CB00007B/459